Acquisitions

Acquisitions

WHERE, WHAT, AND HOW
A guide to orientation and procedure
for students in librarianship,
librarians, and academic faculty

TED GRIEDER

*Contributions in Librarianship and
Information Science, Number 22*

GREENWOOD PRESS
WESTPORT, CONNECTICUT • LONDON, ENGLAND

Library of Congress Cataloging in Publication Data

Grieder, Theodore, 1926-
  Acquisitions : where, what, and how.

  Contributions in librarianship and information
science ; no. 22 ISSN 0084-9243)
  Includes bibliographical references and index.
  1. Acquisitions (Libraries) I. Title. II. Series.
Z689.G695   025.2   77-84762
ISBN 0-8371-9890-9

Library of Congress Catalog Card Number: 77-84762
ISBN: 0-8371-9890-9
ISSN: 0084-9243

First published in 1978

Greenwood Press, Inc.
51 Riverside Avenue, Westport, Connecticut 06880

Printed in the United States of America

10 9 8 7 6 5 4 3

CONTENTS

ACKNOWLEDGMENTS

The many knowledgeable librarians for whom and with whom I have worked; Josephine Grieder and Walter Goldwater, who read the final manuscript for structure; Thomas Crotty, who set up charts and forms; and, particularly, the Council on Library Resources, which provided the assistance that enabled me to undertake this book.

INTRODUCTION

Acquisitions: Where, What, and How is composed of two parts. Part One deals with orientation and presents an overall survey of general acquisitions procedures. To library school students who might be interested in Acquisitions as a career, to nontechnical-services librarians, and to academic faculty, it aims at giving a general view of acquisitions interrelationships in and out of the library and at providing a *survey of acquisitions concerns and activities*. There is necessarily, however, some procedural detail. Part One, in short, describes *where* Acquisitions is in relation to other library activities and to other components and functions of the university community as a whole. Part One further aims at explaining in general *what* constitutes the functions of Acquisitions.

Part Two deals with a number of specific procedures and routines at various work stations within Acquisitions. It utilizes a *how*-to-do-it approach which necessarily goes into considerable detail about bibliographic checking, order work, gifts and exchanges, approval plans, the use of statistics, and a number of other subjects. The user is here specifically referred to "How to Use Part Two" for further explanation. Part Two should be of particular interest to the student or librarian interested in Acquisitions as a profession; but it should as well be consulted by anyone who wants to find out what Acquisitions is specifically all about.

I have tried to make this text a working guide, with sufficient, though not excessive, detail; but some detail is inevitable if anyone is to learn properly how to perform particular acquisitions routines. I do not pretend either that this text is all-inclusive or that some of the points of view expressed do not relate to subjects and practices about which librarians themselves hold differing opinions. My stance toward faculty comes from seven years of full-time university instructional endeavor and from more part-time teaching than I care to remember, at three very different universities. My stance toward the practice of Acquisitions in particular and toward librarianship in general comes from fourteen years in the profession, split evenly between work in Acquisitions and Special Collections.

The thrust of this text in the main supposes the practice of Acquisitions in college and research libraries. But the emphasis here is to some extent only a matter of degree. All acquisitions librarians are, after all, concerned with acquiring books, no matter what the budget or the audience of readers. And the general procedures for buying a book, irrespective of its cost and nature, require approximately similar approaches and controls. Here and there in this text, it may appear that the obvious has been belabored; but work in Acquisitions teaches its professor to take very little for granted. It is my belief that it is far more useful to present a student/librarian with a full range of procedural guides, from which he can select those which will be of use to him, than it is to approach the subject of Acquisitions too generally, thus leaving the student/librarian without a great deal of information which can, in one form or another, be helpful in his thinking about and practicing Acquisitions.

Finally, I must apologize for my frequent use of the masculine pronouns: he, him, and his. Rhetorically, I simply could not cast my sentences to my own satisfaction without using these masculines; and I can only rely for understanding of this kind of problem from anyone who has tried to come to grips in exposition with the attempt at such usages as "he/she," "it," "person(s)," or whatever, as substitutes for these masculine forms. I do not wish to protest my own usage in this matter too much, but feel compelled to note it here, since so many of those with whom I have worked and for whom I have a most considerable professional esteem have been so well entitled to the feminines of she, her, and hers.

PART ONE

Orientation (*Where*) and General Procedures (*What*)

I.1

THE MACROCOSM: OBSERVATIONS ON THE UNIVERSITY COMMUNITY

Within the university, as I see it, there are four groups which may be sorted out: administrators, academic faculty, students, and, for our purposes here, librarians. I am not at this point concerned with that other group—the vast clerical staff upon the collective back of which everyone else appears to ride. Let us look at these four groups in order.

Once upon a time, universities were administered, as were libraries, by scholars who had risen in the ranks and who, reluctantly, finally took over the reins of their institution under pressure of demand by fellow scholars and the student community. Many of these scholar-administrators continued with teaching and research activities. Currently, every university and college administration contains numbers of persons who draw handsome salaries, make fundamental decisions affecting every member of the university family, and, yet, have never spent a day in the classroom and little, if any, time in academic research. Thus in recent years we have seen generals as university presidents, lawyers as deans of student bodies, and youthful junior business executives as administrative assistants second only to the presidential eminence. In one institution with which I am familiar, retired colonels have traditionally held key administrative positions. Certainly there is evidence to indicate that administrators are more concerned with the woodwork of things measurable—football stadia, alumni enthusiasms, money, the numbers of graduates sent out into commercial and technological pursuits—than they are with matters of humanism or pure science.

Under such circumstances, it is not surprising that university administrators tend not to understand the concerns of their faculties very well and tend to view the student body with the suspicion with which the orderly regard the unruly. How university administrators view their librarians is demonstrated by salary ranges. While some progress has been made, and while in some communities librarians have achieved "faculty equivalency" or even "status" (i.e., the drawing of an eleven-month salary that is lower than the nine-month salary of the academic faculty), in a nation where income *is* status the standing of librarians is self-evident.

The relation between the university administration (UA) and the library is largely economic, since it is from the UA that the money comes for books, staff, and physical layout. As a rule the university administration does not give the library as much yearly budget as it requests. So a game is annually played in which the library asks for more than it needs, knowing the amount will be cut and hoping that the cut will not drop the budget below its true needs. If such a relation exists between the library and the UA—in the instance of state institutions, between the institution and the state comptroller—woe be it unto the honest but naïve director of libraries who submits an honest, accurate budget request; for his fair figures will be slashed to the non-survival level. Other than to weigh its requests for money, the university administration will not usually be concerned with the library unless student and faculty opinion seems to indicate that the library is not functioning properly. In this event, the university administration will probably become directly involved, since it, like all other parts of the academic community, views the library and librarians as very much the creatures of the community.

The academic, or teaching faculty is, so to speak, another kind of a cat. For despite its eccentricities and predilections for prima donna roles, the faculty is at least somewhat engaged in distributing some kind of learning and pursuing some kind of search for the truth in some kind of discipline. And whatever his peccadillos, the faculty member who has achieved a doctorate from a reputable institution in a reputable discipline (these qualifications are admittedly pretty exclusive) is a demonstrably intelligent and industrious individual. Acquisitions librarians who have to deal with faculty unpredictabilities sometimes feel as if they were dealing with perverse and malevolent children. But they must remember that patience can educate almost anyone. They should also remember that the professor has concerns far from the intricacies of acquiring books, and that it is his very remoteness from the practicalities of Acquisitions which demands professionals like us. That the faculty has other fish to fry is a good thing; for the library will more or less be left to the librarian, if he can handle the job. Patience, firmness, and competence will keep the faculty happy; stupidity, bureaucratic nit-picking, faintheartedness, lying, silly attempts to deny mistakes (and acquisitions librarians can never afford not to admit to these, since the complexity of their work will inevitably lead to some errors) can produce an ugly foe with an elephantine memory. And the faculty member is not an ally to be sneered at; with all due qualifications, he still stands most respectably at the center of the university community.

Because the faculty of humanities and social sciences uses the library as its laboratory, it is with this faculty that usual library procedures are most concerned. The proliferation of departmental libraries for the scientist and of special libraries for various sciences and such disciplines as dentistry, medicine, law, commerce, and so forth, usually remove the professor of such disciplines from much contact with the librarians in the general library. I might note in passing that law and medical librarians handle clients of economic status and are themselves the recipients of marked economic benefits. All librarians are equal, but some are more equal than others.

Since it is to Acquisitions that requests to build in certain fields are directed, such faculty queries as "What the hell happened to that book I ordered nine months ago?" are to be expected. G&E (gifts and exchanges) can also expect faculty contact from scholars seeking to donate unwanted monographs and assorted issues of journals for tax write-offs. The degree of faculty involvement in the acquisition of library materials varies greatly, of course, from institution to institution and is determined in large part by whether the faculty or the library has chief control of the budget.

Students very infrequently suggest books to buy, and are in general even less aware of the location and activities of Acquisitions than are their professorial leaders. The students who are found in Acquisitions are employees; and these necessarily industrious and bright kids compare favorably with their peers who lounge around circulation desks and misshelve books in the stacks. I have, in fact, seen a number of students who appeared to enjoy working with books, bibliographic routines, and record-keeping, perhaps because such employment engaged their minds.

The Library, and those who work within it, lies, then, at the very heart of the university community. For, whoever its users are—the scientist looking for a recent journal or the latest translation of an article by a Lithuanian co-seeker, the freshman trying to find out what has been written lately about barn burning, the sophomore wanting to read up on fraternities, the graduate student who needs an interlibrary-loan title immediately, Professor X who has forgotten to place required reading texts on reserve, Professor Y who has just discovered that his basic text for his course in spore-forms is out-of-print, or Professor Z who is struggling with the variant-edition problems of *The Woodlanders* for his definitive resolution of the final text—they all, these representative components of the university community, must come to the library. And it is within the library that the librarian moves and works in a microcosm within the macrocosm of university.

In his place in this microcosm of the library, the acquisitions librarian must face the fact that if all goes well, compliments will be few, and if anything goes amiss, complaints will be swiftly forthcoming. He must also face the fact, as must all personnel in Technical Services, that co-workers in other parts of the library—in turn under a variety of pressures from faculty and students—will often be on his neck for prompt attention to particular problems. And any acquisitions librarian will soon discover that many fellow librarians outside his realm are very little better informed about the nature of Acquisitions than are faculty and students.

I.2

THE MICROCOSM:
THE DIVISIONS OF THE
LIBRARY AND THEIR FUNCTIONS

Within the library are the following divisions: (A) the administration; (B) the public services of (1) circulation (variously called, loan, readers services, etc.) and (2) reference; (C) special collections; and (D) technical services. Not to be overly philosophical, all of these four divisions functioning together generally aim at two things: *collection development* to provide the teaching and research resources which the university needs; and *service* to make these resources effectively available to the university community. The methodology of selection which *is* collection development is necessarily considered several times in this text (in I.3-4. and II.4-6., 11.; see also especially II.12.); for, after all, without acquisitions of materials there is no collection development and perhaps no library worthy of the name. The term "service" has, of course, different meanings for different divisions of the library—hence such terminologies as *public, technical,* and *special* (collections) services. I think that if we do not confuse the concept of service by always identifying it in some way with "meeting the public," we can see that any correctly functioning division of a library is in fact a service operation.

Finally, as the following brief discussion of the divisions of the library will probably make clear, I tend to believe that for one reason or another, by nature and/or training, most librarians are better suited to the demands of one particular library operation than to another. This point of view is, of course, subject to debate. But my experience has been that a good bibliographer, serials librarian, cataloger, etc., does not exercise his full potential if pulled off, say, to a reference desk. Similarly, many librarians like the psychological interplays of public services, and would be lost and acutely unhappy amidst the myriad and impersonal routines of Acquisitions, just as a subject specialist invaluable in his collection development role might make a bad and unhappy cataloger. To use analogy, it is difficult for me to conceive of a capable theatrical director who would not look for a particular kind of an actor to play a particular kind of a role.

A.

Any library of any size will have a director and at least a couple of assistant or associate directors who customarily oversee one large area of activity— public services, technical services, personnel and physical plant, and so forth. Several chief administrators of this kind should be sufficient for even a large library, although they tend to proliferate given any kind of congenial soil. Some library administrations also possess rather alarming numbers of executive secretaries and administrative assistants.

Although a good many library administrators derive from the public services and are sometimes only vaguely aware of the functions and budgetary and staffing needs of technical services (let alone the proper procedures for acquiring and processing books), in the past at least these library administrators have risen from the ranks and have been, thus, often more knowledgeable about the details of their work than the president of the university has been about his. More recently, however, there has arisen the somewhat disturbing practice of suddenly jumping candidates in doctorate programs in librarianship into important administrative positions without reference to prior professional experience. The result is administrators with little or no background in the day-to-day practicalities of librarianship. Overall, then, the acquisitions librarian must expect that most of his masters may very well lack any real knowledge of acquisitions techniques and problems, and he must be prepared to explain and defend with patience and tenacity what seems to him to be the terribly obvious.

It is only fair, perhaps, to add that a director of libraries will have not only his own ship and crew on his hands, but university administrators, trustees, faculty stars, student leaders, donors, and extra-university community leaders as well. Thus, it is entirely possible that a director will have less than adequate time for staff rapport, in which event he must still be responsible for appointing capable subordinates to represent him to the librarians. On the other hand, it seems difficult to argue that the primary concern of a head librarian should not be the library itself and the economic and vocational well-being of the librarians therein.

B.1.

The Circulation (or Loan) department, sometimes given the more recent appellation of Readers Services, is the one perhaps most generally and continuously in contact with the public; it forms, thus, a primary battleground where the strengths and weaknesses of any library emerge from the trial-by-fire test of whether or not titles requested by patrons can be produced. If cards for books in hand do not duly appear in the main card catalog (MCC; public catalog, PC), or if books which do appear in the MCC have not reached the library's shelves, Circulation will in turn have Acquisitions or Cataloging on the hook. Circulation, then, concerns itself largely with the logistics of library materials, very simply with keeping the house in order.

Checking large numbers of books in and out, sending notices for overdue books, trying to collect fines for overdue or missing books, reading shelves (if there is ever time for an inventory like this) to correct misshelving, ordering replacements for missing titles, and sending battered books and serials to the bindery—all of these basically simple but multitudinous tasks must be done over and over again, hopefully with good will and accuracy. Because of the mechanical and repetitive nature of many functions of Circulation, this department and many of its procedures lend themselves well to the use of machine systems, which most Circulation departments of size now have or will soon be getting. This development brings with it the responsibility of monitoring some kind of computer control effectively.

In spite of the demands of these various duties, and the large professional literature dealing with them at length, I am not alone in having some mis-givings about how truly professional are even the administrative aspects of Circulation operations. But a large number of librarians are at present en-gaged in this occupation, and I do not wish to understate the tact required in dealing with users of all kinds—students, faculty, staff, extra-university community—in such matters as fines, proper qualifications for access to various kinds of materials, and so forth. Nor do I wish to underrate the responsibility of directing a large staff of stack workers, many of whom are part time, and working out their rather complicated time schedules and assignments.

The reserve book room (RBR)—as a rule a subdivision of Circulation—is the location where students are supposed to find reading copies of required and supplemental texts for specific courses. The idea of the RBR pre-supposes that professors will submit coherent lists of titles to be placed on reserve. Such titles should ideally be submitted on alphabetized groups of acquisitions request forms, with full author, title, imprint, and reprint infor-mation spelled out. The idea of the RBR also presupposes that lists of de-sired titles will be submitted several months ahead of the time for required use so that they can be gathered together, or bought by Acquisitions if necessary, in a routine way, and not in a desperate and often futile last-minute race against the calendar. It is further presupposed that lists will be only for in-print (or reprinted) titles or for out-of-print titles known to be in the library's present holdings, not for five copies of a title published in 1812 and never reprinted. Given competency in the library and given the fulfillment of these presuppositions, the RBR and the acquisitions routines related to its re-quirements should proceed smoothly. Because, however, few faculty ever live up to these expectations, the RBR, and the Acquisitions department in RBR instances, are all too often in needless crises over required but un-available texts. A training program directed at faculty through RBR and Acquisitions seems the only possible solution.

To add a final point here, I think it is important for the acquisitions librarian to bear in mind that the Circulation department can be viewed as a talent pool and a potential source of student help. The head of Circulation employs large numbers of part-time students, as we know; and he or his assistants may be willing to transfer students whose aptitudes rise above the nature of the tasks they customarily perform. No one likes to lose a superior clerical employee; but Acquisitions can sometimes rely on circulation supervisors with altruistic natures and an eye for talent to suggest possible technical services candidates.

2.

The Reference department is the other large public service and is one with which Acquisitions will have considerable contact. Since reference work, like cataloging, is usually emphasized heavily in schools of librarianship, and properly so, the overall nature of the resources with which the reference librarian works should be clear to anyone pretending to our profession. How and how much these resources are called into use varies from one Reference department to another. But all such departments stress guidance and question-answering, and in this sense aim at the same goals as the teaching faculty. Further, in recent years, at least in many college and research libraries, this teaching function has been emphasized by breaking the reference librarian's day into time on the desk and off the desk. That is, question-answering and problem-solving are no longer done in a full-day stint behind the reference desk; so there is what I, as no expert at all, think of as desk time and free time, which is of course free only in the sense that the librarian is not fixed by schedule to desk duty.

However, on the reference desk or off, the guidance and answering services of Reference are on several distinctly separate levels distinguished by degree of difficulty. Reference librarians themselves acknowledge various levels of difficulty in their work by keeping quantitative-qualitative records. That is, they will record the total number of questions answered or problems solved in a given working day, and then break down this total number by the length of time required for each response—under one minute, five minutes, fifteen minutes, over thirty minutes, and so on. I myself break these time periods into *words* related to the nature of questions answered or problems solved: *directional, ready-reference,* and *research,* although the first two tend to overlap.

A directional work effort gives guidance to the location of the nearest phone, duplicating machine, restroom, coke machine, etc., as well as explaining where to find the circulation desk, French literature collections, or the proper elevator for a particular floor. There is a good deal of directional work in Reference. And there is considerable ready-reference activity as well: the identification of quotations, how to compound interest, who Mrs. Grundy is and in what play, the proper way to address a viscount, who was Secretary of State in 1842, and so on. It seems to me to be only civilized to answer directional questions. Whether or not ready-reference questions should be answered at all in college and research libraries has been debated. Whether or not a Master's Degree in Library Science is an essential for directional and ready-reference work has also been debated at length. I myself cannot see why such work cannot be farmed out to career non-professionals.

To assist students and faculty in their study and research activities is, of course, a meaningful part of reference work. The reference librarian's ability to render such assistance has been, I think, greatly enhanced by the free-time concept which permits reference librarians to be in the physical area where the books related to their subject expertise are shelved; to work with researchers as they use the titles in this area; to have access to an office where some thought can be given to research problems; to have access to computer banks for bibliographical searching; and, where collection development is handled by reference subject specialists rather than by bibliographers, to be able to devote time to book selection.

My own view, as a further reading of this text will make clear, is that bibliographers are to be preferred to reference subject specialists as selectors and collection developers, *except* in building the important resources of the reference collection itself. Beyond this, the acquisitions librarian should understand that many reference librarians know little more about acquisitions routines than do the faculty; and, if used as selectors, reference librarians have a propensity for ordering the same title over and over again and for presenting requests in illegible formats lacking correct (or even worse, containing incorrect) and essential bibliographical details.

It is also necessary for those in Acquisitions to understand that by his nature the reference librarian is public-service oriented and very responsive to the moods and demands of his patrons. Hence, he sometimes shows what might be viewed as undue enthusiasm in relaying to Acquisitions reports of real or imagined mistakes in its operations; sometimes attempts to get Acquisitions to render individual services that are neither possible or necessary; and sometimes attempts to change acquisitions routines (by requesting too many "rush" orders, for example) that must be sustained for proper work flow and record control. In such matters, reference librarians, like the academic faculty, must receive some kind of guidelines from Acquisitions and be expected to abide by them. If library schools paid as much attention to the methodology of acquisitions as they pay to the subjects of reference and cataloging, the substance of this paragraph would be happily superfluous.

C.

The special collections librarian (also called a rare book(s) librarian, a curator, etc.) is responsible for the management of the library's various titles and collections which require special attention and handling because of their format (maps, prints, manuscripts, etc.) and/or their value (usually monetary but also related to a number of other complex factors). Like subject specialists and bibliographers, the special collections librarian usually possesses a good academic background as well as some "feel" for books and some knowledge about their history. He is service oriented, in that he continually deals with rather complex inquiries related to historical and bibliographical research and with graduate students, academic faculty, and postdoctoral researchers from other institutions working with advanced problems in their particular disciplines.

Such a librarian may assume a somewhat protective stance toward his holdings; but whoever has seen the ravages that befall the rare or beautiful book that somehow gets into normal technical processing routines will, perhaps, not judge this defensive posture too harshly. The special collections librarian should always, however, regard his collections as research resources to be available to the qualified user, and he should never confuse his own research responsibilities by behaving more like a private collector indulging his whims and passions than like what he is—namely, a professional librarian with responsibilities to a qualified public. On the other hand, it is simply silly for any librarian to regard rules and regulations set up to protect rare and valuable materials as either unnecessary or undemocratic.

Special Collections grows by purchase and gift. The librarian in charge will generate requests for purchases himself, often from dealer catalogs specializing in out-of-print (o.p.) and antiquarian materials. Depending upon library structure, in one institution the special collections librarian may order directly from dealers and have his purchases sent directly to his area in the library. In another institution, one more bureaucratically structured, his requests may have to be sent out and received by Acquisitions. In this latter instance, Acquisitions will have to work closely with Special Collections to insure proper punctuality and handling of the ordering and receiving of such special materials. Everyone in Acquisitions, particularly the gifts (G&E) librarian, should always keep an eye out for rare materials, purchased or donated, that can occasionally get lost in the shuffle and be cropped, bound, and stamped for the stacks or, worse, discarded.

Criteria for what is "special collections material" should ideally be worked out among Administration, Special Collections, and Acquisitions. Guidelines defining acceptable gift materials should also be worked out by the librarians in these three divisions. And the acquisitions librarian should always feel free to call upon the special collections librarian for assistance in making decisions about the value or rarity of particular titles, the value of gifts offered, and so forth.

D.

Technical Services can be divided for our purposes here into the traditional subdivisions of Acquisitions and Cataloging. Since this text concerns itself with Acquisitions in the chapters which follow, I need make only a few observations at this point about the nature of the occupation and those who pursue it. The techniques of cataloging, unlike those of acquisitions, are stressed heavily in almost all library schools; so I will only touch upon cataloging and catalogers below. As this text will make clear as it progresses, Acquisitions and Cataloging are bound together in that it is their joint technical services operation that gets books *into* the library and *onto* the library shelves.

1.

The duties of the acquisitions librarian are to receive requests for purchases of titles from all parts of the university community (he will almost inevitably generate a number of requests himself) and (a) to ascertain that such requests are not for titles already in the library; (b) to verify that such titles actually exist; (c) to determine if Library of Congress resources have cataloged the title, or, failing that, to determine if the title appears in other national or trade bibliographies; (d) to determine the price and availability of a given title; (e) to order requested titles that have passed through procedures a-d, above; (f) to receive and pay for ordered titles; and (g) to send all titles along with all possible bibliographical information to the Catalog department. This rough summary, in fact, represents the approximate skeleton of what the following chapters of this text are all about.

The acquisitions librarian should, ideally, possess the wisdom of Solomon, the patience of Job, the learning of J. S. Mill, and the charm of Alcibiades. He should know books and the book trade—in-print, out-of-print, and reprint (book, mini-print, and microform). A head for figures is essential, since he will be dealing with and juggling large amounts of money and keeping track of a great many fund accounts. He must know, or soon learn, bibliographical procedures with tools in English and Western European languages. And he will have to be industrious or go under, since books keep being sought, bought, and received in a never-ending stream.

The acquisitions librarian will also have to deal more directly with all other parts of the library than will any librarian outside his department; in so doing, he will inevitably come into contact with a very wide range of personalities and educational levels, often in moments of crisis. It will behoove him, on the one hand, not to make overhasty judgments or be overly abrupt and, on the other hand, not to lose himself, and subsequently lose any ability to act promptly, in the incredible amount of nit-picking detail in which any technical services area seems to be inevitably involved. As with other specialties in librarianship, a certain education, temperament, and way of looking at people and things seem to be more suited for acquisitions work than for any other kind.

2.

In the good old days, the cataloger would seize the next title at hand and promptly proceed to describe it as a physical entity, analyze its contents, make appropriate subject headings and added entries, and classify the title so that it would shelve among its fellows according to whatever system of classification was being used (in American research libraries, now almost exclusively Library of Congress). Today, most catalogers in most institutions in the United States seem to do very little original cataloging—once the very cornerstone of their art. The decline of this art seems to be due in large part to reliance on Library of Congress (LC) "copy," whether found in LC-NUC (*National Union Catalog*) sequences or in computer data banks. There must, I believe, be original catalogers at the Library of Congress to produce this copy upon which everyone else relies, although I have never met one.

The general demise of rapid and expert original cataloging is, I think, reflective of a reliance on verification (pre-cataloging) routines in Acquisitions as well as upon machine resources, although perhaps no librarian is much interested in performing tasks which machines can perform correctly and more rapidly. But when catalogers rely heavily upon an outside assistance that is not always forthcoming, some delays are certain and the central art of their profession is in decline. Whatever the causes of the situation as it now exists, almost every acquisitions librarian sometimes longs for the return of the good old days.

For example, the acquisitions librarian is attempting to keep in motion the complexities of the routines required to buy and pay for a certain number of books per day and, at the same time, to send the books he has acquired on to the cataloger with as much verification as is possible from a variety of bibliographical resources. When a cataloger, as occasionally happens, complains about the inaccuracy of the verification of one volume among many—and is prepared to spend some time to prove his point—it may seem to the acquisitions librarian that his cataloging compatriot is being a bit unfair. With the advice to grin and bear it, let us carry on.

I.3

THE MICRO-MICROCOSM: A SKETCH OF FUNCTION AND FORM IN ACQUISITIONS

The most important elements of this brief chapter on function and form are the definition of function (in A., below) and the discussion of form and the Organizational Chart which illustrates form (under B., below). Anyone seriously interested in Acquisitions should look at the definition closely and study the chart carefully. He should understand the terminology used and be able to describe generally the functions of the various sections which form Acquisitions.

In Part Two, II.2.A.2. should also be referred to right at this point for a more detailed chart of the Separates section itself. To have both charts well in mind will be helpful throughout the chapters that follow.

A. FUNCTION

The function of Acquisitions may be summarized in *five* activities, which occur in the following sequence: *selecting*; *verifying* (precataloging, searching); *ordering*; *receiving*; and *recording funds* (encumbering money for titles ordered— books and serials—but not yet received, paying bills for titles received, and keeping track of expenditures for a variety of individual funds/budgets in relation to time of fiscal year and overall, annual budget).

The process of *verification* is taken in the statement of function above to *include* the "holdings check," although in Part Two (II.2.A.5.A-B.) the two procedures are treated in separate, though consecutive, discussions to facilitate exposition. It is important to note, further, that the process of *selection* is the only one of these five activities *ever* taking place outside the function and form of Acquisitions (see I.4-5., below, where interrelationships of selection and acquisitions are considered at some length).

In the jargon of the trade, these five acquisitions activities are more crudely spoken of as "buying a book." For example, at the end of a long day, the head of Acquisitions may say to his weary staff, "Well, we bought a lot of books today." By this he means that a certain number of titles (books and serials) have today been *verified, ordered* in today's mail from a variety of dealers, and the appropriate *funds* encumbered. He also means that a certain number of titles previously ordered on other days have this day been *received,* paid for and expenditures of *funds recorded,* and sent on to Cataloging. *Selection* of titles may or may not have taken place on this particular day and may or may not have taken place within the Acquisitions Department.

B. FORM

The Acquisitions department functions, as we know, to acquire library materials and, by processing them into the Catalog department, to move them to a stage only one major step away from the library's shelves. Interestingly enough, two of the chief sections of Acquisitions are formed to select (to some extent) and verify materials to be *purchased,* but differ from each other in the *form* of the titles with which they work: the Separates section handles monographs/books; and the Serials section deals with various forms of publications intended to be published continually into the future (some librarians still refer to serials as "continuations"). The Gifts and Exchanges section (G&E; but gifts dictate the vast majority of the activities of this section) is formed to verify materials that are *not purchased, and it* works with titles in both monographic and serial format.

The Order section is formed to buy, receive, and record expenditures for the titles for which the Separates section forwards requests. Serials normally does its own ordering work because of the particular problems of payment and record control inherent in the acquisitions of serials (in a number of libraries, Serials acquisitions and cataloging are combined into the form of a distinct section in Technical Services, in an effort to centralize all routines related to acquiring and processing this demanding form of material). That all of these sections exist as *particular forms* is a result of the necessity for *specialization of function* to deal with the different materials and routines in Acquisitions.

In the Organizational Chart, below, the Separates (monographs/books) section has responsibility for the Order section and, through it, the typing pool, the mailroom (shipping, receiving room), and, in conjunction with Serials, for the book-keeping operations. Separates also monitors approval plans which, according to their number and size, can demand a great deal of somewhat painstaking attention. As is usual, Serials supervises the bindery operations (since serials are the library materials requiring the most bindery work) and the Kardex, which keeps the records of all serials ordered and received.

Any chart, such as the organizational one provided here, is a fixed, rather lifeless kind of device. The viewer of this chart has to visualize the heads of all sections and subsections constantly in communication with one another about problems in the operations of their particular sections/forms, with everyone pretty much relying on everyone else for assistance and advice when needed. To visit an active Acquisitions department and see and hear the bustling about and the interplay between various sections is to bring such a chart to life.

ORGANIZATIONAL CHART

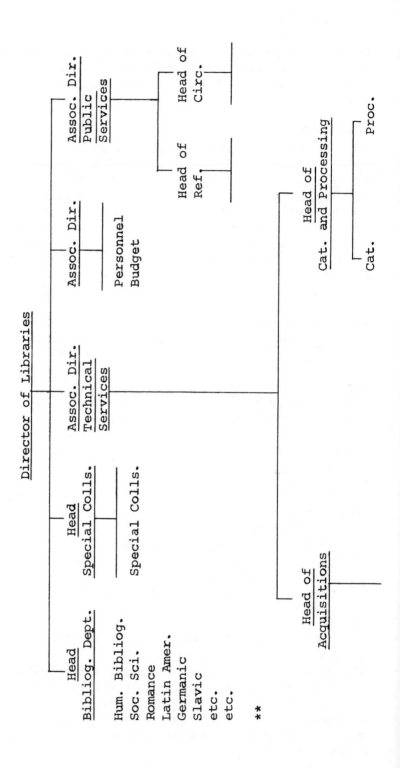

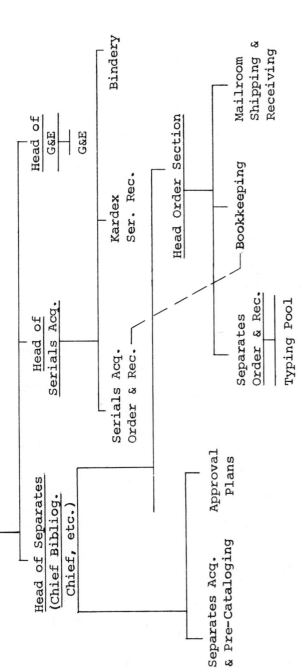

Head of Separates (Chief Bibliog. Chief, etc.)

Head of Serials Acq.

Head of G&E

Separates Acq. & Pre-Cataloging

Approval Plans

Serials Acq. Order & Rec.

Kardex Ser. Rec.

Head Order Section

Bookkeeping

Separates Order & Rec.

Typing Pool

G&E

Bindery

Mailroom Shipping & Receiving

**Line simply omitted if no bibliographic corps; duties assumed by Reference Subject Specialists. This department could equally well be in Technical Services, and should certainly have close liaison with T.S.

I.4

THE LIBRARY BUDGET:
ITS RELATION TO SELECTION
AND ACQUISITIONS

A.

How selection is structured varies from institution to institution, depending upon (a) the organizational form of the library itself, (b) the degree to which the faculty interests itself in acquisitions, and (c) who controls what is commonly though misleadingly called the library's "book budget" for the acquisition of monographs *and* serials (for *who* selects, see particularly I.5.A.1-3.; II.5.; and II.12., below). Budgetary control exists in one of three patterns: (1) some academic libraries have somehow managed to lose all budget control—and, subsequently, most powers of collection development and guidance—to the faculty, producing the consequence of very spotty collections created almost entirely by the particular and often obscure specialties of particular scholars; (2) other academic libraries maintain partial control of funds, reserving some monies for the purchase of reference and special collections materials and some for general collection development, with the faculty controlling the remainder of the budget; and (3) still other libraries retain control over all of their budgets, in which event rational policies of selection and collection development are greatly facilitated.

However the distribution and control of the library budget may have been delegated, it should be obvious that correct selection policy requires an accurate and comprehensive budgetary breakdown. This is essential for balance in buying, since no Acquisitions department should buy disproportionately for any one discipline. Usually, then, whether the library controls all funds or not, Acquisitions suballocates certain percentages of the budget to be spent that it believes are appropriate for various departments and programs, so that there will be a balanced program of collection development. For example, it is common to allocate a general amount for Arts and Sciences and then to subdivide this amount into allocations to individual departments—based upon enrollment (primarily graduate), upon doctoral programs planned for or in effect, and upon the present and projected sizes of faculty. Allocations for other programs would be made similarly—for engineering, agriculture, business administration, and so forth. It is both fair and necessary that guidelines for the distribution of funds be spelled out, as in Tables 1, 2, and 3.

Serials budgets should as well be balanced, based on the strengths of various disciplines and also on their degree of need for serial publications. For example, the science researcher relies heavily upon a serials program for his research; but unless he is in a retrospective science—such as geology, paleontology, and others— he will work largely from current journals as well as from his own experiments and consultation with colleagues, without much reliance on books that are not basic reference tools. The humanities and many of the social sciences, on the other hand, are often very much interested in the acquisitions of retrospective serials to assist them in historical, literary, social, and other research. In the acquisitions of serials, I might note that it is important to distinguish between allocations for new subscriptions to be placed, current subscriptions that are already an annual obligation involving large amounts of money, and backfiles of serials titles (most of which will be out of print and will have to be purchased from out-of-print dealers or as reprints). It should also be pointed out that the costs of serials subscriptions, particularly in the sciences, have been skyrocketing for some years; thus, all requests for new subscriptions should be weighed very carefully in relation to present and future cost, use, and demonstrable, real need.

TABLE   1.

Graduate Students per Discipline: Arts and Sciences, 1977

DISCIPLINE	TERM	
	Fall	*Spring*
Anthropology	17	19
Art	30	28
Botany	33	32
Chemistry	45	45
Drama and Speech	32	30
Economics	14	12
Education	100	104
Engineering	200	212
English	60	56

. . .

TABLE 2.

Graduate Programs: Arts and Sciences, 1977

DISCIPLINE	MASTER'S PROGRAM AND YEAR INITIATED (IF RECENT)	DOCTORAL PROGRAM AND YEAR INITIATED (IF RECENT)
Anthropology	yes	Fall, 1972
Art	yes	no
Botany	Spring, 1974	no
Drama and Speech	yes	projected, Fall, 1977
Economics	yes	Spring, 1973
English	yes	Fall, 1971
French	yes	Fall, 1972
Geography	Spring, 1975	projected, Fall, 1979

. . .

TABLE 3.

Faculty and Projected Faculty: Arts and Sciences, 1977

DISCIPLINE	1977	1978
Anthropology	10	12
Art	16	19
Botany	18	19
Drama and Speech	12	14
Economics	11	12
English	26	32
French	9	11
Geography	5	6

. . .

B.

Let us now suppose the budget of a research library with a student body of some ten thousand, with a graduate program in some depth, and with the proper number of serials subscriptions—estimated by rule of thumb at about 1.5 per full-time student and weighted toward the largest and developing disciplines. Let us also suppose the present collection to be about 800,000 volumes and suppose an acquisitions program now geared to procure 200,000 more volumes in, say, a five-year period. As long as we are supposing, let us further imagine that the Acquisitions department possesses sufficient able personnel, professional and clerical, and financial backup to achieve such a five-year goal. With the disciplines for which it does not buy being excluded (law and medicine, say), the main, central library might submit a budget like the overall allocation of funds on Table 4. Amounts in dollars are only approximate, but are given to provide an idea of proportion, which should be about right for the institution we are supposing.[1] Obviously, the budget for institutions with a larger student body and faculty than we have postulated should be proportionately higher, *provided that* the holdings of such larger establishments are not so comprehensive as to make extensive retrospective collection development unnecessary.

TABLE   4.

Overall Allocation of Funds, 1976/7 and Projection of Funds, 1977/8

BOOKS	1976/7	1977/8
Arts and Sciences	238,000	260,000
Business Administration	23,000	25,000
Engineering	14,500	16,000
Library	56,000	62,000
School of Education	20,500	24,000
SUBTOTAL	352,000	387,000
Serials and Sets		
*Current Serials and Subscriptions	220,000	240,000
TOTAL BOOKS AND SERIALS	572,000	627,000
*S&S (Serials and Sets) Backfiles		
Science and Engineering	66,000	72,000
Humanities and Social Sciences	100,000	115,000
Education and Business Admin.	14,000	16,000
SUBTOTAL	180,000	203,000
TOTAL: BOOKS, SETS, SERIALS	752,000	830,000

*This budget breakdown does not include binding costs, which are chiefly related to serials, although certainly a factor in the total costs of sets and monographs. Almost all libraries under-budgeted for binding. As a rule of thumb, as of this time, probably 18 percent of the total books, sets, and serials allocation should be planned (i.e., requested) for binding on a budget such as that in Table 4: 135,000.00.

C.

A budget breakdown and analyses of faculty and graduate studies like those in Tables 1-4 should be prepared to provide guidelines for Acquisitions, no matter who controls the purse strings. However, a further and more detailed breakdown in such large areas as, for example, Arts and Sciences is essential for orderly and planned purchasing. As one illustration of the many which are possible, Table 5 demonstrates just such a detailed allocation of funds for the same supposed institution about which we have been speaking. It should be kept in mind that in Table 5 we are allocating funds for monographs only. For example, large sets (sometimes *defined arbitrarily* as those planned for more than five volumes to be issued during a period of more than three years) would be purchased from the sets and serials backfile monies, just as payment for current subscriptions and new subscriptions would be paid for out of funds laid aside for the purpose (see Table 4).

TABLE 5.

Arts and Sciences Book Budget, 1976/7

DISCIPLINE	1967/7	1977/8 (PROJECTED)	1978/9 (PROJECTED)
Anthropology	10,700	12,000	13,500
Art	9,500	10,500	12,000
Botany	6,500	7,500	8,400
Drama and Speech	9,500	10,500	13,000
Economics	9,500	10,500	12,000
English	23,500	26,000	28,000
French	10,700	12,000	13,500
Geography	6,700	7,500	8,400
. . .			

D.

If allocations are spelled out as they are in Tables 1-5, they usually get faculty approval (if such is needed) with a minimum of stress. From this kind of spelling out, it is also possible to estimate the number of books that can be purchased for each department—by simply dividing average cost per title into amount allocated. (Projected costs must allow for increases in costs of material.) Of course, such a method of allocation means that Acquisitions must be kept informed of current balances by the Bookkeeping department. Both the monies paid out for titles actually received and the funds encumbered by orders placed, but not yet received and paid for, must be clearly indicated. Each week the head of Separates can, thus, get a clear idea of what monies have been committed, even though the *university* accounting office has not yet formally recorded this amount.

Bookkeeping should be kept up daily. When orders are cancelled, the bookkeeper returns these funds to the appropriate discipline. All that is needed for this kind of record keeping are the following: a statement of the discipline concerned; its allocation; the amount withheld for approval plans; a record of the balance of funds spent or encumbered; and the amount of free funds remaining. If an institution receives books on approval plans (sometimes called blanket-order plans or standing-order plans), it generally keeps a separate sheet for expenditures on these plans to see if the amount each plan requires is correctly estimated each year (see II.6.). What lies behind all of this record keeping—aside from the aim of a balanced program of acquisitions—is the reality that any library monies not spent or encumbered may be lost at the end of a fiscal year. Also, if a library does not spend its money in a given fiscal year, it may not get as much money in the next year's budget (see II.7. for an amplification of the subject of recording and using statistics).

By an important rule of thumb, the acquisitions librarian should try to commit (encumber—that is, order, though not necessarily have paid for) 25 percent over the budget for any given fiscal year by the end of that year. So plans should be laid ahead to spend faculty monies not satisfactorily spent by departments in institutions where the faculty controls its own funds. As a rule, all funds remaining should be put into one bag of money *two months* before the end of the fiscal year, and the Acquisitions department should then spend this money out.

The amount of budget available to select, purchase, and, if necessary, bind monographs and serials will determine the numbers of personnel required to spend the budget. These numbers are in turn determined by the amount of work that can be done by personnel at the various work stations in Acquisitions, and by their salaries. (In II.7. some production figures are cited to show what may be expected of staff handling monographs at the bibliographic-checking work station.)

We must keep in mind, also, that there are three discrete budgets within the budget for Acquisitions: (1) the budget to pay for library materials; (2) the budget to pay for the clerical and professional staff that selects, verifies requests, orders monographs and serials titles, types and files orders, receives and pays for titles ordered, and, finally, records expenditures and sends titles on to the Catalog department; and (3) the budget to pay for the supplies and machines (whether typewriters or computer terminals) with which an acquisitions staff works (see II.4. for G&E, which takes only 2 and 3, above, out of the budget).

I.5

THE SELECTION AND ACQUISITIONS OF MONOGRAPHS AND SERIALS

Here we are concerned with three chief subjects, which follow respectively in A.1-3., below: *who* selects; the acquisitions methods applicable to *current* materials; and the acquisitions methods applicable to *retrospective* materials. The discussion of these three subjects in relation to the acquisitions of monographs is almost entirely applicable to the acquisitions of serials; and this discussion should be kept in mind as an integral part of the further brief discussion of serials in B.

Current materials are, of course, in print. But please do *not* think of retrospective materials as necessarily out of print; they are sometimes out of print and sometimes in print, in original or reprinted format. What we are concerned with, when we consider current and retrospective materials, are the *methods* by which Acquisitions brings them into the library.

A. MONOGRAPHS

1.

If the faculty does all selection, then the library in general, and Acquisitions in particular, is concerned only with processing requests. More usually, there is a cooperative effort between the faculty and the subject specialists or bibliographers in the library; and in recent years the academic faculty seems to have come to expect the library to assume more and more responsibility for collection development, current and retrospective. This willingness of the academic faculty to release prerogatives of selection to the library has been brought about chiefly by the growth of the concept of the librarian as a subject specialist or bibliographer. Thus, almost every college and research library of any size now employs a number of librarians who are not merely keepers and recorders of books, but have a genuine depth of learning in one or more subject fields and, often, competency in non-English languages.

A number of libraries at present expect reference subject specialists to select in their areas of expertise. In theory, such personnel are active about half-time in reference work and half-time in selection. Conversations about selection procedures with various librarians at various institutions, plus some reflection, have led me to conclude that such function splitting in Reference stems from economic motivation, and that library administrators who initiate such policies are consciously or unconsciously trying to buy two jobs for the price of one. It is true, however, that some reference librarians favor such a dichotomy of responsibility, possibly as a form of status building. But selection and collection development demand full-time attention if they are to be pursued in depth; and the quality of selection certainly suffers from part-time treatment. Retrospective work, in particular, suffers from such split-function treatment.

Economics aside, I doubt that anyone would seriously argue that full-time application to selection by trained bibliographers was not the best professional resource for collection development. Administratively, a Bibliographic department can be run on pretty much an independent basis, or can be under the administrative lines of the public or technical services. Whatever its place in the chain of command, a Bibliographic department must have a close, if not formal, liaison with Acquisitions because it must know about and work within the established routines of this department. In some libraries, such a lack of liaison has caused difficulties in Technical Services (for a fuller treatment of the Bibliographic department than can be given in the following few paragraphs, see II.5.).

Bibliographic departments are built around language and subject blocks. For example, such a department might have a bibliographer for humanities, one for social science, and another for science. In addition to bibliographers working primarily with subjects in English, no fewer than four bibliographers would be required in other language areas: Spanish, other romance languages, Germanic, and Slavic. Of course, the more focused his expertise, the better the bibliographer's work will be in his areas of responsibility. And the largest institutions, with wide research interests and course offerings, may have many more language and subject bibliographers—Scandinavian, African, Portuguese, Asian; physical sciences, natural sciences, education, business administration, and so forth.

Duties of bibliographers include close faculty liaison, which should be initiated at the beginning of each academic year by a meeting between the Bibliographic department and every academic department for which it will be selecting. The meeting should be held in each academic department itself, although every faculty member should be encouraged to visit or communicate with the bibliographer working in his academic discipline as frequently as possible. Bibliographers themselves should make it a point to visit individual members of their particular faculties to discover their academic needs and plans. Faculty liaison is further encouraged if there is a "library representative" for each academic department. It is particularly desirable that all book orders from any one department go through this library representative, who can then eliminate inappropriate and duplicate orders and can also get some idea of what his colleagues are doing about acquisitions in their specialities.

The bibliographer is also responsible for knowing the state of the collections in the areas of his responsibility. Studying shelf lists and surveying stack holdings are helpful here. Another duty, if geography permits, is to visit appropriate book dealers pretty much as a matter of routine; certainly, research libraries should send their specialists on buying trips to such centers as New York and elsewhere (see II.10.C. for a description of a buying trip). Finally, the bibliographer should expect to read a reasonable number of academic publications in his field. A list of journals which he should read should be drawn up, probably in conjunction with suggestions from academic departments.

It is a truism, but not one always apparent to library or university administrations, that Bibliographic or Area Development departments are expensive. It costs a good deal of money when librarians assume responsibility for current and retrospective collection development, since qualified bibliographers usually command respectable salaries and since each bibliographer should have at least one full-time, competent clerical assistant. Moreover, the bibliographer's requests for purchases, like those of any professor, have to be put into acceptable form before going to Acquisitions; so typing and secretarial assistance are required as well. Currently, I would say that $140,000 a year is probably a very minimal salary figure to support a Bibliographic department with five librarians in it (for a variety of reasons, I think bibliographers should be required to have an M.L.S.). Of course, if one paid the academic faculty to do the same bibliographic work, the cost would be a great deal higher; but administrators tend not to think this way.

2.

Once we determine who is to handle selection (ideally, perhaps, bibliographers backed by academic faculty and subject-specialist suggestion), the next step is to decide *how* to implement current selection. It should be remembered that the current materials of today become the retrospective, possibly even out-of-print, materials of tomorrow. By its nature, retrospective work costs more than current work in time and money (see II.11. for further discussion of in-print, reprint, and out-of-print titles relevant to our discussion here and in 3.).

There seems to be general agreement today that national bibliographies, when they exist, or Library of Congress proof slips are major keys to current selection. Book reviews in academic journals are not used nearly so frequently as in former days because of the time lag in acquiring academic titles in this manner, since such scholarly resources are notoriously slow in appearing. To work with the literatures of countries for which there is no national bibliography, a bibliographer must rely on various sources—including, hopefully, solid lists of current imprints provided by reliable dealers specializing in the materials of such countries, and L.C. proof slips—which may or may not be comprehensive for some countries and languages.

For nations for which national bibliographies are available—Britain, France, Germany, Spain, the Netherlands, Switzerland, Russia, the United States, among many—two approaches are possible. The bibliographer/selector can receive by airmail the bibliographies appropriate to his area; make his selections from them; give them to an assistant to see that a properly prepared request card is submitted to Acquisitions for each title desired; and see to it that orders for titles are processed out of Acquisitions, by airmail if necessary, in an expeditious manner.

However, because of time involved in producing a request card in the Bibliographic department and putting in motion the various routines of the Order section of Acquisitions (see II.3. for some order routines), many research libraries have gone into approval plans (blanket-order plans, standing-order plans, a rose by any other name, etc.) with dealers in a number of countries. In theory at least, the dealer and his staff understand the nature of academic materials and the needs of particular libraries. As soon as the most recent part of his national bibliography (often the weekly portion) is available, the dealer marks which titles he thinks he ought to send (sometimes distinguishing between titles at once available and those still only in preparation), and he airmails a marked copy to the appropriate bibliographer, who reviews the selections, adds or crosses out titles as he deems necessary, and airmails the bibliography back to the dealer, who then sends the books as available. If current selection is made only from national bibliographies or from comprehensive approval plans utilizing such bibliographies, I see no need for bibliographic assistants to check O.O. (orders-out, on-order) files to avoid ordering titles already on order; such a prompt method of current selection as the one we are discussing will not be in danger of duplicating previous orders (see II.6. where approval plans are considered in much more detail).

Many libraries use Library of Congress proof slips for current selection. This method has several advantages, among them the fact that the slips can be sorted by LC classification into subject blocks and sent to particular area bibliographers, and the fact that sets of LC-style cards can be made by xerography from these slips so that no problem for getting LC catalog copy exists for titles ordered in such a way.[2] The use of LC proof slips requires the generation of requests and the multiple filing of order slips, and thus requires much more busy work than does a successful approval plan. Also, proof slips are *not so comprehensive* a selection source as national bibliographies. Some libraries may, therefore, combine the use of national bibliographies and LC proof slips. Any method of current selection, however, that uses dual or multiple procedures has inherent problems of duplication of effort and of titles ordered, and must be carefully monitored.

If current titles are already being acquired by any kind of comprehensive program (approval plans, selection by bibliographers from national bibliographies, LC proof slips, special current lists supplied by reliable dealers in countries without national current listings, or any methodology combining these resources and procedures), it is important that academic faculty and librarians alike do not duplicate each other's efforts and order the same titles over and over again. For example, if bibliographers are covering academic titles in, say, English literature from *Book Publishing Record* (BPR), *British National Bibliography* (BNB), LC proof slips, or whatever, then the English Department in particular and all other relevant departments should be aware of this fact and should submit requests for current titles in English literature *only* if added copies are desired and necessary (in II.9.A.1. a useful form concerned with this problem is illustrated).

3.

Possible approaches to the acquisition of retrospective, non-current imprints are varied and numerous. In general, such imprints can be divided into two groups: titles that are *almost certainly available* and titles *not certainly available*. Titles with a fairly certain degree of availability are: those listed in the most recent issues of national in-print checklists, such as *Libros en Venta* (LEV), *Books in Print* (BIP), *Verzeichnis Lieferbarer Bücher* (VLB), *British Books in Print* (BBIP), and so forth; *or* they are those published within the last *three* years (allow four years for European titles not in such checklists, except Russian, and six years for academic titles not found in an in-print tool, such titles being referred to as "non-trade" publications); *or* they are those reprinted and listed in an in-print guide, a reprint guide, or a reprint firm's catalog. These retrospective but still apparently in-print or reprinted titles have to be ordered individually from appropriate dealers and obviously cannot be acquired by the acquisitions procedures discussed in 2., above (for o.p. rules, see also II.2.A.3.B.(2), #25).

The reprinting and reproducing of out-of-print books and serials, by a variety of methods, have made it possible for the librarian who utilizes these resources today to make purchases of items he could never have hoped to acquire in the relatively recent past. Here I only mention a couple of the many reprint tools; but certainly such titles as Ostwald's *Nachdruckverzeichnis. . . ,* (which aims at a worldwide listing of reprints and is up to at least 1967 at present) and the serial *Guide to Reprints* should be on everyone's desk, along with the catalogs and listings of all reprint firms in the U.S. and elsewhere (we should all, however, *be aware* that in a number of instances reprint titles are announced and listed but *not* reprinted because of insufficient indication of library interest). Any novice bibliographer or acquisitions librarian should make it a point to *visit and examine* the reference and bibliographical holdings of a large Acquisitions department. A conversation about the nature and use of reprint guides with some experienced acquisitions librarian in such a department will be worth a great many written words.

Methods of reproduction of out-of-print materials other than by book format are varied. An acquisitions librarian will certainly subscribe to such serials as *Guides to Microforms in Print* and *Microcosm* in order to keep abreast of titles in various formats in current and planned projects. Almost any novice will be aware of microfilm, microcards, microfiche, mini-print, and the various machines and aids necessary for the use of each. Winchell (now up to date as Sheehy, *Guide to Reference Books,* 1976, the current convenient replacement of the basic Winchell and its three supplements) is always the handy guide to reference works detailing monographs and serials reproduced in these various forms. Photoreproduction is a possible resource when a copy of a single o.p. title is needed. However, the library itself must clear titles still in copyright, and must then either do its own work from a book in hand or send a letter of clearance and the book to some company specializing in photoreproductive work; thus, this approach is very limited (see also II.2.A.6.E.).

Out-of-print, antiquarian titles that have not been reprinted may be acquired in several ways: by purchasing collections, by advertising desiderata in book-trade media, by asking appropriate dealers to search for materials, and by selecting from the lists of titles offered in the antiquarian catalogs of various and sundry booksellers. At this writing, something of a seller's market still exists in the antiquarian trade after the slow years of the thirties, forties, and early fifties, despite the tightening budgets of the present. This situation, which may change in the future, means that it takes an active policy of acquisitions and of cultivation of dealers to turn up good collections and individual books. If a dealer has a *good* collection at a fair price or a single desirable title, there will be several institutions with which he can place it; and he will first approach those whose needs he knows and with whom he is on good terms. Many dealers will, in fact, approach a particular person in Acquisitions with whom they have rapport. One person in Acquisitions may very well *be* the entire library so far as an antiquarian dealer is concerned; and this is the person to whom the dealer will direct offers of material (see II.11.C. for more about the antiquarian, the o.p., trade).

Collections, and booksellers who specialize in putting them together, can be found in almost any part of the United States. But a good deal of the o.p. book trade is located in the vicinity of New York City. Good will and buying trips to New York and surrounding areas to become acquainted with dealers specializing in antiquarian material should always be a part of any acquisitions program aiming at serious retrospective collection development. Almost all dealers who work with college, university, and research libraries have specialties; and acquisitions librarians must be familiar with a number of such dealers in order to know whom to ask for what. Directories of book dealers can be helpful in this matter, despite the fact that dealers come and go with the years; and any antiquarian bookseller or acquisitions professional can guide the neophyte to the most current national and international listings (for example, *Book Dealers in North America,* known familiarly as "Sheppard's" and published every couple of years by that firm; Sheppard also publishes *Dealers in Books in the British Isles*; and so on).

Some libraries also send acquisitions and bibliographic personnel abroad to familiarize themselves with overseas dealers, their establishments, their services, and the scope of their holdings in the materials with which they work. Properly pursued, purchasing abroad can sometimes be even more rewarding then purchasing in the United States. In fact, to develop programs of acquisitions in some countries, those not geared to Western European or North American concepts of service, such visits are almost a necessity. I do not believe that academic faculty are greatly to be relied upon for purchasing abroad, since scholars are sometimes startlingly uninformed about the book trade and even about the holdings and the development programs of their own libraries. Further, such scholars understandably lack a knowledge of acquisitions procedures, and can cause great confusion throughout the library when they try to relay information and materials from overseas.

Buying collections is obviously more feasible for smaller libraries than for those with larger holdings: for if over 20 percent of a collection duplicates a library's, purchase is not economically feasible unless duplicates can be turned to profit by their sale to a dealer or by exchanges with or sales to another library. Such trades or sales are tricky and time-consuming propositions. Sometimes, however, it has proven feasible for certain groups of libraries to buy collections in cooperation with one another and to distribute the titles acquired where they are needed and do not cause problems of duplication of holdings. As only two examples of such cooperative projects, the University of California library system was able to purchase the 100,000-volume Ogden Library and the 50,000-volume Isaac Foot Library, and was able to distribute them among the various participating libraries of the university.

Advertising for individual o.p. titles is an acquisitions technique pursued by some libraries, although an expensive one in staff time and, thus, in these times of diminishing personnel, perhaps something of a luxury. After all, to prepare lists for a dealer to place in *The Library Bookseller* or the *Antiquarian Bookman* (both of which will take lists directly from libraries themselves) requires setting up particular routines and having sufficient personnel to handle them: someone must select titles to be advertised; someone must type lists of these titles in an orderly format; someone must set up standards for accepting or rejecting offers of titles advertised; someone must apply these standards to each title offered; and so on. Other libraries prefer to ask dealers with whom they work in other aspects of collection development to search for o.p. titles, and they do not advertise in journals at all. Whether or not he uses its advertising services, any acquisitions librarian worth his salt will read every issue of *Antiquarian Bookman* with attention (I myself feel this way about the *Book Collector* as well, but this is perhaps too fine a point).

However they are organized, search routines for o.p. titles must be governed by several considerations: (1) only items that someone seriously wants should be searched for; (2) probability of success must be an important factor in determining whether or not to search; (3) requests for searches must go to the proper dealer and be given to him exclusively for a specified period of time; (4) unsuccessful searches must be terminated at some point in time because it is both senseless and extravagant to pursue any particular title forever; and (5) *no* title that is going to be very expensive if searched for and found should be placed with a dealer *unless* Acquisitions definitely plans to purchase that title when it is located and offered. This last consideration is important; for to place a search with a reliable and conscientious dealer and to refuse it as too expensive, when located and offered, is a very bad business indeed. More than one acquisitions librarian who should have known better has greatly vitiated a dealer relationship by such a tactic. The usual antiquarian directories are of some assistance in determining what dealers to use for searches. But the proper dealer for particular searches is often determined by a long process of trial and error, and the final decision about which dealers to use for what is really a bit of departmental lore, passed along from one librarian to another. In essence, what works is best; it is a fact that some search dealers will work very well for one library and not for another.

Selection from antiquarian/o.p. catalogs for the acquisitions of retrospective materials is, I think, the most interesting and pleasurable of collection development activities. And many famous collections in both private hands and educational institutions have been developed by this pursuit. Irrespective of the degree to which he is himself engaged in selection (and some degree is almost inevitable), I take it simply as fact that any acquisitions librarian worthy of the profession will study such catalogs as part of his daily routine and will be familiar with a wide range of the dealers who issue these keys to the world of books (see II.11. for more about the book trade). Such catalogs and the routines for working with them form a part of the workload of any active department; so whether or not he generates requests from them himself, the acquisitions librarian must understand these catalogs as a particular kind of resource for retrospective collection development.

Three rules may be given for the proper handlings of antiquarian catalogs. The *first rule* is that the catalog must be recent. Catalogs of any interest at all have few, if any, desirable items left much longer than *two weeks* after their first mailing; and professional and clerical time used in selecting and ordering from catalogs that are not pretty much "hot off the press" (for example, catalogs sent from overseas by surface mail) is usually spent almost entirely in vain. "Advance" and airmail copies from dealers are, thus, most desirable; and such copies are sent *only* to the acquisitions librarian who dealers know will act promptly.

The *second rule* is that antiquarian catalogs which qualify under the first rule must be acted upon promptly—promptness is essential in selection, in the holdings checks in the MCC (main card catalog; public catalog) to eliminate duplication, and in orders for desired titles being placed by airmail, cable, or phone. Obviously, if a catalog of recent issue goes to Professor X and sits on his desk for a month, it then fails to qualify under rule one, and there is no point in processing it by rule two. Thus, a record should be kept of the date when a catalog is referred to a selector; and it should be hand delivered, not mailed, to the selector, and recalled after a few days (see II.9.5. for two forms to spell out and control selection from antiquarian catalogs).

The *third rule* is that the quantity of items selected must be weighed against the factor of time required to process such a quantity. In other words, if a selector marks so many items that a monumental holdings check is required (for which there may or may not be immediate staff time), the whole element of promptness is lost and few titles will be acquired as a result. For this reason, limiting selectors to marking, say, no more than twenty-five titles in a catalog seems advisable (with the usual allowance for occasional exceptions), *unless* selectors can themselves provide prompt and *experienced* personnel time for extensive holdings checks.

B. SERIALS

Serials are open-ended publications, intended to be issued from some beginning point in time and indefinitely into the future. Some regularity is implied in the term "serial," but *regularity of issue* (daily, weekly, monthly, quarterly, etc.) *is not an essential characteristic in the* definition of a serial. "Serial" is, then, the all-inclusive term for the kind of open-ended publication about which we are speaking. But some librarians, who should know better, persist in juggling the term "periodical" with that of "serial." The term "periodical" contains a definite emphasis on regularity of issue; but "serial" is much to be preferred for clarity and precision: for example, periodicals, magazines, literary journals, little magazines, scholarly journals, newspapers, monographs in series, and so forth *are all* serials, with varying degrees of frequency and regularity of appearance and varying kinds of audiences, from cinema buffs to Nobel physicists. If it gets over the basic concept of the serial as a publication intended to be continued indefinitely into the future, this text will not have been in vain. *Monographs in series,* for example, tend to be issued irregularly (sometimes almost eccentrically), but are nonetheless serials. I emphasize monographs in series here because they form a significant portion of the serials subscription load carried by research libraries and *must* be understood *as serials.*

1.

Like monographs, serials lend themselves to either current or retrospective acquisitions approaches. But any new subscription (order) placed for a current serial publication is very much unlike an order placed for a monograph—a subscription is for a title intended to continue indefinitely, whereas an order for a monograph is a one-shot, single transaction. Similarly, orders for sets, no matter how monumental or how long before the final volume appears, are for titles with some expected terminal point of publication. It is important to note further that a number of current serials have a long history of publication (often with title changes over a period of time), and that the acquisition of a current serial may involve not only the work of placing a subscription, but also decision making about acquiring the previously published backfiles of the serial and the retrospective acquisitions procedures necessary to do so.

The bibliographies and guides used in serials selection and verification differ somewhat from those used for monographs; but it is really the problems of *cost* and *control* that have led to the Serials Section as a work station to deal with serials materials. The initial cost of a serial subscription is only the tip of the iceberg, so to speak; for an initially inexpensive current subscription can involve large sums of money as the years roll by. Serials also have, as we know, built-in costs of binding and binding procedures far beyond such costs for monographs and sets. The decision to place a subscription for a current serial is, thus, not one to be taken lightly; it is to be weighed carefully in relation to demonstrable academic need, the present and planned program of academic development in the university, and the budget available and projected for the acquisitions of new titles and the sustaining of present and future costs for subscriptions already in effect.

Current subscriptions are placed with agencies which specialize in handling them, since no Acquisitions department of any size has the staff or time to control the logistics involved in placing serial orders individually with individual publishing bodies. Such subscription agents will provide various services—placing orders, grouping bills so that they can be paid at a convenient time (usually on an annual basis at the beginning of the library's new fiscal year), checking on and supplying missing issues, etc. These services predictably cost money and vary in efficiency, facts to consider in selecting serials agents. There are a number of large and reliable firms acting as serials subscription services, and any serials librarian can indoctrinate a neophyte in the merits of each and the services they provide. Approval-plan agents/ dealers usually expect, it should be noted, to handle the subscriptions for new serial titles as they appear in their assigned areas of coverage.

Agents of one kind or another, therefore, control the extra-library logistics of subscriptions as a paid service. Within Acquisitions itself, the control for serials (really a record control for the ordering and receiving of titles) is largely in the Kardex. The Kardex is simply a series of cabinets in which (on cards in large numbers of pull-out trays) the subscription record and the receiving record of all issues of all serials subscribed to are recorded under the established entry for each title (usually LC). Kardex control may be summarized by the questions which the personnel working with it can answer: Has a subscription been placed, and if so when? When might the first issue of a new subscription be expected? When can the next issue of any particular serial be expected to arrive? What is the present and the anticipated cost in the future of a subscription to a particular serial? Where in the library are the issues of a particular serial title located?

2.

Retrospective serials (serials backfiles) have, like monographs, antiquarian/o.p. dealers specializing in their acquisitions. Serials are not, however, treated by the in-print guides available for monographs; so the serials librarian would approach the acquisition of a backfile in several ways. He might, first, approach the publishing body of a current serial to see if it has, as sometimes happens, retained backfiles for sale. If this approach does not work, he will then check reprint guides and reprinters' catalogs to see if the backfile desired has been reprinted. If the reprinted backfile seems expensive or if the backfile seems not to have been reprinted, the serials librarian will next contact the dealers specializing in retrospective serials: there are a number of such dealers in the United States and elsewhere, some of them very large and highly efficient firms (any competent serials acquisitions librarian in a large Acquisitions department will know about these firms, their merits and deficiencies, and the nature of their services). By means of the *three* sequences of action enumerated above, the serials librarian can determine whether or not a backfile is available at all and, if available, in what format(s) and at what price(s). He can always, of course, put the search routines we have discussed in relation to monographs into operation for a serial backfile that is not immediately available.

Sometimes, both a reprint of a serial backfile and a backfile from an o.p. dealer will be available. There is then the process of weighing the reprint price against the price for the backfile, in which the possible binding costs and the condition of the backfile must be considered. Cost is a consideration in all such comparative instances, just as cost is an important overall factor in serials operations in general. Certainly, fairness of price asked must also be weighed in considering any backfile purchase, whether or not there is only one option for its acquisition. Because serials librarians place far fewer orders for current titles or retrospective materials than those placed for monographs by the separates librarian (as a rough comparative ratio, we could estimate fifty or more orders for monographs to each order for a serials subscription or backfile, depending of course upon budgetary allocations within given institutions), the serials librarian has more time to consider cost and need for each acquisition.

I.6

PROCESSING: BUYING (ORDERING) AND PAYING (RECEIVING) ROUTINES, WITH A SKETCH OF A DAY'S WORK IN ACQUISITIONS

A.

Processing requests for particular titles, as we all pretty much understand now, may simply be defined as *buying* and *paying for a book* or serial. *Buying* a title requires several steps: (1) a *holdings check* to see if the library already possesses a requested title, where a title already in the library is located, and, given all considerations, whether or not a duplicate or multiple copy may be desired; (2) *verifying* the title (precataloging by LC searching, machine searching, or other bibliographical searching) to determine whether or not it has been cataloged by the Library of Congress, by another library listed in the NUC *(National Union Catalog),* by another library contributing to a data bank to which there is access by terminal, or (failing the preceding) by some non-U.S. national library; (3) *ordering* the desired title from the appropriate dealer (this step is not necessary for approval-plan titles, which are acquired as explained in I.5.A.2. and in II.6); and (4) *filing MOF slips* (multiple-order-form slips) to record an order so that it will not be duplicated unintentionally and so that funds for an ordered title can be encumbered by the bookkeeper. The buying function for monographs is largely the responsibility of the head or chief of the Separates section, just as buying serials is the responsibility of the head of Serials acquisitions.

Paying for a title likewise has several steps: (1) it must be received in the mailroom and sent from there to be received in the Order section or the Serials section; (2) *MOF slips* comprising the order record must be *retrieved*; (3) the *title* must be checked to be sure that what has come in is what was ordered (the proper book, the proper edition of the book, and so forth); (4) the number of *pages and volumes* of monographs and pages of issues and volumes (and number of volumes) of serials must be *checked* for correctness and completeness (*collated*); (5) the title and its price must be put on an invoice or a bills list, and that *invoice* must be *paid* and funds spent must be *recorded* properly by the bookkeeper; and (6) the *title* must be *forwarded* to the Monographs or Serials sections of the Catalog department, accompanied by work slips from the MOF and the form of the original request (request card, LC proof slip, etc.) *containing all appropriate bibliographical information* turned up by the holdings check, LC searching, computer searching, or any other bibliographical searching routines that may have been used. The paying function for monographs is largely the responsibility of the head of the Order section, just as paying for serials is the responsibility of the head of Serials acquisitions.

Because the acquisitions of serials has some particular techniques and problems inherent in the nature of the species, such materials are, as we now know, usually dealt with by a separate Serials section within Acquisitions. In fact, everyone in an Acquisitions department must clearly understand the nature of serials and serials work if confusion is to be avoided and serials kept under proper bibliographical and logistical control, just as everyone must understand the Kardex and its function of serials control (see I.5.B. for definition and statement about these serials subjects). Kardex control and Serials section procedures free the Separates section to deal with the multitudes of monographs and "short" sets which pour into any active Acquisitions department, and can only be controlled by rather technical and time-consuming sequences of filing slips, pulling slips, and recording expenditures in a rational and planned manner (computers will, hopefully, one day do away with the need for human hands for these sequences). If everyone in Acquisitions understands the nature of monographs, sets, and serials, then monographs going astray in the Serials section and serials wandering somehow into the Separates section can be detected and redirected into the proper channels and routines.

B.

A sketch of the day's work of a head of Separates (chief bibliographer, etc.) may at this point provide a brief summary of subjects treated in this and previous chapters of this text. It should be emphasized that the head of Separates will be mostly concerned with the *buying routines for monographs*, mentioned in A., above (and in more detail in II.2.). Monographic *paying* routines are those of the Order section in large part and have been mentioned in A., above (and are considered in more detail in II.3.). The Serials section, as we know, both buys and pays for its own materials.

The head of Separates, who may also be known as chief or head bibliographer (he could conceivably double as the head of Acquisitions), can perhaps be described as one who lives in a world of budgetary figures, with a plethora of curiously mingled mail, innumerable fund numbers, hosts of the bibliographies and booktrade guides necessary in the verification of United States and foreign titles, and with ceaseless streams of three-by-five-inch request cards and LC proof slips. He will also have to solve order and receiving problems and oversee whatever approval plans are in force. He will have, or should have, a substantial number of people working for him.

If the Order section is large enough to require a professional, the chief or head of Separates may not have to get deeply involved in its routines; but he will have to know a good deal about them in order to solve the problems that arise constantly, and he will normally have the final administrative responsibility for the Order section (see Chart in I.3.B.). He will also have to juggle work assignments and see that everything gets done properly and that the constant flow of paper and books into and out of his area of responsibility goes as smoothly as possible. Further, he will have to train bibliographic assistants (also called checkers, searchers, etc.); keep track of sick days, holidays, and other minutiae of work schedules; and deal with the bibliographical and book trade detail associated with requests for current and retrospective titles.

Many of these responsibilities and duties are considered in much more detail in the how-to-do-it chapters in Part Two of this text. Some mention here, however, of some of the activities of head or chief of Separates on a given day may bring his functions a bit more to life. He will usually start by opening his mail, which will include quantities of flyers and brochures announcing new books, serials, and reprints; antiquarian catalogs from various dealers; and letters related to problems with orders, or letters offering materials, and so forth *ad infinitum.* Announcements of new and forthcoming titles may be forwarded to other librarians or academic faculty, although a great many such flyers are discarded after a glance; antiquarian catalogs, if recent and if in the mainstream of on-going collection development programs, may also be forwarded. There will be some letter writing as well, since letters generate letters.

As the chief (head of Separates) attempts to deal with his incoming and outgoing mail, the mailroom personnel, of which there should be at least three in sizable operations, will be opening packages, cartons, and boxes of monographs, sets, and serials; matching received titles with order invoices; placing each group of titles listed on a particular invoice on book trucks by invoice arrangement, with the invoice folded neatly into the first book listed on it; and wheeling tidy arrangements of monographs into the Order section of Separates and tidy arrangements of serials to the Kardex, where the recording personnel will take over. The receiving, staging, and expediting procedures of the mailroom are vital to orderly accessioning of materials; and its personnel should be intelligent and carefully and correctly trained, probably by the chief bibliographer or the head of Acquisitions with some assistance from the serials librarian. Administrators commonly underestimate and underpay mailroom personnel—an economy that can in the long run cost a great deal of money in wasted time and much unnecessary confusion.

Once his own mail has been disposed of, the chief will begin to plan bibliographic checking procedures for the day. Since he has an elaborate chart before him on his desk—a chart presenting a detailed picture of monies spent to date—he will "batch" requests with an eye to spending the various funds in the various budgets in his charge in a balanced manner from month to month. Ideally, all requests should be processed as soon as they come in (*rush* requests are almost always expedited; but these should be few in number and only marked "rush" in cases of demonstrable and immediate need); but in actual fact, the volume of incoming requests, amount of staff time available, and funds remaining for acquisitions in particular budgets— all affect the time at which any group of requests can or should be processed.

Any experienced chief will know at a glance about what percent of any particular group of requests will already be in the library; so he will give his bibliographic assistants quite a few more requests than he expects them to verify, knowing that the holdings check will show a number of unwitting requests for duplicates. Such a duplicate is noted as a "lib has" and is returned by the chief to the requestor to inform him that the title he has ordered is already in the library. At this time the chief will also return handwritten requests (as he does any kinds of handwritten lists) and will ask selectors to provide typed information on individual request cards. He will also return, for further information, requests that are unclear, incomplete, or erroneous. And it is very important that he return all requests (with the possible exception of those for "rushes") for titles that will come in as a matter of course on approval plans, along with a form explaining specifically any approval plans so that future requests that would only duplicate titles coming in on such plans may be averted. As a matter of fact, titles that arrive from approval plans are usually already cataloged and on the shelves before Professor X gets around to ordering them (see II.9. for several samples of forms to explain why a request is being returned to the sender).

The chief will know that bibliographic checkers/assistants can usually be expected to verify (pre-catalog, search) some twenty to thirty requests in a four-hour period, in addition to discovering "lib has" (duplicate) requests that turn up (see II.7., where these figures are worked out). When a bibliographic assistant's day is over (a four-hour stint of checking is about all any assistant can efficiently survive), he turns in his verified and "lib has" requests (in neat groups, with titles not in the library again subdivided by particular fund and by main entry alphabetically within fund group and "lib has" and problem requests in other groups), and he exits into the outside world. His boss, the chief, then reviews verified requests for accuracy;

those that are o.k. go to the typing pool to have MOF's typed, are batched by names of dealers, and sent out at day's end. Work that is not o.k. is put into the checker's tray to be reviewed and corrected the next day.

Apparently "lib has" requests are also reviewed to be sure that they truly represent requests that will duplicate library holdings and are *not* from departments outside the main library desiring an added copy for their own research holdings, in addition to copies located elsewhere. Then too, verified non-duplicate requests may turn out to be o.p. and not reprinted, according to the appropriate books-in-print tools for various countries and the reprint guides which are routinely consulted by bibliographic checkers. Such apparently o.p. titles will be returned to the requestor to see if he wishes any particular o.p. title placed on search with a dealer. The chief will know, however, that certain titles which do not normally appear in guides to in-print titles are probably in fact still available, and he will try certain dealers or the issuing bodies of such publications before proceeding to o.p. routines.

If a library possesses a bibliographical corps or another group of subject specialist selectors, say from Reference, the chief himself may not do much selection from antiquarian catalogs (discussed in I.5.A.); but he will be responsible always for seeing to it that antiquarian and o.p. selections from these catalogs are sent out promptly. Keeping track of expenditures and budgetary funds is as much a part of his work with approval plans as it is with antiquarian and current requests generated outside these plans. And he must further monitor approval plans to be sure that titles acquired from them conform to the selection guidelines to which the various approval-plan agents have agreed, that library subject specialists and faculty survey new approval-plan arrivals promptly, and that the last approval-plan arrivals leave the shelves of Acquisitions and go on to Cataloging before another new group of approval titles comes in.

Further time will be spent in liaison work with the Catalog department, making sure that catalogers receive all proper precataloging records of, and understand what bibliographical work has been done in Acquisitions with, every book processed through Acquisitions. Other time will be spent, usually in a pleasant manner, with dealers who have something to sell, ranging from items and services that amount to only a few dollars to those involving very large sums of money. And attention must always be paid to other librarians and academic faculty who rightly or wrongly believe that their needs, wants, and requests are not being attended to properly. I would observe as well that even if Acquisitions is not heavily concerned with selection for collection development, it still ought to have at least one "bookman" subject specialist to deal with the numbers of problems that demand his kind of knowledge about o.p., antiquarian materials. Such a specialist would also be useful as a translator and intermediary between the special collections librarian and other professionals with whom the special collections librarian might attempt to communicate.

Finally, the chief, like any other section or department head or librarian involved in procedures where numbers of tasks performed or amounts of money are concerned, *must* keep daily written records for the specific purposes of (1) constructing manuals to guide all of his personnel, (2) justifying his requests for staff and supplies, and (3) writing his annual report which all heads of sections and departments must prepare, and the more figures in this report the better (see II.7.B.4. for a suggested format of the annual report).

Before leaving the subjects of this chapter, I must stress that the sketch above in no way pretends to describe in full the techniques and activities of a day's work in Acquisitions or the kinds of problems, and their attempted solution, that can take a good deal of thought and energy. Part Two deals with a number of acquisitions techniques in some detail and more than merely suggests the routines of acquisitions. But I hope that a reader will by now at least have *some* feel for what Acquisitions is about.

I.7

HARDWARE; AND COOPERATIVE ACQUISITIONS: TWO COMMENTARIES

A.

Only a few years past, the history of attempts to automate library technical services and public records was a dreary one. In the mid-seventies, however, several successful automated programs emerged from the stresses and strains and enormous expenditures of the trial period. We need not here be concerned with machine or computer controlled records for such public services as Circulation, which lend themselves to mechanical or computerized operations of varying degrees of cost. But we must realize that machine systems will materially affect the activities of any Acquisitions and Cataloging departments that go into them. Overall, we should attempt to take a positive attitude toward advancements in technology and reflect that any librarian whose activities can be satisfactorily replaced by a machine has demonstrably not been doing work of much professional consequence.[3]

If acquisitions requests can be put into a computer terminal for a holdings check, much time over that required for a manual check of the MCC (main card catalog; PC, public catalog) will be saved. If the O.O. (orders-out, on order) file can be checked as well by computer terminal—as it can be, to cite only one example, in the Stanford Ballots system—a very considerable time gain is possible. In addition to such time gains when these facilities are available, verification (precataloging, searching) routines are obviously implemented if acquisitions personnel has access to a large body of computerized bibliographical and cataloging information. For example, if a requested title is found already cataloged in the OCLC (Ohio College Library Center) data bank, it is easy enough to punch in a request for a set of catalog cards for that title, and the set will be forthcoming shortly. If a title is not found in a machine search of such a data bank, the title can be punched into the bank from LC or NUC entry sources, and sets of cards can *then* be requested. Original cataloging can as well be punched into a data bank and card sets can be requested and run off in the same way.

As of this writing, the OCLC computer-shared cataloging system is the largest in the country, with over 100 libraries participating, and still growing; and there are occasional independent systems, such as the rather sophisticated Ballots at Stanford. But for a library starting into computer technology from scratch, OCLC probably offers the easiest way to begin, upon the commitment of the necessary funds. Its file at present contains about one million entries, roughly half from LC (the MARC records comprising "all" English-language monographs and sets—not serials—cataloged by the Library of Congress since 1967) and half from the various participating libraries. Obviously, with such a large number of contributing libraries, OCLC data banks of bibliographical and cataloging information will grow considerably larger in time and increase proportionately in usefulness. Serials cataloging information and serials control (receiving records, claiming missing issues, and so on) are said to be in the works at present, as is a fiscal record system.

Some libraries may not need computer resources for acquiring and cataloging; but all can profit from a detailed computer listing (printout) of weekly or monthly acquisitions expenditures *if* the library does not already have a system that works economically and satisfactorily. Any fiscal-record system should show: (1) the initial annual amount of the budget for any discipline given funds, with the amount of money encumbered from the previous year deducted (encumbered funds are those from which books have been ordered but not yet formally paid for by invoice); (2) a progressive picture from week to week or month to month of the amount of monies spent and encumbered; and (3) the percentage of funds and amount of funds remaining—that is, funds neither encumbered nor spent—on the same weekly or monthly basis. I emphasize budget control figures, however produced, because some libraries do not have entirely satisfactory methods for presenting, on a regular basis during the fiscal year, a clear financial picture of the state of the funds for any given discipline. Such a shortcoming is incompatible with rational and fair programs of collection development, which presuppose a budget fairly arrived at for all disciplines (see I.4. and II.7.) and a budget under firm control.

The ideal merits of machine procedures are, thus, clear. But we should note that whenever a computer terminal enters into acquisitions operations, a whole new work-flow procedure will have to be set up to take the machine procedure into account; and a procedural manual will have to be worked out for processing titles through the terminal. Titles not appearing in computer files will, of course, still have to be searched manually. Moreover, when Library A discovers that Library B has contributed cataloging information for a particular title to a shared system, considerable professional work in cataloging—adjusting classifications, descriptions, and so forth—may still be necessary in Library A before that particular title can be processed onto its shelves. The costs of expert time for such adjustments of cataloging information in shared systems should not be underestimated.

On the other hand, the record keeping of acquisitions expenditures (see II.7.) seems to me to be a definite and positive plus for machine operation. Of course, any technology is all to the good if it can alleviate the chores of serials paying and claiming along with alleviating the routines, for all titles, of pulling apart MOF's, filing MOF's, retrieving MOF's, keeping permanent fund-slip files, etc. The alleviation of such manual chores and routines by the use of machines presumably lies in the near future.

Finally, a less positive aspect of the hardware question is that cost-accounting comparisons between what it costs to acquire and process X number of books annually in a totally manual acquisitions system, and what it costs in that *same* system to acquire and process the *same* X number of books annually (allowing for increases in the prices of materials, staff salaries, machine rentals, etc.) after that system has been computerized, seem to be peculiarly difficult to come by. Any annual report will give costs for monographs and serials and staffing in Acquisitions. But salaries for hardware personnel and machine costs have a tendency to show up on budgets other than those for the library, and sometimes in a vague manner. Hardware personnel salaries and machine costs (rental, repair, supplies, etc.) are, moreover, substantial; and not to relate these expenses directly to the costs of library operations is really not playing the game fairly. Furthermore, costs for machine systems are not flexible. Once an institution gets locked into such a system, it is generally at the mercy of whatever cost increases will inevitably appear in that system. One may fire, perhaps rehire, clerical or professional software; hardware does not lend itself to quick responses to budgetary fluctuations.

Hardware people (software) sell their product so hard that they sometimes influence traditionalists to strike unduly negative stances. I think we may conclude, however, that if anyone argues the better-service concept of hardware, he seems usually to stand upon firm ground. If he argues the money-saving capacity, or the economy of hardware, his footing seems less sure.

B.

Cooperative acquisitions is at present the subject of much professional conversation and literature and the object of increasing professional activity. For our purposes here, I think we can arbitrarily distinguish the *theory* from the *facts* of cooperative acquisitions. The *theory* is that several libraries will agree to form a single unit to acquire titles costing more than a particular, agreed-upon amount of money or concerned with a particular subject, and that only one member of this unit will then acquire any title coming within this cost-subject definition—the acquiring member at the same time assuming responsibility for giving whatever access to that title is deemed appropriate by standards fixed by all libraries in the unit. The *facts* of cooperative acquisitions are the procedures required to convert theory into reality and the *cost* of these procedures, and the *usefulness* of their end result. The *purpose* of cooperative acquisitions is to save money in these times of spiraling costs of library materials.

How well the facts of cooperative acquisitions relate to theory and the achievement of purpose can become entangled in philosophy and controversy. Let us here, then, simply set up a couple of greatly simplified *hypothetical* situations and, by observing some of their procedures, see if we can draw any conclusions about cost and usefulness.

1.

In a metropolitan area with excellent public transportation, a group of college and research libraries of varying size decide to go into a cooperative acquisitions program. A number of meetings are held to establish the framework of the program. Logistics indicate that more money will be required to initiate the program than the group can generate; so public monies, state and federal, are sought and duly obtained. After the organizational structure has been set up, the group must agree upon guidelines for specific materials to be acquired, agree upon each individual title conforming to these guidelines when it is suggested for acquisition, agree in which particular institution each particular title will be located, and produce some kind of a public union list to describe and indicate the location of all titles thus acquired.

The fact is obviously that all of the procedures described above, including those required to get the program organized, will require a good deal of time from a good many librarians, who must spend time traveling to and from meetings, deciding upon particular acquisitions and locations for them (within a committee format that lends itself to time-consuming colloquy), reporting their activities to their own institutions in verbal and written form, and so forth. If one contemplates this time as money—and it *must* logically be so regarded—the cost of this travel and decision making is very high. Beyond this is the cost of compiling the union list—professional and clerical library time, commerical printing, publishing, binding time, etc. It may be argued that public monies will absorb this cost. But what if these monies cease?

The very substantial cost of this hypothetical program of cooperative acquisitions aside, what is its true usefulness? This question can be answered, perhaps, by another question—which can also serve to conclude our look at this program: would not *all* of the materials acquired by this procedure be of the greatest utility if, instead of being dispersed, they were concentrated in the largest library with the largest supplementary research resources?

2.

In a particular geographical area, several large academic libraries, separated from one another by a hundred or so miles, decide to band together to pool information about and provide mutual access to their substantial holdings. This is a most constructive occurrence, but one which will cost, not save, money. Can this group, then, save money by means of cooperative acquisitions?

Any answer to this question would have to consider the costs in time (as money) discussed above; the additional expenses for librarians traveling longer distances; and, much more importantly, the not inconsequential cost of transporting, over longer distances, users to cooperative materials or materials to users. It is also fairly certain that the individual academic faculties which use each of these cooperating libraries would strenuously object to not having those library materials significantly related to their researches directly on hand. Cooperative acquisitions would, in this event, be limited to materials of a peripheral nature and probably of low use.

3.

The facts of cost and usefulness are, we can see, important in thinking about cooperative acquisitions; and time costs for the services of librarians should certainly not be overlooked—at least not in the present day, when staffing needs for libraries are being looked at very closely by administrators. And, further, true costs for such programs should not be obscured by the presence of public monies, which may or may not be forthcoming in the future.

PART TWO
Specific Procedures (*How*)

II.1

HOW TO USE PART TWO

Part Two of this text is a sequence of "how-to" chapters. Any how-to-do-it approach has inherent in it a how-to-*use*-it approach as well. For example, the chapter on the "Checking Manual" not only aims at showing how to make such a manual, but also at providing a *use*-ful guide to the bibliographies, checking routines, and other procedures described therein. A number of the details and routines described in the various chapters of Part Two overlap, to some extent, the content in the more general approaches and descriptions of Part One. Experience teaches us, however, that almost nothing can be taken for granted as learned in acquisitions work if it is touched upon only once.

The Checking Manual is complete and somewhat detailed (it is actually a book within a book) in order to give considerable information not only about checking procedures, but about bibliographical and trade tools and special problems as well. I think that the "Order Procedures: Summary" (II.2.A.8.) *within* the Checking Manual (this "Summary" is really a pamphlet within a book within a book) should also be pointed out here as an important source of information—for the faculty, the university community, and nontechnical services librarians—about correct acquisitions procedures. Such a pamphlet, adapted to individual institutions and distributed within them, will save everyone in the faculty and in the library community a great deal of trouble by explaining how to order library materials correctly.

The Checking Manual itself may seem rather traditional in point of view and, perhaps, overly explicit. But I have found that it is usually better to give too much than too little in a text, and that information in such a manual can be useful to refer to when the memory for a particular procedure or the recollection of the nature of some bibliographical resource needs reinforcement. Further, I have seen a number of order procedure manuals, but relatively few checking manuals. And since checking routines in Acquisitions involve not only buying a title, but verifying (precataloging, searching) it to expedite processing in the Catalog department, I believe that the subject of bibliographic checking is very important indeed.

In the other chapters of Part Two, I have tried to include sufficient guidelines and information to enable a user to understand the subject in hand without becoming entangled in a web of detail. At the same time, I have tried to stay with practical suggestions and illustrations related to actual working situations in Acquisitions. Any reader may find both omissions and areas of disagreement; but I hope that everyone will find something of use.

Unfortunately, the subject of Acquisitions in our schools of librarianship seems all too often to fall into either an animated discussion of the practices and policies of the county public library (bestsellers and censorship) or into a most peculiar medley of theoretico-historico-philosophico-antiquarianism (with apologies to the shade of Jonathan Swift); and neither approach has more than tangential relevance to the actual practices and purposes of Acquisitions. How to master these practices and understand these purposes is, of course, the subject of our preceding and following text, which I hope will make clear several basic points about the nature of Acquisitions: it does not tolerate a casual approach; it requires a fairly good memory and some small aptitude for arithmetic; it demands a thorough mastery of a considerable amount of detail; and every day it necessitates a number of prompt and generally correct decisions. Acquisitions is hard work. There are many easier and less interesting vocations in the way of the world.

II.2

HOW TO MAKE A
COMPLETE *CHECKING MANUAL*

In the Checking Manual that follows after these introductory comments, my statements to the reader of this text are italicized, as they are here, to separate them from the text of the Manual itself (which is in regular type face). A checking (procedural) manual of some kind is essential for any kind of effective acquisitions operation. A manual should aim at (a) defining terms; (b) orienting a beginning librarian, bibliographer, or bibliographic checker in the uses of the basic tools of the trade; and (c) clarifying the procedures involved in the functions of buying and paying for the monographs and serials acquired for the library. If a manual is complete, it should serve both as a procedural guide and as a reference work for answers to questions and solutions to problems arising in the daily exercise of acquisitions routines.

Furthermore, all acquisitions personnel should be familiar with the manual and should have some exposure to the techniques applied in all sections of the Acquisitions department, so that everyone can proofread, and correct if necessary, request forms, bibliographic notations, typed MOF's (multiple order forms), etc. Any uninformed and merely mechanical performance of any acquisitions routine can lead to serious and repeated errors.

Such a manual is also, as a matter of practical fact, both a continuing examination device for training personnel and a weapon of self-defense. For example, if there is no formal typed or printed exposition of standard procedures, no administrator or supervisor can ever be exactly sure how far along his beginners are progressing or how much his more experienced staff has learned. Further, if a clerical or a professional employee cannot read and understand a properly constructed manual, he can be quickly detected and weeded out of Acquisitions, where he manifestly does not belong.

The manual as a device for self-defense simply prevents anyone from having to answer any particular question innumerable times. If the problem evoking the question is dealt with by the manual—and it certainly should be—the questioner can simply be referred to the manual by another question: "Have you read the manual?" Responses to this question would be (1) "No," to which the reply would be, "Then do so"; or (2) "Yes," to which the reply would be something such as, "Then you will remember that this subject is discussed in the section on 'Definitions of Terms,' which you had better review again."

This Checking Manual can be viewed similarly as a guide for any institution with personnel geared to perform the tasks and understand the procedures described. It can also be viewed as a resource which can be modified to almost any degree by any acquisitions librarian in almost any acquisitions operation. Occasional comments in this manual are intended to remind the reader that behind any Checking Manual is a real Acquisitions department; within some existing institution; with real, living human beings carrying out the various procedures and dealing with the various problems which are the day-to-day concerns of any Acquisitions department of any size.

Any manual will occasionally have to be modified or changed. It is best kept, therefore, in a press or clamp binder, so that title pages may be removed and inserted, and other sections changed as need be. Side tabs can be attached as easy guides to sections referred to frequently. Moreover, every bibliographic checker, as well as all other key personnel, should have a copy of the manual; and there should be extra copies around. Lack of sufficient manuals is all too common and professionally indefensible.

A Table of Contents listing the various sections of the Checking Manual follows below. Any manual should contain a treatment of the subjects enumerated in this Table of Contents, although orders of arrangement and expository approaches will vary. After the Table of Contents, there follows an exposition of the subjects of the different sections in the order listed. These sections use illustration and example to deal with various procedures and problems and solutions. Any acquisitions librarian will learn much about his trade, and remember it, by preparing a satisfactory manual geared to the needs of his particular institution.

CHECKING MANUAL: TABLE OF CONTENTS

A.1. INTRODUCTION

The primary function of the Acquisitions department is to purchase books, periodicals, and other library materials in support of the academic and research programs of the university. To this end, the routines and procedures outlined in the following pages have been developed to assist the department's staff to perform the book-buying function in a uniform and efficient manner. The following pages comprise, therefore, the basic operating manual of the Bibliographic section. As such, they should be consulted constantly for the answers to any questions arising out of acquisitions operations concerned with the purchasing of monographic library materials or with related activities. Problems not answered in the manual should be taken to the chief bibliographer. The organizational charts following this introduction (A.2.) will be of assistance in determining to which section of Acquisitions questions of particular kinds should be directed.

Since the manual is kept up to date, all bibliographic checkers should feel free to bring suggestions for revision or changes of established procedures to the chief bibliographer. Until changes are officially approved, however, the manual should be followed carefully by all checkers and other staff. All staff in Acquisitions are expected to be familiar not only with bibliographic checking, but as well with order procedures (see especially Section A.8.).

Questions concerning departmental problems outside the scope of this manual—about personnel rules, supplies, equipment, etc.—should also be directed to the chief bibliographer.

A.2. ORGANIZATIONAL CHARTS

The two charts that follow are somewhat different in nature. Both should be in a manual; but what I say here preceding the charts, which would need little explanation in the manual itself, is for the reader who may have to be able to draw up such structural summaries. Chart 1, the "Acquisitions Department Organization Chart," represents an outline of the various sections and chains of command in the Acquisitions department as a whole. Note that Chart 1 uses the terms "department" and "section," whereas Chart 2 uses "section" and "unit." Terminology varies from library to library (and I have varied it here for illustration), but should be consistent within each. Both charts have brief characterizing notes about duties of departments, sections, and units.

Chart 2, the "Separates Section: Table of Organization," represents the Separates (monographs) section only and shows rank of professional and clerical personnel (individual names should also be shown after rank in such a chart); the full-time staff (1.00); the part-time staff (.50 or less); and abbreviations for fund sources from which salaries are drawn (SR: regular staff budgeted for anticipated permanent positions; GA: general library assistance funds; and WS: work study funds).[4] *Total FTE (full-time employee or employment) will obviously vary as budgets increase or decrease and as special funds to purchase materials may come in from year to year. The job slots in Chart 2 are for a library system where professionals rank from L-1 to L-4 (note that there is only one professional in the Separates section) and for nonprofessionals who qualify as library assistants (LA) from LA-1 to LA-4. There is as well an STC, to indicate a clerical typing specialist, and a number of "St." slots to be filled by student assistance on a part-time basis.*

Any librarian in Acquisitions should be able to construct such charts and explain the functional interrelationships which they represent. All staffs are better oriented if they can see exactly where they fit and how. A chart such as 2 can be made with plastic tabs which take paper inserts and may, thus, be changed as the personnel and FTE allowances for various departments, sections, and units change.

1. ACQUISITIONS DEPARTMENT ORGANIZATION CHART

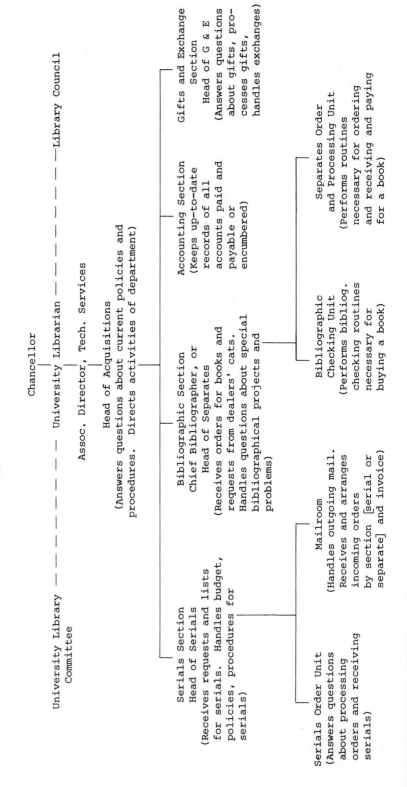

University Library — — — University Librarian — — — — — — — Library Council
Committee

Assoc. Director, Tech. Services

Head of Acquisitions
(Answers questions about current policies and
procedures. Directs activities of department)

Serials Section
Head of Serials
(Receives requests and lists
for serials. Handles budget,
policies, procedures for
serials)

Bibliographic Section
Chief Bibliographer, or
Head of Separates
(Receives orders for books and
requests from dealers' cats.
Handles questions about special
bibliographical projects and
problems)

Accounting Section
(Keeps up-to-date
records of all
accounts paid and
payable or
encumbered)

Gifts and Exchange
Section
Head of G & E
(Answers questions
about gifts, pro-
cesses gifts,
handles exchanges)

Serials Order Unit
(Answers questions
about processing
orders and receiving
serials)

Mailroom
(Handles outgoing mail.
Receives and arranges
incoming orders
by section [serial or
separate] and invoice)

Bibliographic
Checking Unit
(Performs bibliog.
checking routines
necessary for
buying a book)

Separates Order
and Processing Unit
(Performs routines
necessary for ordering
and receiving and paying
for a book)

2. SEPARATES SECTION: TABLE OF ORGANIZATION,
with personnel rank, name,
time, and fund slots indicated

SEPARATES SECTION

Head: L-3 (SR) 1.00

Standing Order Plan Unit

LA-1	.50 SR
St.	.25 WS
Total FTE	.75

Typing/Secretarial Pool

Assigns order numbers, types MOF's for Library requests for books and serials. Sorts and handles department's correspondence; supplies.

LA-1	1.00 SR
STC	1.00 SR
LA-1	.50 SR
LA-1	.50 SR
Total FTE	3.00

Separates Order & Receiving Unit

Screens all outgoing purchase orders for non-serial orders. Receives non-serial orders, etc.

LA-2	1.00 SR
LA-1	1.00 SR
LA-1	1.00 SR
ST.	.25 GA
ST.	.25 GA
ST.	.375 GA
ST.	.125 GA
ST.	.25 GA
ST.	.25 GA
Total FTE	4.50

Bibliographic Checking Unit

Verifies and checks against holdings all requests for monographic materials; prepares offers for orders; request quotations; searches, etc.

LA-4	1.00 SR
LA-2	.50 SR
LA-1	.50 SR
LA-1	.50 SR
LA-1	.50 SR
LA-1	.50 SR
LA-1	.50 SR
LA-1	.50 SR
LA-1	.50 WS
LA-1	.50 SR
St.	.50 SR
St.	.25 GA
Total FTE	6.25

A.3. DEFINITIONS OF TERMS: THE
REQUEST CARD AND SOME USEFUL NATIONAL
AND TRADE BIBLIOGRAPHIES

Several forms follow here. The first, A., represents the front of a simple *library request card. If such a card, which* has nothing on the back, will do the job, there is no point in manufacturing something more complex. The second form, B.1., represents the front of a detailed library request card. It is constructed by an Acquisitions department that expects all of its staff to know a good deal about technical services terminology and processing. For our purposes here, it is certainly useful as a tool to define terms with which experienced personnel should be familiar. The third form, C.1., represents the back of the same detailed library request card. Request cards, like MCC cards, are three-by-five-inch size; so these three forms are enlarged.*

In relation to C.1., it should be noted that anyone interested in Acquisitions should be well acquainted with the national and trade bibliographical tools listed thereon, even if library procedures of a particular institution do not require the frequent use of these tools. Neither the use of computer resources as backup nor the use of LC proof slips for current selection, with their built-in LC cataloging, will ever completely replace the use of bibliographies as instruments for verifying (precataloging) routines or original professional cataloging, particularly in research institutions engaged heavily in retrospective collection development.

I give some definitions related to the front of the detailed card in B.2. and some definitions related to its back in C.2. But I will leave it to the serious student or reader to familiarize himself in depth with the tools mentioned. Most of these should be mastered in reference courses in schools of librarianship. Any listing or description of bibliographical resources is, of course, subject to continual change and updating.

Please note in D., below, that the Acquisitions department which uses this manual also expects its bibliographic checkers, as well as its professionals, to understand and use the catalogs of national libraries and the national and trade bibliographies of the various countries (and languages) with whose materials the Acquisitions department is concerned. The instructions to checkers in D. spell out their bibliographic responsibilities.

A. SIMPLE CARD

LIBRARY ORDER REQUEST FORM

To: General Library	For: (name of departmental library, if any)
Date Requested:	Date Needed:
Author (surname first)	
Title & Edition	
Place, Publisher, & Date	
Series & Volume No.	
Bibliographical Source & Item No.	
Searching & Verification Record (for library use only)	Price per copy (use local currency)
	Number of copies (if more than one)
	Requested by: Phone No.

B.1. FRONT OF DETAILED REQUEST CARD

23 24 25	26	27	Call No. 16
_ UNV _NYP _OP			

ORDER NO.
30

Author (last name first) or periodical title
1

Date ordered
29

Title
2

Dealer
28

L.C. Card No. 20

17 18 19
_ AC _AV _DNC

Series
3

Destination
21

Place 4			Publisher 5	Date of Pub. 6
Edition 7	No. Vols. 8	No. Copies 9	List Price 10	Estimate 11

Reserve Books
Course _____   22

Secondhand Dealer 12	Catalog No.	Item No.

Semester

Fund (see Procedure Manual)
13

Recommended By
14

Authorized By
15

B.2. DEFINITIONS OF TERMS ON FRONT OF DETAILED CARD

The definitions which follow in this section are for the terms and abbreviations of terms appearing on the front of the library request card, B.1., above. The back of the card is represented in C.1., below, and definitions of terms on the back of the card follow in C.2. The *numbers* on the representations of the front and the back of the detailed request card *provide the key* to the definitions below, which generally follow the order in which a checker might encounter the terms, and what they define, in the process of the holdings check and verification. Procedural instructions, wherever particularly important, are added in some of the definitions.

1. "Author"

The author is the person or body chiefly responsible for the content of the book. When that responsibility is divided among three or fewer joint authors, the first author mentioned is the name used, although all joint authors should be noted after the title entry. If there are more than three authors or contributors, the collector or editor of the material may be considered the author, depending upon his importance in compiling the book.

The name of the author, whether personal or corporate, determines the filing of the information about the title. This name is called *the main entry,* except in serial publications which *usually* take the title as the main entry. However, serials published as particular organs of sponsoring bodies take the name of the sponsoring body as the main entry.

2. "Title"

The title is the particular name of any written work. It appears on the title page of the book, along with author and imprint (place, publisher, date of publiction). Serial publications, as noted under "author," above, often have only a title entry, which is, then, *the main entry* for the serial.

3. "Series" (and Series Note)

A *series* is a kind of serial issued as a number of separate monographs, which can stand alone as independent works but are usually related to one another by subject, issuing body, etc.; a series is issued in a successive number of volumes with a collective title and is planned to be continued indefinitely, like any serial. The two types of series of greatest importance are *monographic* and *publishers'* (which are explained in A.9., the section on serials, series, and sets).

The *series note* appears in parentheses in the "series" space on the card and gives the name of the series of which the title in the series is a part. It is important to observe that *both* the main entry and the series note must be checked in the MCC during the holdings check. If, during the process of verification, a bibliographer discovers that a title is a part of the series, he then makes a series note on the request card and *rechecks* the MCC under the series title.

4. "Place"

The place is the name of the town or city where a work was published. If the town or city is obscure, its state or country may occasionally be added for clarification. A gazetteer is available in the department. Place, publisher, and date of a publication comprise what we call the *imprint.*

5. "Publisher"

The publisher is the person, firm, or corporate body taking the financial responsibility for bringing the book to the purchasing public. If the publisher's full title is long, the checker need give his short title only, penciling out extraneous words.

6. "Date"

The date is the year in which the book is published or printed, as specified on the front of the title page. Sometimes a formal bibliographical resource will show the date of publication in brackets [ ], meaning that the date was taken from some place other than the front of the title page. An "open entry" on a date of publication (1918-   , as an example) indicates a publication begun in a particular year, but still continuing. Such a publication would be a monographic set or a current serial title.

7. "Edition" (Simplified Statement)

An edition is any one of the forms in which a literary text may be issued by an author or a subsequent editor. As each edition is issued it is required that several new plates be made for the printing press. A rerun of old plates only slightly revised is called a reprinting, or impression. A first edition is *not normally* recorded on a request card, *unless* it is required to point up a request for the first appearance of an important literary work. Editions subsequent to the first edition may be indicated by a number (2,3,4, etc.) or, in some instances, by the abbreviation "enlgd." or "rev." Reprints are to be so indicated by "repr." in the edition space of the request card and other special notations (which are illustrated in the sample cards at the end of "Order Procedures: Summary" in section A.8.).

8. "No. Vols."

This space is used only when two or more volumes are to be ordered; if a "1" has been recorded in this space, it should be penciled out. Sometimes the numerical format of a set differs from its physical format, in which case both formats should be recorded—for example, "14 vols. in 10."

9. "No. Copies"

The number-of-copies space is used *only* when more than one copy of a title is wanted; any recorded "1" should be penciled out. Any request for multiple copies should be called to the attention of the chief bibliographer. It is important to remember that under our system, it is not possible to request two or more copies for two or more *different* destinations on one, single request card; and a separate card must be made for each such destination of location in our libraries.

10. "List Price"

This is the cost of a title as confirmed in a dealer's catalog or in a current trade bibliography. Non-domestic titles will normally show the list price in the currency of the country where the title has been printed. The converted price in U.S. currency will appear in the "estimate" space. A price confirmed by a citation in a recent catalog or trade bibliography should have a *check* penciled over it to indicate such confirmation. If the price is *not* confirmed, it is placed in the "estimate" space. If a requestor has typed the price for an *in-print* title in the "list price" space, but the bibliographer does not confirm the price (see "Verification," A.5.B.), a *circle with an arrow* to the "estimate" space should be placed around the amount in the "list price" space.

11. "Estimate"

As noted under "list price," above, the price of the title will show as an estimate when the list price is not confirmed. Search titles are normally estimated at $15.00 *per volume,* unless common sense dictates a higher price.

12. "Secondhand Dealer, Catalog No., Item No."

This space is filled in when out-of-print titles are ordered from booksellers' lists or catalogs; the bibliographer should be certain that the "dealer" space (28) is filled in as well. If for any reason, a title from a catalog is ordered from a dealer other than the one listed in the "secondhand dealer" space, *all* information in this space should be penciled out.

13. "Fund"

The annual budget allocated for the purchase of monographs is divided into library and departmental funds (which are explained in some detail in the "Order Procedures: Summary" in A.8.). All bibliographers are expected to understand funding, and the differences among all kinds of library funds and cataloged and DNC (do not catalog) departmental funds.

14. "Recommended By"

The name of the requestor of the title should appear in this space.

15. "Authorized By"

The signature of the person responsible for the fund charged on a request card should appear in this space. The library representative of an Arts and Sciences department (A&S) should authorize all cards on his department's A&S funds; a departmental chairman must authorize all titles requested on his departmental funds (research or grant funds). Any A&S card requested on a discipline other than the one to which the person making the request belongs must be referred to the department which will have to buy the title. Such cards, as well as any others presenting funding problems, should be given promptly to the chief bibliographer. He may decide to purchase a dubiously funded title from general library funds at his disposal, since a degree of faculty good will enters into play here.[5]

16. "Call No."

The call number is a device (alphabetical in LC procedure, numerical in Dewey) composed of a classification number, according to subject, and an author number. The call number identifies each book uniquely by subject and, of course, determines each book's shelving location in the library. Each catalog card in the public catalog (the main card catalog) will have a call number on it—usually the Library of Congress alphabetical classification used in most research libraries like ours. The *shelf list,* a card catalog with titles in the library listed alphabetically by call number, is maintained in the Catalog department; since the shelf list gives the most detailed information about the library's holdings for any title, it should be consulted whenever more information than is available in the main card catalog is required.

   17. "AC"

This abbreviation stands for "added copy," and this space should be checked *in red* whenever an exact duplicate of a title already cataloged or on order for a *cataloged fund* is desired. All requests for AC's are reviewed by the chief bibliographer, since such requests are not approved automatically.

   18. "AV"

An "added volume" is one which fills in a series, serial, or set; for the "fill in" volume to qualify as an AV, it must be for a title in which all volumes are cataloged under one call number. When such an added volume is requested, the AV space should be checked *in red.*

   19. "DNC"

These letters stand for "do not catalog," the notification that the material being ordered will not be cataloged, but merely stamped with ownership and forwarded to the requestor. Since DNC cards are always for books for departmental (nongeneral library) collections, they are normally processed by the bibliographic checker specializing in departmental request cards. For DNC procedures, see Section A.6.

   20. "LC Card NO."

In this space goes the order number which the Library of Congress has assigned to the set of catalog cards for a particular title. In the entries in LC catalogs, this number appears in the lower right-hand margin and should be recorded on the request card whenever it is encountered in the usual routine of checking (never check an extra tool merely to obtain an LC card no.).

   The first two digits of the LC number indicate the year in which the title *was cataloged*; then follows a hyphen and the card-set number (for example, 63-67384). Do not worry about the ISBN number or confuse it with the LC card number.

   (*Check with the Chief Bibliographer on this subject, since our photographic and OCLC routines have about eliminated our ordering of LC card sets.*)

   21. "Destination"

In this space is indicated a destination *different from* that which is normal for books purchased on the fund given. For example, "Reference" indicates that the title will be shelved in the Reference Collection rather than in the general collection of the library; "Chemistry" indicates that the title will shelve in the chemistry section of the physical sciences library along with geology and physics titles, rather than in the main collection of the library. "Repl." in this space indicates that the Circulation department is requesting a title to replace one that is missing (any "Repl." is also an AC for Catalog department purposes).

22. "Reserve Books"

In this space go the number of the course and the semester in which a title will be used. All such requests should have been submitted *first* to the Circulation department and *must have* the initials of the reserve books librarian in the "authorized by" space. Reserve books are always ordered "Rush." The bibliographer must make sure that "rush" *in red* is at the top of the card (see 26., below).

23. "UNV"

The "unverified" space is checked when a bibliographer cannot find the book listed (see 24., below) in a source for verification of entry, although he may have ascertained that the title actually exists by consulting a publisher's or dealer's catalog or some non-verifying retrospective bibliography that doesn't establish entry (*and* so indicated this fact on the tracing of his work on the back of the request card).

24. "NYP"

The "not yet published" space is checked by the bibliographer to indicate that a current title (one announced as printed in the current year or to be printed in the future) has been found in current publishers' ads or publishers' announcements, but has *not been verified* in a verifying source (where the title was found is indicated in the tracing of his work on the back of the request card).

25. "OP"

An o.p., "out-of-print" book is one no longer available through regular trade dealers, since the publisher's stock is exhausted. Domestic titles printed more than 3 years previously; foreign titles printed more than 4 years previously; Russian titles not having been ordered from the latest issue of *Novye Knigi*; non-trade titles (issued by corporations, foundations, associations, etc.) printed more than 6 years previously—all such titles are *arbitrarily* assumed to be o.p.

It is important to note, however, that any U.S. or British or non-English-language titles presumed to be OP by the above rules of thumb *must then be checked* in an appropriate in-print catalog, where such is available, before a final decision can be reached: BIP then PBIP for domestic imprints; BBIP for British books; *Libros en Venta* for Spanish-language publications; and so forth.

26. Priority of need. Search. Quote.

a. In the left hand portion of the wide space at the top-front of the request card are placed *in red* such terms of priority of need as "rush," "rush to order," and "soon," whenever they are appropriate (these terms are defined in the section on priorities in the "Order Procedures: Summary" in A.8.). Requests to "Search" or "Quote" are also stamped or printed in this same location.

b. *Search.* If a title is out of print, it is normally searched with the appropriate out-of-print dealer as specified in the "Dealers" section of this manual (A.11.). The price of a "search" is estimated at $15.00 per volume, although this estimate is highly variable and will be changed in a number of instances by the chief bibliographer. Science books and titles ordered on departmental funds are normally *not* searched. Questions concerning search problems should be directed to the chief bibliographer.

c. *Quote.* A quote to a dealer or publisher asks if he has a title in stock and, if so, its price. Quotes may also be sent to request imprint information; but, at present, the bibliographer must himself put such a request *in brackets* after the title sought. For example, in addition to the Quote notation at the top of the card, after the title entry on the card he would pencil in "please give place, publisher, and date of publication." A quote may also be sent when the number of volumes in a set seems doubtful or when a title looks like it might be very expensive. The bibliographer should not, however, have to quote very frequently; and there is *no point* in quoting a title unless it seems probable that a dealer's response will give more information than is available on the request card itself or from the usual bibliographical sources.

27. Miscellaneous format notation

In the right-hand portion of the wide space at the top-front of the request card are placed the terms "photoreproduction," "microfilm," "score," "record," "map," or any other term necessary to identify the special form of the item being purchased. Such a term should not be placed so far to the right that it will obscure the call number.

28. "Dealer"

In this space goes the name of the firm/dealer to whom the order, search, or quote will be sent. See the "Dealers" section of this manual (A.11.) for a general listing of these dealers.

29. "Date Ordered"

In this space is typed the date when the multiple order form (MOF) is typed and the order sent to the dealer. It is filled in by the typist, *not* the bibliographer.

30. "ORDER NO."

In this space goes the purchase order number assigned to an MOF for each title ordered. Whenever a title has been ordered but not permanently cataloged, it is important that this number be recorded if it shows up during the holdings check (Section A.5.A.), since it provides the key to the order record for the title to which it has been assigned. Bibliographers do not assign order numbers themselves: they are assigned in sequence as each day's MOF's are typed, batched according to dealer, and sent out by the Order section.

C.

In this section, it is not intended to discuss or define the terms on the back of a detailed card, C.1., in great detail. The aim is rather to represent the blocks of information on the back of a detailed card and they say a few words about these blocks, so that the bibliographer will be aware of how these blocks are organized.

Of course, the details of C.1., like those of B.1., above, are representational only and could have a different and/or simpler arrangement or, as in the simple request card, A., could be omitted entirely. However, Acquisitions will always have to use trade tools for the in-print and out-of-print determinations which govern the approach to an acquisition. Moreover, data banks, such as OCLC, will not verify all titles acquired, particularly retrospective; and LC and other bibligoraphies will have to be used in the verification of these.

C.1. BACK OF DETAILED REQUEST CARD

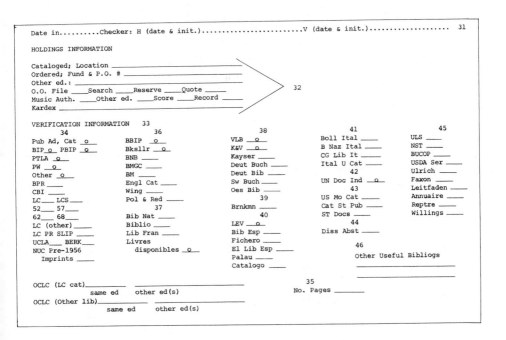

```
Date in.........Checker: H (date & init.).......................V (date & init.)..................... 31

HOLDINGS INFORMATION

Cataloged; Location _____
Ordered; Fund & P.O. # _____
Other ed.:                                              > 32
O.O. File _____Search _____Reserve _____Quote _____
Music Auth. _____Other ed. _____Score _____Record _____
Kardex _____

VERIFICATION INFORMATION   33
      34                 36              38              41            45
Pub Ad, Cat _o_      BBIP  _o_       VLB _o_       Boll Ital ____   ULS ____
BIP_o_ PBIP _o_      Bksllr _o_      K&V _o_       B Naz Ital ____  NST ____
PTLA _o_             BNB ____        Kayser ____   CG Lib It ____   BUCOP ____
PW  _o_              BMGC ____       Deut Buch ____ Ital U Cat ____ USDA Ser ____
Other _o_            BM ____         Deut Bib ____        42        Ulrich ____
BPR ____             Engl Cat ____   Sw Buch ____   UN Doc Ind _o_  Faxon ____
CBI ____             Wing ____       Oes Bib ____         43        Leitfaden ____
LC____ LCS____       Pol & Red ____     39          US Mo Cat ____  Annuaire ____
52___ 57___              37          Brnkmn ____    Cat St Pub ____ Reptre ____
62___ 68___          Bib Nat ____       40          ST Docs ____   Willings ____
LC (other) ____      Biblio ____     LEV _o_              44
LC PR SLIP ____      Lib Fran ____   Bib Esp ____    Diss Abst ____
UCLA___ BERK___      Livres          Fichero ____
NUC Pre-1956           disponibles _o_ El Lib Esp ____     46
  Imprints ____                      Palau ____      Other Useful Bibliogs
                                     Catalogo ____   _____
                                                     _____
OCLC (LC cat)_____  _____    35
            same ed   other ed(s)       No. Pages _____
OCLC (Other lib)_____  _____
            same ed   other ed(s)
```

C.2. DEFINITIONS OF TERMS ON BACK OF DETAILED CARD

31. Date and personnel information

The typist opening the mail stamps the appropriate date in the "date in" space before distributing the cards to the chief bibliographer. Cards not coming through the mail are stamped with the "date in" by the student assistant filing request cards into holding drawers. When request cards are "run," the date-in is important as an indicator of older cards, which would probably be run first. It sometimes happens that holdings checks are done *only* to weed duplicate requests out of request-card backlogs and that verification is left until later; if there is a time lag between date of a holdings check and the date when verification for a request card begins, the holdings check may have to be done again. Initials are vital to indicate who is responsible for what procedures with a card; in the event of error, mistakes can be pointed out to the checker making them.

32. "HOLDINGS INFORMATION"

The terms in this portion of the request card are discussed in detail in the "Holdings Check" section of this manual (A.5.A.).

33. "VERIFICATION INFORMATION"

The procedures for the bibliographic verification (pre-cataloging) of particular kinds of titles are discussed in some detail in this manual's section on verification (A.5.B.) and bibliographic procedures for the imprints of some major European nations. What is at present intended is that the bibliographer be given a brief, general view of the tools with which he will do most of his work.

On the back of the complex request card, a *zero* has been placed by the trade bibliographies or other resources which *confirm price* and such order information as *in-print availability* but which are *not* accepted as *verifying entry.* The bibliographic titles with *no zero* by them are those which *do verify entry.* These are largely national bibliographies. It is important to note that some Acquisitions departments accept *only* LC-NUC sources for verification. Of course, if a title does not show up in these sources, it must usually be pursued elsewhere.

In numbers 34 and following, I will give only a brief explanation of guide numbers and bibliographical groupings in sequence. The reader-student must use Sheehy (Guide to Reference Books, 1976) *and a personal and thorough examination of the bibliographies mentioned to learn the nature and use of each. It should be obvious that with time certain tools change in nature and some disappear; others, like the resource of a terminal to a computer data bank, will appear. Also, what bibliographies and trade tools "verify" to the satisfaction of a Catalog department differs from institution to institution.*

34. U.S. Bibliographies: Trade, National, Library Catalogs, and OCLC

These U.S. tools fall into two groups within this block: (1) the in-print and trade tools providing current publication information, but not used as verification sources as indicated by the zeros by them; and (2) the verification tools which follow under them.

The trade tools, such as *Books in Print* and *Paperbound Books in Print,* give important initial price and availability information for current and retrospective publications. *Publishers' Trade List Annual,* to which BIP may be viewed as a kind of an index, often provides more publishing information, especially for sets and series, then BIP or PBIP. PW can be of use for statements about forthcoming books, particularly fictional and creative titles; and "other" sources can be helpful at times, for it is hard for a bibliographer to deny the existence of a book he cannot find verified anywhere when a professor stands before him, as happens, with the book in his hand.

Additional publishing information for the book trade can be found in the domestic and foreign publishers' catalogs kept in large numbers in alphabetical file in Acquisitions. These are consulted when in-print tools fail to give sufficient information; such catalogs can be very useful on occasion, but we try to limit their use because it can be time consuming. If such a catalog is consulted, its title and date should be noted by the bibliographer. (We also have large files of antiquarian catalogs, which often contain elaborate bibliographical descriptions, for special retrospective consultation.)

The *national U.S. bibliographies* that follow vary in approach: BPR gives the monthly and annual U.S. domestic publishing record by subject approach, and CBI gives *all* English-language titles, wherever published, in monthly and cumulative issues—establishing LC entry (and giving order numbers for card sets). The extension of the LC-NUC catalogs continues beyond 1968, of course, into the present, although the OCLC computer system covers from 1967 to date and theoretically replaces LC catalog verification from 1967. *Book catalogs of individual libraries,* such as those from the University of California at Berkeley and at Los Angeles (to cite only two among a number of such publications), can be very useful in providing sound cataloging for retrospective titles and subjects they cover; if the library book catalog has *added entries* as well as main entries, it can be very helpful in getting from an added entry to the verifying main entry.

We are familiar with LC proof slips as double-agent tools: for selection and for self-verifying devices with built-in LC entry verification. OCLC is a fact of verifying life for both domestic, U.S. imprints and non-domestic imprints. For the information of the Catalog department, verification distinguishes LC cataloging material in OCLC from cataloging done by other cooperating libraries and records other cataloged editions in cases where only editions different from that of a requested or received title show up in OCLC—in which case "other ed" information will have to be penciled in. (*See also,* Section A.5.B.1.b-c. for further commentary on OCLC and on the *National Union Catalog Pre-1956 Imprints* as verifying resources.)

Bibliographers must be familiar as well with "other useful bibliographies" (46), particularly of the sequences of catalogs for U.S. publications of the nineteenth century, for which there is not room on the card. Retrospective sequences of verification sources for some of the other major nations, with whose publications we work, *are* on the card.

35. "No. Pages"

In the process of verifying *any* o.p. book, the bibliographer should record its number of pages in the event it should be decided to reproduce rather than search a particular title. Page numbers are also useful in determinations of variant or new editions. However, a special search should *not* be made solely to determine pagination; the bibliographer should remember also that the pagination of multi-volume sets is not recorded in LC and many other catalogs.

36. British Bibliographies: Trade and National

The publications in this group are put out by British publishers or institutions. *British Books in Print* is the equivalent of our BIP. The *Bookseller* may be viewed roughly as the equivalent of PW, and of more popular interest than bibliographical value.

Pollard and Redgrave's *Short-Title Catalogue of Books* carries British printing from its beginning up to 1640, and Wing's *Short-Title Catalogue* carries it from 1641 to 1700. The *British Museum General Catalogue of Printed Books* is particularly strong from 1814 to date, although it is also strong for earlier British imprints and worldwide holdings in general. The BMGC is at present being successfully brought up to date; it represents the British equivalent of the LC Catalogs and those of the Bibliothèque Nationale. The BMGC is supplemented in coverage by the *English Catalogue,* from 1801 to 1966, which contains some unusual listings not to be found elsewhere, and by the *British National Bibliography,* which is much more current than the BM listings and has weekly, quarterly, and annual cumulations approachable by subject (the British Museum has recently been renamed the British Library). There are, as with any other literatures, a large number of specialized catalogs and bibliographies as guides to specific periods and genres.

37. French Bibliographies: Trade and National

Livres disponibles is the author-title listing equivalent to BIP. The catalog of the Bibliothèque Nationale is the basic French tool. At present, the BN catalog has struggled into the W's since its birth in 1897. *La Librairie Française* is the cumulation of the *Bibliographie de la France* and is useful from 1933. *Livres du Mois* is roughly the equivalent of BPR and can also be used as a selection tool, as can *Biblio,* which parallels CBI for English-language publications by its monthly appearance and annual cumulations which list titles in French on a more or less complete, worldwide basis.

38. German Language Bibliographies: Trade and National

Verzeichnis lieferbarer Bücher is a useful German BIP, by author, title, and catchword; K&V (Koehler and Volckmar) is also a ueful trade BIP for German. (*Currently, we use only VLB.*) Kayser's *Vollständiges Bücher-Lexikon* brings German bibliography from 1750 to 1910 (Hinrich and Heinsius cover earlier periods). *Deutsches Bücherverzeichnis,* the East German publication, brings German bibliography up to date and is supplemented from 1945 by the West German *Deutsche Bibliographie,* which cumulates from a weekly issue with a monthly index into larger volumes. Both recent German national bibliographies are supposed to cover all publications in German in Austria and Switzerland. Austria is also specifically represented by *Oesterreichische Bibliographie* from 1945, and Switzerland by *Schweizer Buch* from 1901.

39. Netherlands National Bibliography

This is Brinkman's cumulative *Catalogus van Boeken* for the Dutch from 1846.

40. Spanish Language Bibliographies: Trade and National

Libros en Venta is the Spanish BIP; *Fichero . . .* may be viewed as a kind of Latin-American CBI. Palau's *Manual,* followed by the *Catálogo general . . . ,* *Bibliografia Española,* and *El Libro Español,* in that sequence, will bring Spanish-language bibliographies up to date, although with some gaps and irregularities. It might be noted that the Berkeley and UCLA book catalogs are very useful for Spanish-language titles published prior to the date of the publication of these library catalogs.

41. Italian Bibliographies: Trade and National

Catalogo dei Libri Italiani in Commercio (1970) is a kind of dated and non-inclusive BIP in this area. And other Italian bibliography is replete with gaps, arrears, etc. But Pagliaini's *Catalogo Generale . . . ,* supplemented by the *Bollettino . . . Italiane* and the *Bibliografia Nazionale Italiana* will bring matters pretty much up to date. An Italian Union Catalog, *Primo Catalogo . . . delle Biblioteche Italiane,* was planned to cover 1500 to about 1957; but tricks of nature, human and physical, have held it back. Italian bibliography and the Italian book trade are difficult subjects.

42, 43. Document Indexes

Bibliographic checkers will not normally be working with the four indexes in 42 and 43, since documents are processed by the Documents department and these indexes are its recording and ordering devices. In the event that need arises for cataloging individual pieces for the central or branch or departmental libraries, verification procedure will put the title into the usual resources to see if another library has cataloged it or, at least, if entry can be established. If a request for a document drifts into Acquisitions unbeknownst to the chief bibliographer, whoever comes across it should give it to him right away; he will then consult with the documents librarian about handling procedures. Hallmarks of documents are their publication by national or international governmental bodies: U.N., UNESCO, any other such body; the U.S. Supt. of Docs., USGPO, AEC, any other federal agency, any state agency, etc.

44. Dissertation Abstracts

Requests for copies of dissertations should be referred at once to the chief bibliographer, since they pose special problems. He will, by agreement, forward them to the bibliographer in ILL (interlibrary loan) in the Reference department. On the theory that Acquisitions *cannot* do everything for everybody, ILL will provide correct LC entry, order, and cost information if it is decided to purchase a dissertation.

45. Serials Bibliographies

Since the serials bibliographers normally verify serial titles, bibliographers working with monographs will not often use the tools in this group. At the least, however, everyone should be familiar with the U.S. *Union List of Serials,* its supplementary and continuing companion, *New Serial Titles,* and the *British Union-Catalogue of Periodicals* and its supplements. If a request has a title listing only, the monographs bibliographer can often quickly verify it as a serial by consulting these basic sources, and can then turn the request over to the serials librarian, with the customary checking record to that point penciled in on the back of the request form. All serials ordering and verifying tools listed under 45, and a good many more, are available in Serials for examination.

46. "Other Useful Bibliographies"

A number of retrospective bibliographies other than those it is possible to list on a request card—and the new resources that constantly appear—can be useful in tracking down elusive titles. If one of these is used, the bibliographer should write its title, with the appropriate checking marks, in space 46 and give the year, volume, and page citations so that the information can be rechecked if need be. Because Sheehy gives a good description of most of these, there is no point in elaborating them here. However, any bibliographic checker will certainly be asked from time to time what other tools were used in the effort to track down a retrospective or current title. Before this more or less pleasant occurrence, he should know how to use at least Evans, Shaw and Shoemaker, Roorbach, Kelly, the *American Catalog,* the *U.S. Catalog,* and Blanck for domestic imprints; Lowndes, Collier, and Watt for British; Quérard and Lorenz for French; and Heinsius and Hinrich for German. And he should make a note of and look at any *new* resources to familiarize himself with them.

D. WORK SHEETS

Checkers please note that after preliminary indoctrination, each one of you will be expected (a) to study Sheehy (*Guide to Reference Books,* 1976), of which a number of copies are available in the department, and (b) to use your notes from this invaluable resource when you orient yourself in our bibliographic center for all national library catalogs and national and trade bibliographies with which you will be working. *All* checkers will be responsible for understanding each tool listed on our request card—not only its specific chronological coverage, but its frequency of issue and cumulation (if appropriate) *and* its approach; that is, author, title, subject, or one or any or all of these.

Beyond this, any checker working in areas beyond those outlined on the request card is expected to know the trade and/or national bibliographies relevant to his work.

Finally, all checkers are to prepare a typed (double-spaced format with triple spacing between entries) *work sheet,* using Sheehy and his own notes from personal investigation of titles, for *each* country/language area on the request card (and other countries and language areas as appropriate) for insertion in this manual directly after this statement. Each sheet is to be headed by the country/language area (France, Germany, U.S., U.S.S.R., etc.) and is to be placed by heading in alphabetical order. These work sheets will be reviewed by the chief bibliographer or his assistant before being put in the manual. Each country and/or language area is to be on a separate sheet. Sheehy ("National Libraries" and "National and Trade Bibliography") is to be the guide *plus* individual notes on the particular titles cited.

The sequence on each sheet (some countries/language areas will require more than one) will be as follows and titled as follows: (1) "National Library Catalog(s)," if any; (2) "Retrospective Bibliographies," from earliest to most recent; (3) "Current Bibliographies," from earliest initial date of publication to latest initial date of publication for still-continuing tools; and (4) "Other Useful Guides."

A. 4. INTERPRETING THE MAIN CARD CATALOG (MCC; PUBLIC CATALOG, PC)

A.

Three introductory points about the MCC should be noted before proceeding to look at a schematic individual catalog card (in B.) and some examples of particular types of cards (in C.). These points are (1) what the MCC is *physically,* (2) what the MCC *tells* a user, and (3) what *should be remembered* as basic filing rules in searching for information in the MCC.

1. *Physically* the MCC is a series of cabinets containing catalog cards of a uniform size (nearly always three by five inches). Each card has been constructed as a guide to give some particular information about a particular title in the library. Each card is headed and filed alphabetically by a single entry: main entry (author or title), added entry, and subject entry.

2. The MCC *tells* a user (a) the library holdings of monographs by particular authors and of serials, (b) the subjects dealt with by these various holdings, and (c) the number of copies of these holdings available in the library system and their location in that system (main library, branch library, departmental library, and so forth). For serials and sets, the MCC also indicates issues and volumes available, as the case may be. The classification number on the card—the call number—enables a user to find a particular book in a particular location on the library shelves where all other titles on the same subject (sometimes sub-arranged by time periods) will normally be found.

3. It is obviously not possible here to go into ALA or LC filing rules, but a bibliographer *should remember* that entries are filed word by word and letter by letter within words. He should also remember that filing for *identical headings* (entries) is by person, place, thing, and title, in that order; and identical entries for the same *thing* are filed by main entry, added entry, and subject entry in that order.

B. LIBRARY OF CONGRESS CATALOG CARD

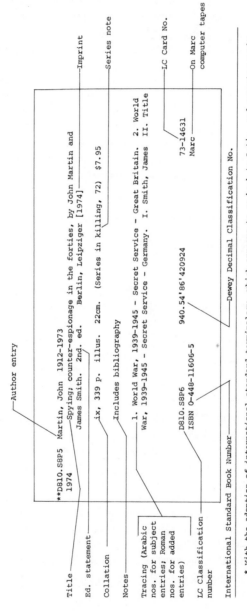

* With the adoption of international standard terminology, which appears to go back to Latin, and computer marks, the new LC cards will look somewhat different, with a slash after title and before author, a colon after place of publication, a dash separating author from imprint, etc.

**The typed LC classification number assigned by the individual library appears here; it may differ somewhat from the printed LC number at the bottom of the card. Special letters by individual libraries may appear before or after this number, such as "f" for folio, "R" for shelved in reference, "mf" for microform, etc.

C.

EXAMPLES OF TYPES OF ENTRY IN THE MCC (SCHEMATIC ONLY)

I. *Separates* (monographs)
A. Main Entry by Author

1. *Personal single author*

E743
S54

Sherwin, Mark
    The extremists . . .

2. *Personal joint author*

Two men are responsible for this book. Main entry is for name appearing first on the title page. E.A. Hoebel, the joint author, will be brought out in the added entries.

E99
E99
W3

Wallace, Ernest
    The Comanches, by Ernest Wallace & E. Adamson Hoebel. Norman, University of Oklahoma Press, 1952. . . .
        1. Comanche Indians.
    I. Hoebel, Edward Adamson, 1906 - joint author. II. Title.

3. *Personal author, pseudonymous*

Eliot's assumed name is better known than her real name, and is preferred as the main entry.

PR4681
A3
H3

Eliot, George, pseud., i.e. Marian Evans, afterwards Cross, 1819-1880.
    The George Eliot letters . . .

4. *Editor*

E.B. Spiess is responsible for editing this group of papers by many hands. His editorial responsibility as editor gives him the main entry.

QH431

Spiess, Eliot B.   ed.
    Papers on animal genetics . . .

5. *Corporate author: government bodies*

   A group of persons working in a governmental agency is responsible for, and considered the author of, the publications of that agency.

   TLZ5064
   A8
   U53
   R

   U.S. Library of Congress. Science and Technology Division.
   Space science and technology books . . .

6. *Corporate author: congresses*

   Congresses, conferences, institutes, and conventions are considered corporate authors responsible for their publications resulting from meetings.

   S590
   I5
   1960

   International Congress of Soil Science.
   7th, Madison, Wisconsin, 1960.
   Transactions . . .

7. *Corporate author: societies*

   Societies, museums, universities, and similar groups associated for a purpose are given responsibility for the publications of their organization.

   QAI
   A5

   American mathematical society.
   Progress report on the society's scholarships . . .

B. Main Entry by Title

1. *Anonymous works*

   F.W.C.'s true name cannot be determined.

   TP548.95
   S4
   S43

   Sherryana, by F.W.C. . . .

2. *Anonymous classics*

   Epics and romances from the early classical and medieval times are so entered.

   PJ7715

   Arabian nights.
   Scheherezade. Tales from . . .

3. *Sacred Texts*

   These include such literature as the Bible, Koran, and Talmud.

   BS195
   K5

   Bible. English. 1964. Martin.
   The Holy Bible . . . translated by Prelate Henry Martin . . .

C. Secondary Entries

main entry

PE1402
W47
1849

Whately, Richard . . .
Elements of rhetoric . . . .

1. Rhetoric. 2. English language—Rhetoric.
I. Title

secondary entries

1. *Subject entry*
   From tracing, in red. *

   Rhetoric
   Whately, Richard . . .
   Elements of rhetoric . . .

2. *Subject entry*
   Second subject entry from tracing, in red.

   English language—Rhetoric
   Whately, Richard . . .
   Elements of rhetoric . . .

3. *Title added entry*
   Entry not in red.

   Elements of rhetoric
   Whately, Richard
   Elements of rhetoric . . .

D. Multiple Copies

1. *Two copies*
   Both in main library

   DP184
   D3
   2c.

   Davies, Reginald
   Spain in decline . . .

2. *Two copies*
   Both in main library, copy 1 in Reference, copy 2 in the stacks

   PR5880
   C6
   2c.
   c.1 Ref

   Cooper, Lane
   A concordance . . . .

*Not to get into reasons to any degree, subject and author and title added entries are now usually simply black. The whole matter of the real need for such entries has been discussed at great length in the professional literature.

3. *Three copies*
  c.1, in physics
  c.2, enology
  c.3, main library

TK7815
M25
3c.
  c.1 physics
  c.2 enology

Malmstadt, Howard
  Electronics for scientists . . .

4. *Two copies of a set*
  c.1, vs. 1-4, 6 only in main library
  c.2, vs. 1-6, in physics

QC20
S6
2c.
  c.1 lacks v. 5
  c.2 physics

Sommerfield, Arnold
  Lectures on physics . . . 6 vols. . . .

II. *Serials*

A. Main Entry under Title *or* Issuing Body: To Show Holdings, Location, On Order Status, etc.

1. *On standing order*
  "-date" is the indication that library receives each number as issued.

QK1
N58

New Zealand journal of botany.
  v.1-date; 1963-date . . .

2. *Location*
  c.1, main library, 1906-12, v. 17-date
  c.2, main library, v. 17-date
  c.3, lacking, probably discarded
  c.4, poultry husbandry, vs. 53-64 only
  c.5, agronomy, v. 55-date
  c.6, soils, v. 55-date, file incomplete

QC984
C39
5c.

  c.2 v. 17-date
  c.3 lacking
  c.4 v. 53-64 poul. hus.
  c.5 v. 55-date agron.
  c.6 v. 55-date (file in-
  comp.) soil & plant
  nutrition

U.S. Weather Bureau
  Climatological data . . .
  1906-12; v. 17-date
  v. 17(1907)-date . . .

3. *Special information*
   The latest issue is in Reference; earlier issues in stacks. But library keeps last two years only.

U1	Military review
M5	1954-date . . .
	latest in Ref.
	library has last 2 years only.

B. Main Entry under Personal Author (monographs in series)

1. *Class. by individual author* and series call no. used from 36-date, when series was put on s.o.

   For the user, all cards for titles in this series will follow the series card *if* the title has been separately cataloged, as has Dziewanowski's book. The searcher *would also* find the main entry under author, with the usual additional entries, subject and added.

series card

DK4	Harvard University
H37	Russian Research Studies . . .
	v.36- under this call no. Earlier vols. cat. under individ. author. See following cards for call nos.

author card

JN6769	Dziewanowski, M.K.
A5	Communist Party of Poland.
K62	Cambridge, Mass., Harvard Univ. Pr., 1959.
	xvi, 369 p. 24 cm. (Russian Research Center Studies, 32)

A.5. BIBLIOGRAPHIC CHECKING PROCEDURES (BCP): HOLDINGS AND VERIFICATION

A. HOLDINGS CHECK

The request card format being assumed for the procedures described in the holdings check is that of the forms diagrammed in II.2.A.3.B.-C., above

1. PURPOSES

The holdings check has *two purposes*. The *first purpose* is to determine whether or not the library owns or has on order any editions of a requested title. A title not in the library system is usually ordered, provided that it is properly funded and from an authorized selector. If a request is for a later edition of a title already in the library, the later edition is ordered only if significantly different from the earlier. Earlier editions, reprints, and added copies of a title already in the library are not routinely ordered (however, see 2.B., below, for departmental requests).

The *second purpose* is to record on a request card/form whatever bibliographical and/or order information is available about a requested title from the MCC or the O.O file. This bibliographical record provides the information that forms a preliminary part of the process of verification (precataloging), to which most Acquisitions departments are committed. After completion of the holdings check, the process of verification begins for those titles which the library wishes to purchase.[6]

2. PROCEDURES

The procedures, the routines, of the holdings check are simply the various sequences of activities of the bibliographic checkers aimed at achieving the purposes stated in 1., above. These procedures will differ, depending upon whether requests are for titles to be cataloged for the library system and purchased from monies from the library budget or are requested by departments and to be purchased from their own monies (from grants, etc.) and to be placed in these departments for the special use of their own faculties.

A. Procedures for Requests for the General Library System

1. Preliminary Treatment of the Request Card
Upon receiving the card, the checker should be sure that the "date in" space is filled in and that he places his initials and the date of the holdings check in the "H" (for holdings) space on the top-verso (back) of the request card.

2. The Main Card Catalog (MCC; or PC, public catalog)
a. Initial Procedure
(1) At the MCC the checker determines whether or not there is a main entry established for a requested title; whether a work is without author

(serials, books prepared by more than three authors, etc.) and thus requires main entry by title; and whether there is a corporate or governmental agency entry established for works produced by corporations, companies, governmental agencies, and similar bodies.

(2) If a checker finds an MCC entry for a requested title or for the author of a requested title, he should first be sure that the form of entry on the card matches that in the catalog. To make such a match requires correcting the request card wherever necessary—for example, giving full names for all authors and *being sure* that complex corporate entries are word-for-word the same. The checker also makes the appropriate check marks, as described in the following paragraphs. It is important to be certain that all titles given as a series note on the request card are also checked in the MCC. If such a note is found in the MCC, the checker must then attempt to determine if the particular volume requested is in the library (see 5., below, for the Kardex; see also Section A.9., serials, series, and sets in this manual).

b. "Lib Has"

(1) If the same edition of a requested title is already cataloged and located in the main library system, the checker writes "lib has" vertically on the heavy vertical line at the left-front of the request card. Under "Call No." in the upper-right-front of the request card, he pencils in the call number of the title. On the back of the card, he fills in the "Date In," and the "H" spaces, using abbreviated form of date, and he gives his initials. A check mark is placed in the "Cataloged; Location" space, nothing more remains to be done except to return the card to the "lib has" box in the bibliographic section.

(2) In contrast to simple "lib has" cases, there are a number of less clear-cut instances—such as requests for added copies, variant editions, departmental copies, etc. These are *not* "lib has" cases, since "lib has" requests are defined as only those instances with the following characteristics: (a) the title requested is destined for the Main library; (b) the Main library has the exact edition requested, or has it on order; (c) the title requested is not marked as an added copy (AC). Statements *c* through *f,* below, deal with these particular cases.

c. Added Copies (AC's)

(1) *It is important to observe* whether or not a check mark appears in the AC space on the front of the request card. If the AC space has a check mark, it indicates that the requestor knows that the library already has one copy or more of the title. He is, however, suggesting that we buy a duplicate, added copy. But he must still justify his request. The checker completes his work, and the chief bibliographer then contacts the requestor.

Entry and other bibliographical verification are taken from the card in the MCC. The next step is to determine if the book/title is available and, if so, how much it costs. The procedures for determining availability and price are not our concern here under the holdings check, but can be found under

"Definitions of Terms" (Section A.3.) and "Verification" (Section A.5.B.).

(2) Some departments have their books cataloged before being sent to the departmental library; others do not. With the exception of physics, which has run out of departmental space, departmental books are shelved in departments.

It is *very important* to remember that if a department requests that a book purchased on its own funds be cataloged before being shelved in the department, such a book is normally purchased, even though it is also in the main library. Whether or not the requestor has marked the card "AC," the book will be bought. If the requestor has failed to do so, the checker *must* mark the card "AC" to call it to the attention of the chief bibliographer—along with all of the usual indications of call number, the placing of a check mark in the "Cataloged; Location" space, and so forth.

d. Other Editions

(1) If the library has an edition of a title other than the one requested, it is usual, *except for literary works,* to order only a later edition with significant changes in content. When the library has such a different edition, the checker pencils "lib has" *if* the request is for an earlier edition.

(2) If the request is for a later edition which appears to be different from that already in the library, the checker does not pencil "lib has." Instead, to the left of the main entry of such cards, he places a check with a small zero in the angle of the check (✓) to indicate the holding of another, but not the same, edition. Whether or not the checker decides the variant edition requested is a "lib has," he pencils in the call number of the edition already in the library in the upper right-hand corner of the card; but "see" is penciled in before the call number to indicate that the call number is not for the identical edition requested on the card.

(3) On the back of the request card, the dates of checking and the checker's initials are given as before. A zero is placed in the "Cataloged" space. Location is, as before, assumed to be in the main library unless otherwise indicated; and only a location other than one in the main library need be indicated. However, in the "Other Edition" space, such imprint information as the publisher and date of publication of other editions (unless there are too many to make such a listing reasonable) is given.

(4) It is also *important* to remember that the checker is expected to record the imprint, the number of volumes in an edition, and the translator and editor, if any are noted on the catalog card in the MCC. The number of pages for an edition held by the library should also be recorded, unless the number of editions already in the library make such a procedure unreasonable. If the checker is uncertain about a "Lib Has" decision, a question mark after the "Lib Has" will bring the card to the attention of the Chief Bibliographer.

e. Lib Does Not Have, or Another Edition Wanted

If the library does not have a particular title or if another edition of a title is to be ordered, the checker first brings the main entry into conformity with any in the MCC, as explained in a., above, placing a check with a zero in the angle ⌐ by the main entry to show that the library has the form of entry but not the title requested, *or* placing a zero by the main entry if the library doesn't have it at all. In either case, there will be a zero in the "Cataloged" space on the back of the card.

f. *Requested Title On Order*

(1) If a check of the MCC reveals that a requested title or another edition of it is on order (see also 3., The O.O. File, directly below), the rules governing "Lib Has" decisions or decisions to buy requests for different editions are in effect. *Please note,* however, that the checker writes "on order" instead of "lib has" on the vertical line to the left-front of the request card. A check mark by the main entry shows an edition identical with that requested is on order; a check with a zero in the angle shows that the form of the main entry is in the MCC. Since a book only on order cannot have been cataloged, there is nothing in the call number space. On the back of the card, dates and initials are as before; and a zero is placed in the "Cataloged" space. Any necessary editions statements are entered as before. The "Ordered" space is checked, and the fund and purchase order number of the title are written out.

(2) It is important to *note* that the intended destination of a title requested and the location of cataloged titles already recorded in the MCC govern "On Order" decisions and return of cards to requestors just as they do in "lib has" cases. In instances of difficult decisions, "On Order?" will always call the card to the attention of the chief bibliographer.

3. The O.O. File (Orders-Out, On-Order)

As you can tell from f. (1), above, the kind of library for which this manual is relevant files O.O. slips in the MCC. This is a good policy for a well-run operation. Students and faculty can always check on the progress of orders, and titles that have been ordered and received but not cataloged can be given cataloging priority if necessary. The MCC, thus, becomes an O.O. file as well from whatever date O.O. cards first began to be filed in the MCC.

Search and quote slips are not filed in the MCC, only in the O.O. file, since to put them in the public catalog would only confuse users running across them. Reserves with antiquarian dealers are similarly only in our O.O. file in Acquisitions, since we might not get these titles.

a. After the MCC, the O.O. file is checked, but *only* for titles presumed to be out of print and for *reprints* of titles that may have been announced but not yet forthcoming. Such titles are arbitrarily defined as follows: (1) American trade imprints more than 3 years old; (2) American non-trade imprints more than 6 years old (a non-trade book is one not issued by a commercial publisher, but by a society, an association, an academic department of a university, etc.); (3) foreign imprints, except Russian, more than 4 years old; and (4) Russian imprints more than 1 year old.

Since we began filing O.O. slips into the MCC 1 Jan. 1975, *only* titles printed before 1975 need be searched in the O.O. file still maintained in Acquisitions.

b. The use, when necessary, of the O.O. file should be recorded on the back of the request card by the usual check for a title found there, a check with a zero in the angle for another edition of the title found there, and a zero for a title not found there. If a requested title is in the O.O. file as on search, on quote, or on reserve (requested from an antiquarian catalog), the appropriate spaces on the back of the card should be marked, and needed additional remarks should be penciled in. On the vertical line at the left-front of the request card, where "lib has" is written for such cases, the checker should record "on search," "on quote," "on reserve," or "on order" (for reprints ordered a number of years back but not yet out), as the case may be.

The discovery in the O.O. file of editions other than the one requested demands the same judgments that govern "lib has" and "on order" decisions, to determine whether to continue to process a card or to return it to the requestor.

4. Procedures for Music Checking

The music-authority file is consulted when scores or records are ordered; but since the music cataloger is the one who consults this file, it need not concern bibliographic checkers except as a point of information. The music O.O. file is a special part of the O.O. file itself; at present it is checked only after the music cataloger has established a form of entry for requests and has returned them to the chief bibliographer to be ordered. Since music, like documents and serials, presents special problems, many music librarians customarily order their own materials.

5. The Kardex

a. The Kardex—which holds the acquisitions records for all serials currently on subscription ("standing order"), such as "periodicals," monographs in series, and some monumental sets—is consulted if a checker suspects that a requested title represents either a title in a series (which may or may not be on subscription) or any other kind of serial publication that may or may not be at present subscribed to. If a series/serial appears in the MCC as a closed entry (i.e., with initial and terminal dates, such as "1958-62"), there is no need to check the Kardex. If, however, an *open entry* of any kind appears (for example, "1958-"), this is the mark of a serial title (or, possibly, a large set) still being published; and the Kardex should be checked. If a series note is on the request card or if evidence of serial publication turns up during the holdings check, always look for such a title in the Kardex. If a serial is not found there, place a zero in the "Kardex" space; if a serial, but not the volume requested, is found in the Kardex, the usual check with the zero in the angle will so indicate this fact in the "Kardex" space, with the additional notation of "many numbers but not the one requested."

b. All titles that turn out to be serials should be given to the serials librarian without further checking. Everyone should be on the alert for such hints of serials as the following: words like "handbook" and "annual"; open entries; words on a request card indicating a desire for a standing order (subscription); a very high edition statement in the "Edition" space; and so forth. (For a discussion of monographs in series and other serials—and some sets—that might turn up in the Kardex, see Section A.9., which should be consulted particularly by checkers doing verifications.)

B. Procedures for Departmental Requests

1. All titles purchased on departmental funds normally shelve in the requesting department and fall into two categories: cataloged, and DNC (not cataloged). (For the routine used with DNC titles, see Section A.6.). Departmental books that are to be cataloged are subject to the same procedure as books to be purchased for the main library system *except* that such departmental orders are not normally regarded as "lib has," since the books are usually wanted by the requesting department whether or not other cataloged copies are in the general library or in other departmental libraries.

2. An up-to-date list of cataloged and DNC departmental funds is kept in the bibliographical section, along with other forms related to departmental order procedures. Unless a checker has been specifically assigned to departmental requests, he should give any he discovers to the Chief Bibliographer.

C. Booksellers' Catalogs

1. Out-of-print titles from a booksellers' catalog may be requested in different ways. For example, a department may send typed request cards *and* the catalog to the chief bibliographer. In this instance, a holdings check is run on the cards in the usual way (as described in A., above), and the cards and the catalog are then returned to the chief bibliographer who will have the titles reserved. If there are *fewer than five* such cards, the bibliographic checker also verifies the cards and stamps them "rush to order" before returning them to the chief bibliographer.

2. On the other hand, faculty members and subject specialists selecting from catalogs may simply mark desired titles in the catalog itself, because such a procedure can greatly speed up ordering time. If fewer than five titles are marked in a catalog, the chief bibliographer will usually have cards typed and give them to a checker for the procedure noted in A., above.

3. If more than five titles are marked in a catalog, the procedure requires the use of a "catalog data sheet" on which the checker fills in: the name of

the bookseller; the number of the catalog; the date he receives it from the chief Bibliographer; and his initials.[7] After checking carefully through the catalog for requestor selections (a procedure normally done the same day a catalog is received), the checker fills in the date on which he is doing the holdings check, and he lists in numerical sequence the catalog numbers of all titles for which a holdings check will be done. He should write no more than two columns lengthwise on each side of the catalog data sheet and should use more than one sheet if necessary.

a. Information gathered in the holdings check is *recorded in the catalog itself*; and the checker should be certain to *use the same procedures* at the MCC and *make the conventional marks* that he uses when processing regular request cards: filling in full names, when available; making any necessary changes in form of entry; recording call number and imprint information for a requested title when another edition is in the library; marking a zero for a main entry not in the library at all; marking a check with a zero in the angle when the author (or other main form of entry) of a requested title is found in the MCC but the title itself is not; and recording "lib has," "on order," and "on search" information whenever necessary.

4. The checker must also record what information he has found in the O.O. file by notations which he, or anyone else, can interpret at a glance. Further, on the catalog data sheet, he must make the following marks by each item number he has listed there: a zero for a main entry not in the library; a check with a zero in the angle when the main entry, but not the title requested, is in the library; a check with a zero in the angle with a "dif. ed." after it to indicate that a different edition from that requested is already in the library; and the familiar "lib has," "on order," and "on search" notations wherever such information is appropriate. A question mark after any notation by a number will alert the chief bibliographer to a problem, about which he will have to make the final decision.

5. When a checker decides that the library does not have the title requested, he circles the number of the item *in red on the catalog data sheet.* He *does not circle* titles which are noted as "lib has," or "on order," or as questionable. But he *does circle* the numbers of titles which are on search, with the notation on the catalog data sheet to cancel the search for such titles if received by order from the bookseller catalog in hand; he will later transfer this notation to the request card (see 7., below).

6. *It is very important* that all checkers be most careful to record in red, by its number on the catalog data sheet, the price of any title costing over $50.00 in a bookseller's catalog, since such purchases require special consideration. This is the last part of all of the available information needed by the chief bibliographer as he reviews selections from booksellers' catalogs before passing them on to the Order section librarian, who will telephone, cable, or airmail to reserve all desired titles.

7. The final step in the holdings routines for such catalog titles is that cards

will be typed for all titles successfully reserved (titles ordered and available), after which the checker who did the holdings check will be required to transfer all holdings information from the bookseller's catalog to the typed cards before returning them to the order librarian. At the time of this transfer, the checker is expected to check the typed cards for accuracy against his notations and the entries in the bookseller's catalog itself. This insures correct MOF's that will finally be typed from these cards and sent out as formal orders for reserved titles.

D. The Holdings Check: A Few Basic Points

1. In our MCC collected works are filed in front of individual titles.

2. Well-known works of literature have one title under which all variant titles of that work file. *Gulliver's Travels* is a notable example.

3. Modified letters such as ä, ö, and ü file as "ae," "oe," and "ue." The Scandinavian ∮ files as "oe."

4. An author's letters and edited editions of his individual or collected works go under his name, *not* under the editor's name, although book dealers tend to enter such titles under editor in their catalogs.

5. Biographies and bibliographies have main entry under the person(s) writing or compiling them.

6. Compound Spanish names normally require checking under both parts of the surname. If in doubt about foreign names and their filing, see *ALA Cataloging Rules.*

7. If a name entry says "pseud. . . . see" another name, *be sure* to give full entry for *name referred to,* as well as doing a holdings check under it.

8. If a card has a complicated corporate body as the main entry, a title check in the MCC will sometimes solve the problem.

9. If only the initial(s) of the first names of an author appears on a request, be sure to check all names that fit under the initial(s), not just under initials themselves.

10. We normally return cards/requests for which only the last name of an author is given if the name is a common one, difficult to track down (Johnson is a good example).

11. Give requests with obviously insufficient entries directly to the chief bibliographer, and do not waste your time on them. He will return to requestor.

12. Be sure to know the proper request format for joint authors and the rules for a work by three or fewer authors and by *more than three* authors.

13. If a checker is in doubt about a problem, he should not hesitate to consult another bibliographer.

14. Remember to give all state, U.S., U.N. documents—any documents in fact—to the chief bibliographer promptly and directly.

B. VERIFICATION

The request card format being assumed for the procedures described in verification is that of the forms diagrammed in Sections A.3.B.-C., above. See also 2.C., below, for the front of the same card format.

After the holdings check is completed, requests for titles to be purchased are ready to be verified. These requests will be for books not in the library, or for AC's or AV's; but "lib has," "on order," "on search" (to a large extent), and other various requests (as spelled out in the holdings check, A., above) will have been eliminated. Verification, which can be roughly equated with pre-cataloging, actually aims at two things: (1) *pre-cataloging* a requested title; and (2) obtaining information for correctly *buying* (ordering) a requested title. *Pre-cataloging* endeavors to establish main entry by LC rules and, as well, record other correct entry information—title, imprint, relation of a title to a series if any, and, if necessary, information about particular editions.

The *order information* essential to *buying* the book is as follows: (1) establishing (or estimating) the price; (2) determining whether the book is in print or out of print; and (3) selecting the appropriate dealer based on the place of publication and the assumption of the book being in or out of print. *Polishing the request card* before submitting it to the chief bibliographer or his Chief Assistant is an important part of this order procedure.

As a rule of thumb, we expect four hours of bibliographic checking time to deliver between 20 and 25 *polished* (completed) request cards. *Unlike* many Acquisitions departments, we expect our checkers to comprehend fully *both* precataloging and ordering routines.

1. PRE-CATALOGING A TITLE

A. Preliminaries

(1) Before beginning to precatalog a title, the bibliographer should check for the following: (a) sufficient imprint information to verify and order the title within a reasonable period of checking time; (b) evidence that the title is a state, U.S., U.N., foreign, etc., document; (c) authorization by proper library representatives; (d) titles that might be serials, since, as you know, the Separates section does not deal with such materials in depth; and (e) the date of publication of the requested title, as a guide to whether or not it is still in print.

(2) A request lacking sufficient imprint information may be put into one or two tools, *but* should be given to the chief bibliographer if not quickly verified. All documents should be given *at once* and without any effort at verification to the chief bibliographer, who will forward them to the documents librarian. All requests not properly authorized by the appropriate library representative—there is a list of library representatives at the end of the Checking Manual—should be given *at once* and without any effort at verification to the chief bibliographer, who will refer them for possible approval.

(3) Possible serial titles can on occasion be checked out in ULS, NST, or BUCOP, if such titles fail to appear in the monographic resources used during the normal routines of verification.

(4) *Before beginning* the process of verification, the bibliographer should make a decision about whether or not a requested title is o.p., since this basic fact will govern our choice of dealers (placing the title with an in-print jobber, searching for it through an o.p. dealer, and so forth).

B. OCLC

Since we are at least in an initial investigatory phase with this computer development, it will be the *primary* LC source choice for verification of current imprints now received from our bibliographical/approval-plan procedures for English-language and Western European languages. Our first results for imprints no more than two years old seem to be good. Also, all checkers seem to enjoy calling up, or attempting to call up, pictures on the moving screen. While we are working up cost/production figures for this resource, we will, thus, use it always as a first choice for titles within the last two years in the language areas stated above. On a selective basis, some checkers will also put such imprints from 1967 on into this resource. *All statements* that follow about priority of use of various bibliographies must be qualified in the light of this present development in the Acquisitions department, which is *formalized* in this preliminary addendum on the subject in this manual and will be amplifeid as we compile more facts and figures.[8]

C. National Union Catalog Pre-1956 Imprints
(and Later Cumulations)

It is obvious that this resource is of considerable pre-cataloging value now (into the letter "s" in 1977/8) and will be of more value when completed in, say, 1980. For pre-1956 imprints, and reprints of them, it is an obvious, initial LC verification resource, as are the NUC cumulations bridging from 1956 to the 1967 beginning of OCLC coverage, which is considerably supplemented by NUC cumulations.

D. Books in Hand

There is no point in pursuing the *books in hand* that come in as current imprints on our various approval plans beyond our own MCC and LC resources.

E. Books Not in Hand

Since we attempt to verify all *books not in hand* before ordering them, sequences of procedures for putting such titles into non-U.S. bibliographies are largely applicable to this kind of title. Subject to the qualifications of the comments in B. and C., above, the statements about verification that follow below *largely concern this kind of title.* These sequences are spelled out by the format of the back of the detailed request card (considered in "Definitions of Terms," Section A.3., which every bibliographer must know).

The usefulness of these sequences is emphasized here, since we are heavily into retrospective collection development—an area in which formal LC sources and OCLC have a number of limitations and in which library catalogs, such as those of UCLA and UC-Berkeley, among others, have considerable initial value relevant to LC entry format.

(1) If the holdings check reveals that the main entry for a requested title *does appear* in the MCC, the bibliographer considers the entry established and immediately puts the title into the most logical verifying bibliography, U.S. or foreign. This procedure inevitably dictates that the Catalog department will have to do more original cataloging than is practiced in institutions dedicated to total LC routines. But this is our policy at present—subject to formal change.

(2) If the holdings check reveals that the main entry for a requested title *does not appear* in the MCC, the bibliographer varies his procedure by first consulting bibliographies that use LC form of entries, depending of course upon their span of coverage in relation to the imprint of the title requested: those bibliographies noted in B-D., above; BPR (domestic imprints only); and CBI (English-language imprints only)—all described further under "Definitions of Terms," Section A.3., above.

a. Sometimes only the main entry (say, the author entry), but not the title of the book itself, is located in an LC-entry resource, in which case the book is then put into (searched for in) the appropriate national bibliography. A bibliographer should *not* put any such book into *more than three* LC sources and should not spend undue time before consulting the logical national bibliography for the title of the book being sought.

(3) Each bibliography used, the specific years consulted within it, and the record of findings (or non-findings) in it should be noted down *at the time* that the bibliography is in hand. The marks used in verification are the same as those used in the holdings check, but are placed *over* each bibliographical element verified.

a. On the front of the request card, a check is placed over all elements verified: the author (or main entry); title; each part of the imprint (place, publisher, date); and price. If any of these elements has not been determined during the process of verification, it is left unchecked to indicate no findings.

b. On the back of the request card, a check and the appropriate year are placed beside an individual bibliography when the title is found therein. A zero, and the years consulted, indicates that a title was not found in a particular source within a particular span of time. Verifying bibliographies not appearing on the back of the request card are penciled in on the bottom of the card in space 46, and the appropriate marks for the years searched are indicated.

(4) If an *edition different from the one requested* is found, a zero is placed on the back of the card beside the appropriate bibliography; the year where the different edition was located is recorded; and in an open space on the back of the card, the information about the different edition (author, title, imprint, etc.) is penciled in. A line from the zero to this penciled information should make clear which bibliography contained the information recorded.

(5) If the process of verification reveals that change of main entry is required or that a main entry is part of a monographic series, any change of entry or series note must be printed on the front of the card; and any *erroneous information should be erased or greened out.* Also, the entry or series note must be *rechecked* for holdings in the MCC and, for o.p. or reprinted titles, in the O.O. file. All such rechecking *must* be indicated by a *second series* of the usual marks to indicate the tracks of the rechecking procedure. If the changed entry does prove to be in the MCC or O.O. file, the usual "lib has," etc., rules apply (as explained in the holdings check, A., above).

(6) If a requested title turns out to be a *serial*, it is given to the serials librarian, unless it is an individual monograph in a series not subscribed to— in which case it is given to the chief bibliographer, who will check with the serials librarian about purchasing the title individually or considering subscription to the series as a whole.

(7) *Reprints* should be treated as new editions; but if the most recent date of publication cannot be verified, the original edition should be. (For reprints, also see Section A.6.)

(8) If an *edition other than the one requested* is the only one which can be verified, then the "Unv" space at the top-left-front of the card is checked *in red* with "ed." *in red* after it. On the back of the card, an edition statement of what *was* found and the bibliography where found must be clearly indicated. If an edition is not verified at all, a *red checkmark* goes in the "Unv" space.

(9) The bibliographer can change the imprint on a request for an *in-print title* if he discovers another edition of a title requested, *provided that* there is no change of editor (or translator or other basic editorial components). This procedure will facilitate verifying and ordering. However, it can *never* be followed for o.p. titles selected from a bookseller's catalog, since such a dealer offers only the copy he specifies in his catalog and would be confused by a request for a bibliographically different title.

(10) *Very recent books* and books presumed to be N.Y.P (not yet published) can be a problem and difficult to verify at all. Requests for such titles will be of two kinds: (1) those lacking adequate bibliographical information (most frequently, an imprint); and (2) those with adequate bibliographical information.

a. Cards lacking adequate bibliographical information are often for books selected by faculty/subject specialists from lists put out by book jobbers, who often advertise new titles by various publishers without giving the imprints of those publishers (the aim of this unfortunate practice being to force libraries to buy from the jobber listing the title in his own advertisements). An NYP title lacking imprint should be put into in-print guides if available and into any available forecasts of new books.

If this procedure *does not* turn up further publication information, such cards should be returned to the chief bibliographer. He will then quote (ask information about place, publisher, date, price) these cards to an appropriate dealer (one from whom Acquisitions normally orders such materials, *not* from the jobber listing or advertising the title without imprint) or return them to requestors for further bibliographical information.

If this procedure *does discover* that a title is still NYP (in preparation and not yet published), entry should be verified, if possible; order information (imprint, price) should be added; and the title should be ordered as NYP from the appropriate in-print dealer.

If this procedure reveals that a book has *already been published,* the title should then be put into the appropriate bibliography for verification; should this title still not show up in current bibliographies, it may be marked unverified and ordered.

b. Cards with adequate bibliographical information should be put into appropriate, usually current, bibliographies for verification. If the titles requested do not show up in a current tool, the bibliographer should consult a publisher's catalog or in-print catalog (PTLA can be useful on occasion here) if one is available. On the basis of what he does or does not find in these tools, the bibliographer will order the book as either unverified or NYP—remembering at all times that any available information is helpful to the chief bibliographer when he must decide whether or not to order such titles at once, to quote them, or question a requestor about bibliographical accuracy.

(11) As has been noted in the discussion of the holdings check, A., above, the library usually orders *later editions* of titles already on the shelves *only* if these editions reflect significant changes in content—*except* in the instance of literary works (including classics, i.e., Greek and Roman literature). Since all, or all significant, editions of a particular literary work may be desired, the checker should record the number of pages in a literary title requested when another edition of it is already in the library. Presumably, the number of pages in the library's copy will already have been noted down during the holdings check.

As a rule, any work requested by the classics department is purchased if the editor, translator, or commentator is different from those for titles already in the library. The same is often true for such major literary figures as Shakespeare, Goethe, Corneille, Dante, and Cervantes (see also Section A.6. for collection policies for variant editions). The final decision is that of the chief bibliographer; but the bibliographic checker must give him sufficient information about pagination, imprint, editor, etc.

(12) *Pamphlet materials* costing less than $3.00 should be put into *only one tool* and ordered as unverified if not discovered there. The bibliographer may recast the entry for such an unverified title if his experience so dictates.

2. ORDERING A TITLE

A. *To order or search* for a requested title, it is necessary to have a price (established or estimated); to decide whether a book is assumed to be NYP, in-print, or o.p.; to know the imprint if at all possible; and to determine to which dealer an order (for in-print titles) or a request to search (for o.p. titles) should be sent. Lacking such order information, the checker will have to decide whether or not to quote and to whom to quote. If he decides not to quote, he will have to decide whether to order unverified or return a request as a problem for the chief bibliographer.

B. Before submitting cards for revision to the chief bibliographer or his chief assistant, the bibliographic checker must *review* and *polish* his cards. He should be sure, first of all, that checks have been placed over all of the various bibliographical elements verified, and that the front of the card gives an accurate history of the checking that was done. Of course, the bibliographical history on the back of the card should accurately reflect that on the front. By glancing at the front and the back of any particular request card, the chief bibliographer should be able to follow *easily* all of the procedures of the bibliographer who worked with the card.[9] If such is not the case, something is wrong with the bibliographical procedure followed. Some routines for polishing the front of a request card for order detail are given directly below.

C. Polishing Details on the Front of the Request Card

The same scheme of the *front* of the request card, which we used before (A.3.B.), with numbers added as guides, is given again below. The numbered statements that follow this scheme use these guide numbers as reference points.

				Call No. 16
23 24 25 _ UNV _NYP _OP	26		27	

Author (last name first) or periodical title
1

Title
2

Series
3

Place 4	Publisher 5		Date of Pub. 6
Edition 7	No. Vols. 8	No. Copies 9	List Price 10	Estimate 11

Secondhand Dealer 12

Fund (see Procedure Manual) 13

Catalog No.	Item No.

Recommended By
14

Authorized By
15

ORDER NO. 30

Date ordered 29

Dealer 28

L.C. Card No. 20

17 18 19
_ AC _ AV _ DNC

Destination 21

Reserve Books
Course ____ 22

Semester

(1) If the overall bibliographical record seems accurate, the bibliographic checker should then be sure that the main entry is clearly legible for ease of MOF typing and filing. He should also be aware that if there are two or three joint authors, only the name of the first will be placed in the author space; but the name of each joint author should appear after the title entry, preceded by a comma and the word "by." If a work is by *more than three* authors, it is usually entered under title, with an author statement listing only the first author and the words "and others" following the title in brackets—that is, "by John James Smith [and others]." If the author is the editor or compiler of a work, the terms "ed." or "comp." appear after his name in the author space.

(2) The title should be complete enough to make sense, and will be followed by the names of joint authors, editors, translators, and compilers when appropriate. Editor and translator statements are *essential* for the correct ordering of any critical editions.

a. When a title is a reprint or facsimile of an earlier edition, an imprint statement about the earlier edition follows the title within brackets—that is, "[London, Smith, 1888]." (Reprints are considered again in the manual in Section A.6.B.)

b. If only one volume of a multivolume set is desired, the volume should be specified after the title—for example, "Notable Labor Radicals, Vol. 2 only." Similarly, if any edition will suffice or if a requestor wants *only* the latest edition or a new edition *only* (if one is forthcoming), this information is supplied in brackets after the title.

c. When words begin with unnecessary capital letters, our practice is to place a slanted line (/) through such letters to tell the typists not to capitalize them. If a title (or any other element) on a request card has been typed all in capitals by a requestor, our practice is to place two short horizontal lines (=) *only* under any letter which is to be capitalized by the typist.

(3) Series notes should be easily legible, with holdings checks clearly indicated. If a series note is too long to fit into the series space on the front of the card, the word "over" within *green* parentheses should lead the typist and reviser to the back of the card, where the note should have been completed.

If a title is one in a series being received in the Kardex, the bibliographer must stamp "Separate: Copy of Order to Serials" in the second-hand dealer space (12), in order to inform Kardex personnel that when the title arrives it should be given to the separates order librarian.

(4, 5, 6) Well-known cities need no further identification of place; if there is any doubt, however, the bibliographer should indicate country (or state) as well.

a. Short titles of publishers (if not ambiguous) are generally sufficient. If no publisher is given in a verifying source, a horizontal line is drawn to indicate this fact; such a line also indicates that place of publication is not given. If a foreign publisher is distributed by a U.S. dealer, the foreign publisher's name should be followed *within* brackets by "dist. by" and the U.S. distributor's name.

b. The date of publication should be the latest in print unless a particular critical edition in the humanities (possibly the social sciences) is requested. Checkers should also be careful not to select a title with a different editor or translator from that requested without first consulting the chief bibliographer. If a later edition of a requested title proves to be available, it may be necessary to change the requested imprint entirely.

c. As noted before, *never* change the imprint for out-of-print titles offered by or reserved with antiquarian booksellers, since they have only the imprint they offer for sale.

d. If a bibliography records a date of publication within brackets (meaning that the publishing date does not appear on the front/recto of the title page) or if it records a copyright, these should be similarly indicated in the date space—for example, [c. 1963]. If a bibliography records a title as a reissue, two dates should be noted—for example, "1964 [c. 1933]." Any uncertain date should be followed by a question mark—for example, "1965?"

e. If a set was published over a period of years, both the initial and terminal dates should be recorded—for example, "1922-1931." An open entry for a set (1855-   , 1926-   , etc.) indicates that at the time the bibliography recorded the publication the set was still continuing. In such cases, a later bibliography, if such is available, might have to be consulted to determine the total number of volumes in the final publication.

(7) First editions are not noted *unless* of interest in describing a literary work or a notable, landmark book in some other discipline. Any other statement indicating that a title is other than a first edition should be noted: revised edition, "rev. ed."; enlarged edition, "enlgd. ed."; subsequent edition, "2" or "3" or "4," etc.; reprint, "repr."; facsimile, "facs."; and so forth.

(8) The number of volumes for a title is indicated only if there is more than one. If a "1" appears in the volume space, it should be greened out. (For more about multivolume sets of considerable size, particularly those not yet completed, see Section A.9. on serials, series, and sets.)

(9) The number of copies is indicated only if more than one is requested If a "1" appears in the copy space, it should be greened out (also see 9 in "Definitions of Terms," Section A.3.).

(10, 11) Bibliographic checkers must be sure that foreign currency prices are converted, that the amount in foreign currency appears in the list-price space and the converted price appears in the estimate space, that a check is placed over the price if it has been confirmed, and that the price is in the estimate space if not confirmed. (See 10-11 in "Definitions of Terms," Section A.3. for other details on this subject.)

(12) It is in this space as well that requests for separates ordered in the Separates section, but also listed in the Kardex, are stamped "Separate: Copy of Order to Kardex," as stated in (3) above. Almost all documents are

at present ordered by the documents librarian; if, for any reason, Separates orders a domestic or foreign document, the second-hand dealer space is stamped "Separate: Copy of Order to Documents," so that the document will be received in Separates and the records will be cleared there. (See also 12 under "Definitions of Terms," Section A.3.)

(13, 14, 15) There must be a fund on each card. Cards indicating A&S funds (see the discussion of funding in "Order Procedures," Section A.8.) should have been authorized by the library representative of the A&S department paying for the title. As a rule, the name of both requestor and authorizer will appear on a card. The bibliographer doing departmentals (DNC or cataloged) should be sure that the chairman of the department buying the title has approved each purchase.

(16-27) Each place on the request card indicated by these numbers has been discussed earlier (under the same numbers in "Definitions of Terms," Section A.3.). Here, we need to note only a few points.

a. First, if a call number without a "see" before it appears on the front of the request card, the AC or AV space (17 or 18) must be checked (unless the card is a "Lib Has").

b. Second, dealers used must be selected from the dealers listed in the "Dealers" listing in this manual (Section A.11.) *unless* the request card is for a title offered or reserved for the library by particular booksellers. If a title is reserved from a bookseller's catalog, his name will appear in both spaces 28 and 12; the catalog number, and the number of the item in the catalog in which the title is offered, will appear as well. If the request card is in response to an offer, "letter of" followed by the date of the offer and any essential reference numbers will appear in red in space 12. We have hand stamps for many of our standard dealers, and these should be used when available.

c. Third, the "L.C. Card No." space (20) is a historical relic, first replaced by our own procedures for producing camera copy and now replaced by OCLC routines. Do not look for or record LC card order numbers.

d. Fourth, if a title is not found in a verifying bibliography, it must be checked *either* as unverified or as NYP; it should *not* be checked *both* unverified and NYP. However, a card can be checked both unverified and o.p.

e. Fifth, if a request is checked o.p., it will also be noted as a "search" in space 26, estimated at $15.00 per volume, and placed with a search dealer from the list in this manual—unless it is a request card in response to an offer from or a reservation for a title in a bookseller's catalog. The present policy is *not* to put unverified titles on search.

D. Submitting the Cards

When completed and polished cards are turned in to the chief bibliographer or his chief assistant for revision, they should be grouped by dealer. Further, "search" titles should be grouped separately from in-print titles, and "quote" and problem cards shold also be kept in separate groups.

C. VERIFICATION FLOW CHARTS

Some flow charts are useful; some are not. Nevertheless, many librarians seem both fascinated by such charts and much impressed by those who construct them. Such being the case, below are three types, which are susceptible to the usual amount of variation. Charts 1 and 2 may be of some use as samples. Chart 1 traces a title from the time it arrives in the library as a request through the point of its being ordered. A chart like 3, a type which is somewhat fashionable in some circles, can ultimately become so complex that simply to push a truck of books along possible lines of work stations, and demonstrate what to do with these various books at each step along the line, may be more useful to both clerical and professional personnel.

1. Placing A Separates (Book) Order

The entire operation may be thought of as having two discrete phases as follows:
    1. Receiving and precataloging the request
    2. Placing the order for the requested title

Placing the Order

	Mail Room	Typist	Chief Bibl.	Student Holdings Checkers	Verification Checkers	Separates Order	Student Filers

1. Request card received
2. Distributed to Department
3. Distributed to Chief Bibliographer
4. Distributed by Chief Bibliographer to Student for Holdings Check, or filed in "Request Card Hold File" for later action.
5. Holdings checked
6. Cards returned to Chief Bibliographer
7. Unwanted duplicates returned to requestor
8. Cards to be verified distributed to verification checkers
9. Cards verified according to procedures in Checkers Manual
10. Cards returned to Chief Bibliographer for revision
11. Cards revised
12. Cards distributed to Typists for Multiple Order Form
13. MOF typed
14. MOF distributed to Separates Order Section for typing proofreading
15. Typing proofread
16. MOF is distributed as follows:
    a. Canary: LC
    b. Salmon: Accounting Section for encumberance
    c. Buff: Sent to Cat. Dept. to be filed in Public Cat.
    d. Purchase order mailed out to vendor
17. Remaining portion of MOF forwarded to Student Assistant for filling, awaiting receipt of order
18. MOF filed to await arrival of book
19. Request card filed to await arrival of book

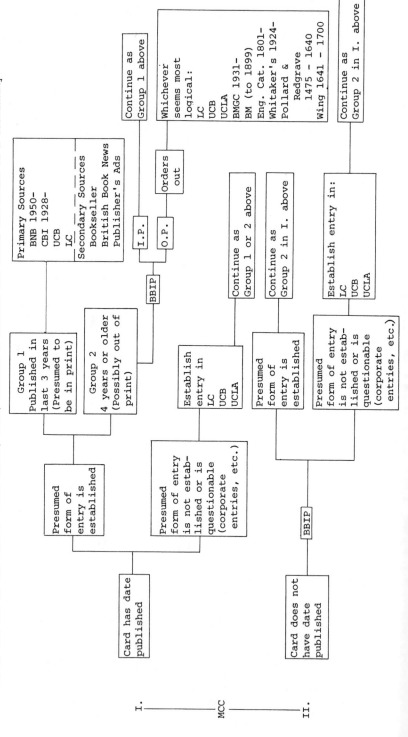

2. Verification Procedure: British

[This chart relies heavily for entry and total verification on the book catalogs of the libraries of the University of California at Berkeley (UCB) and Los Angeles (UCLA). If a terminal is presupposed, it would appear right after the "Card Has Date Published," and "Card Does Not Have Date Published" blocks on I. and II. of the chart. This chart, then, follows a routine for books not found in a terminal.]

3. SEPARATES VERIFICATION PROCEDURE: USING A TERMINAL AND OTHER RESOURCES

This chart is somewhat simplistic. Many such charts use diamond shapes for questions, boxes for procedure, etc. You might wish to try a hand at making a fancier chart, so to speak. Please note that books can be cycled into a terminal for only so long a time and that some books will eventually have to receive original cataloging.

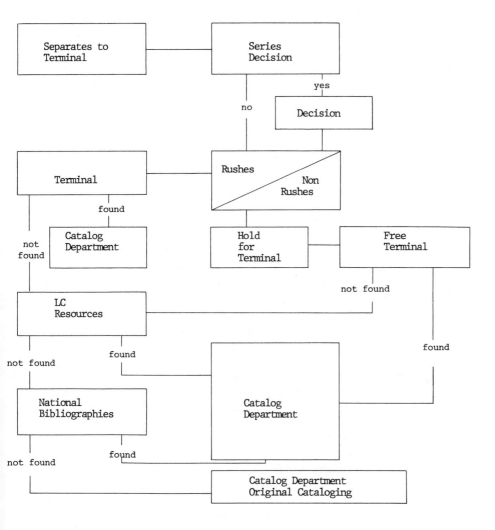

A.6. DEPARTMENTAL REQUESTS; AND SPECIAL PROBLEMS: VARIANT EDITIONS, VARIANT EDITIONS COLLECTION POLICIES, REPRINTS, AND PHOTOREPRODUCTION**

Any manual should have sections spelling out the routines for special kinds of requests and for particular bibliographical problems that arise in the course of daily business in particular institutions. For example, with the proliferation of special libraries related to particular disciplines in most large research institutions—and with the appearance of small departmental research collections purchased from state, federal, and other grants and endowments—it may be necessary to spell out what to do with requests for titles purchased from such funds and intended for such departmental, special libraries, and how to set up routines to facilitate the acquisitions of such titles. Likewise, more specifically bibliographical questions concerning policies for variant editions, reprints, reproduction of copy, and so forth may have to be spelled out, since such questions involve both acquisitions and ordering techniques. I do not propose to elaborate all possibilities, here, since they vary from institution to institution, and will give only a few samples as possible guides for dealing with particular repetitious problems.

A. DEPARTMENTAL REQUESTS: DNC (DO NOT CATALOG) AND CATALOGED

1. DNC

A. At present, titles requested on DNC departmental funds are not checked in the MCC or O.O. file, the departments assuming responsibility for not ordering duplicates of their uncataloged holdings. If DNC titles are ordered by library personnel, the O.O. file should be checked in order to prevent some such library department as, say, Acquisitions from ordering unnecessary duplicates.

B. The only other work to be done with these cards is to check the O.O. file for titles costing over $50.00 and to polish ragged entries for filing convenience. If DNC requests from academic departments appear to be likely candidates for addition to the main library system, the chief bibliographer can request the departmentals bibliographer to order any such titles that have not already been acquired for the main library.

2. CATALOGED

A. Cataloged departmental requests are processed like any other requests for books to be cataloged, *except* that the title is ordered for the

---

**Bibliographic Checkers *please note* comments under photoreproduction, E., below.

requesting department even though there are a number of copies located elsewhere. If bibliographic procedures reveal, however, that the requesting department already possesses one copy of a requested title, another copy is not purchased unless the department has checked the AC space on the request card.

B. In this last instance, the request will be returned as a "lib has," unless the chief bibliographer wishes to check with the requestor by phone. Further, departmental requests are not put into acquisitions routines unless such requests are signed by the appropriate departmental chairman.

B. VARIANT EDITIONS

1. As has been noted in the section on the holdings check, the library does not normally purchase earlier editions of scientific works when a later one is already cataloged in the MCC. In other words, the latest available edition of a scientific work is almost always to be preferred.

2. Earlier editions of literary works or scholarly editions of important titles in the humanities are ordered from time to time, even though a number of other editions of the particular title may be in the MCC. We are currently, for example, acquiring as many as we can of the significant scholarly editions of works by the Greek and Latin authors.

3. In the event that another edition of the requested title is in the MCC, the bibliographer doing the holdings check should record the page numbers, the imprint, the number of volumes, and the editor and/or translator (if any) of this other edition, because such information is necessary for whoever has the responsibility for decisions to purchase variant editions.

4. As explained in the section on the holdings check, whenever any variant edition of a requested title appears in the MCC, its call number with a "see" before it is the key which alerts the chief bibliographer to the fact that a variant edition problem exists. The call number without a "see" in front of it means, of course, that the request is a "lib has" (unless it is for an AC or an AV). Reprints are also viewed as "lib has" duplicates if the library already owns the original edition of the reprint.

5. A knowledge of the details explained in the paragraphs above, and of the sections in this manual on "Definitions of Terms," "Holdings Check," and "Verification," should enable the bibliographic checker to solve most variant edition problems himself. In cases where the final decision is unusually difficult, the procedure at present is to return the request card to the requestor with a "lib has ____ ed." notation, and let him resubmit a request for the particular edition if it is one he specifically desires. The chief bibliographer will backstop decisions on these matters.

C. VARIANT EDITIONS COLLECTION POLICIES

The statements below on this subject are greatly simplified. Large research libraries have vastly more expanded, complex programs.

We have, at present, several separate categories of policies for variant-edition collecting. These are as follows:

    1. Major Authors Project
    2. Drama Project
    3. Browsing Collection Project
    4. Social Science and Scientific Works
    5. Reference and Popular Works
    6. Translations
    7. Scholarly, Definitive, and Monumental Editions

1. MAJOR AUTHORS PROJECT

This project is maintained by the subject specialists, faculty, and various acquisitions personnel. There are *four programs* at present in this project, which are as follows:

    A. Major Authors "All Editions"
    B. Major Authors "Lifetime Editions"
    C. Major Authors "Works"
    D. Major Authors "Scholarly Editions"

Each is enumerated below. No distinction is made between works in poetry or prose.

    A. Major Authors "All Editions"

      We collect all editions for the following authors:

        (1) William Butler Yeats
        (2) Ezra Pound
        (3) T.S. Eliot
        (4) Henry Miller
        (5) D.H. Lawrence

Paid for from English A&S funds (in some few cases the library humanities fund will assist), these materials are shelved in Special Collections. We *do not* collect all "printings" or "impressions" or "states," but significant edition variations only. Important bibliographies may be shelved with this material.

B. Major Authors "Lifetime Editions"

We buy any edition, not already in the library, published during the lifetime of the following authors (Hume and Locke are funded A&S Philosophy; all of the others are A&S English):

18th Century		*19th Century*			
Hume	-1776	Borrow	-1881	Ruskin	-1900
Locke	-1704	Byron	-1824	Scott	-1832
Pope	-1744	Browning	-1889	Stevenson	-1894
Sterne	-1768	Eliot	-1880	Tennyson	-1892
Swift	-1745	Hardy	-1928	Wordsworth	-1850
		Hunt	-1859		

C. Major Authors "Works"

For selected twentieth-century authors, we collect a copy of each work that the author has written. In reality, this is "title" collecting, rather than "edition" collecting. First editions are preferred; although if a first is difficult to acquire, any edition may be acceptable. These titles are paid for from A&S English in most cases. The authors collected are listed in the "Major Authors Works" sheets, kept at the chief bibliographer's desk since they are constantly being added to by the English department. Please be familiar with these sheets and the authors included therein. Books acquired in this program will be shelved either in Special Collections or the stacks, depending upon such factors as desirability, price, condition, etc.

D. Major Authors "Scholarly Editions"

The works included in this program are those having scholarly, academic merit. Both in-print and out-of-print materials are relevant to these editions; and the program applies to any author in American or English literature— scholarly editions, definitive editions, critical works about, academic bi- ographies about, bibliographies, etc. Funding is obviously A&S English. Two examples are as follows:

(1) A new scholarly edition of a Ben Jonson work that we have in some other edition. The new edition has a new critical introduction.

(2) A twentieth-century definitive edition of a Ruskin title that we have in another edition is found in a bookseller's catalog. We would buy this as a scholarly work, even though Ruskin is a "Lifetime Editions" author (B., above). This material may or may not be shelved in Special Collections, depending on such factors as price; desirability; condition; date; whether or not it is criticism about, or the actual work of, an author; and so forth.

2. DRAMA PROJECT

This program will be worked out in the near future along the guidelines laid down in the "Major Author's Project" above.

3. BROWSING COLLECTION PROJECT

Material destined for the browsing collection, whether it is ultimately intended for the stacks or not, may be acquired in whatever in-print edition it is available.

4. SOCIAL SCIENCE AND SCIENTIFIC WORKS

We collect some early, landmark editions in these disciplines; but this aspect of acquisitions is largely a matter for the chief bibliographer and the academic departments concerned. What is important for everyone to remember is that we *routinely* acquire updated scientific works in the disciplines with which we work.

5. REFERENCE AND POPULAR WORKS

Encyclopedias, dictionaries, handbooks, travel books, etc. are collected in earlier and later variant editions as suggested by subject specialists, faculty, and other interested and informed parties.

6. TRANSLATIONS

If it becomes available, we usually purchase an English-language translation for any *non-creative* academic title present in the library only in a foreign language.

7. SCHOLARLY, DEFINITIVE, AND MONUMENTAL EDITIONS

Generally, approaches to the acquisitions of such editions follow the procedures discussed in "Major Authors Scholarly Editions," above.

D. REPRINTS

1. PROCEDURE

A. Descriptive information indicating that a reprint is being ordered follows in brackets the title requested. Delete such information if the verified reprint entry includes similar information. *Only* reprint-edition information appears in the place, publisher, and date spaces on the card. "Repr." appears in the edition space, as usual. If the reprint edition cannot be verified, the original edition should be; the usual LC, OCLC, or other bibliographical record tracing the original should appear on the back of the request card.

B. Even if the original of a reprinted title is verified, the card must still be marked as an unverified edition. A request for a reprint of an earlier edition of a title already in the library is returned to the requestor as a "lib has orig. ed."

2. EXAMPLE OF VERIFIED REPRINT EDITION

Shaw, John F   , 1789-1845
    History of the State of Massachusetts [Repr. from Ed. of 1869,
    ed. by R.B. Smith]
N.Y.   Barnes and Noble   1963
Repr. $7.50

E. PHOTOREPRODUCTION: O.P. BOOKS

As we know from 1.5., above, there are today very large numbers of more or less comprehensive programs of reprinting—completed, under way, or planned. Before contemplating the purchase of a photoreproduction of any particular title from any one company, the Acquisitions Librarian must determine whether or not that title is already available in another or a similar format: it might be included in some large reprint project already in his library but not formally cataloged in the MCC; planned but not yet forthcoming as an inclusion in a reprint series already subscribed to by his library; or already reproduced and available at lower cost on an individual basis of purchase from some other reprint company. Also, whatever is noted briefly below is only very approximate and subject to changes at any time in cost, legal regulations, procedures, etc.

Until a few years ago out-of-print books could only be obtained after an arduous and usually expensive search on the o.p. market. Now, aside from the great number of series of reprint projects under way or planned, many such books are available on a *one-shot* basis on microfilm or as printed copy from University Microfilms, Ann Arbor. The decision to request such copy will be made by the Chief Bibliographer in consultation with requestors. Budget is, of course, a factor.

University Microfilms carries a stock of about 100,000 titles as listed in its catalog, *Books on Demand.* These titles are priced as paperbound; hard cover is about $3.00 per volume extra. *Books on Demand* is kept with the other reference and bibliographic tools in Acquisitions.

1. BINDING

Paper or cloth bindings are available from U.M. We order cloth for library purchases, paper (unless otherwise specified) for departmental purchases. Check the latest catalog for binding costs which must be penciled in along with estimate of reproductive cost.

2. PRICE

A. As listed in *Books on Demand.*

B.* Title not listed in BOD and estimated at roughly 12¢ per page, plus binding cost if cloth binding is desired, plus search fee. Check latest catalog for these costs. The $25.00 search fee initiated ca. 1974 necessitates a more careful approach to this one-shot method of acquisitions. If we are considering a clothbound copy of a 300-page monograph by this method (not to speak of charts, graphs, etc., which are a problem in themselves), we are talking about a substantial sum of money.

*As of 1976, the procedure outlined in 2.B., above, is *not valid.* Please refer *any title* not in BOD directly to the Chief Bibliographer, who will handle requests for one-shot reproductions of o.p. titles by discussing the facts of life with the requestors of such.[10]

A.7. APPROVAL PLANS

The brief statements below are simply to orient bibliographic checkers and give them a general familiarity with approval-plan procedures. For an in-depth expansion of the subject of the approval plan, see II.6.

A. HISTORY

The Approval Plan is an arrangement with selected vendors to send new books in certain subject fields to the library, where subject specialists can review them for acquisition. We will probably expand into foreign-language areas in the future. (*Checkers* should *be sure to note B.4.C., below.*) Our two present plans are for English-language titles only. These plans were begun in a limited way in July, ____ and expanded in January, ____. The vendors who supply the library with these materials are _X_ and _Y_.

Y supplies books dealing with the Biological and Physical Sciences:
        Chemistry
        Engineering (Civil, Mechanical, Electrical, etc.)
        Geology
        Mathematics
        Physics
        Science and Technology
        Biological Sciences

X supplies books dealing with the Humanities and Social Sciences:

Anthropology	History
Art	Philology (Classics, French, etc.)
Drama	Philosophy
Economics	Political Science
Education	Psychology
Fiction, Poetry,	Religion
Avant-Garde Lit.	Sociology
Geography	Speech

All American publishers are represented in the Biological and Physical Sciences plan. *All* American university presses and *some* trade publishers are represented in the Humanities and Social Sciences plan. A complete list of these trade publishers is given in the approval-plan manual which is at the desk of the Approval-Plan Assistant.[11]

B. PROCEDURE

1. REVIEW

The books are unpacked and placed on the approval-plan shelves by mailroom personnel, in the usual invoice order under the designations of humanities and social sciences or biological and physical sciences. Each book has an individual "processing slip" made out by the vendor. Mailroom Assistants date each of these processing slips. Reviewers—faculty, subject specialists, etc.—are required to comb new titles *weekly*. If a reviewer fails to review his material during the week, the approval-plan assistant reminds him on Friday afternoon. If a reviewer still fails to show up by the end of Monday, the chief bibliographer and the approval-plan assistant will process the backlog the first thing Tuesday morning.

2. PROCESSING

A. Bibliographic information: the dealer's processing slip is used as our work slip. For library purposes, the processing slip is augmented by more complete bibliographic information taken directly from the book in hand—including proper entry (personal, corporate), title, publisher, place, date, LC or OCLC search record, and series information.

B. Funding information: subject-specialist or faculty reviewers may assign preliminary funding information. Sometimes a jacket blurb will offer additional assistance. Whatever the case, a fund decision should be made for each title and noted on the processing slip before any bibliographic checking is undertaken. In the fairly common event of doubtful funding by reviewers, the approval-plan assistant must check with the head of Acquisitions or the chief bibliographer.

C. Holdings check: the processing slip is used for holdings notations; bibliographic procedures are the same as for all requests.

D. Verification: the processing slip is used for verification notations; bibliographic procedures are the same as for all requests. However, it is *important* to note that OCLC is our only immediate resource for the verification of titles as recent as those arriving on approval plans. LC resources will, of course, supply verification for corporate entries for any other than a recent, first meeting of a corporate body, and often will supply main entries for translations (in the case of translations the entry used for the foreign-language original is used).

E.Serials: possible continuations of such types as monographic series, symposia, colloquia, etc., are reviewed, at the request of the approval-plan assistant, by the serials librarian. When this kind of serial is approved, the series entry is verified and the card is typed by the approval-plan assistant. Titles in a series not approved for continuation/subscription are processed as separates. Backfiles for a title in a series which comes in on an approval plan—several more or less recent volumes to initiate a serial subscription at the first issue or volume—are ordered by the approval-plan assistant in the usual manner, if so requested by the serials librarian.

F. Rejects: volumes which are rejected by reviewers or turn out to be duplicates of library holdings are returned to the vendor. The reason for rejection is noted on the processing slip, the second copy of which is retained by the approval-plan assistant. The listing of the title on the invoice is greened out so that the volume will not be paid for by the library. When the reject shelf fills up, the approval-plan assistant types a mailing label (about twenty-five books per package, with $300.00 insurance) and sends the books with the label to the mailroom personnel who will return them to the vendor.

3. FINAL PHASING

A. The processing slips are given to the typists for the typing of permanent request cards.

B. On the return of these cards from the typists, the approval-plan assistant shifts all holdings and verification information from each processing slip to the front and back of a card, and revises typing if necessary.

C. The assistant then returns all cards to typists for MOF's, leaving the processing slips with cards; the slips will be discarded by the Order section personnel when they work on approval materials.

D. The completed, full truck of approval-plan titles is left at the Order section station; typists give MOF's to separates receivers to be read and put in each volume along with the appropriate checking/request card; separates receivers then distribute the record and fund-keeping parts of MOF's and send the book truck to the Catalog department, along with the checking card and the catalog work-slip portions of the MOF.

4. MISCELLANEOUS

A. Statistics are kept for all approval-plan titles received, so that monthly and annual figures can be compiled for this operation—titles received in various disciplines, expenditures in various disciplines, etc.

B. A "work chart," such as the one below, summarizes procedural flow.

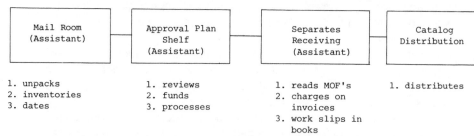

Mail Room (Assistant)	Approval Plan Shelf (Assistant)	Separates Receiving (Assistant)	Catalog Distribution

1. unpacks
2. inventories
3. dates
	1. reviews
	2. funds
	3. processes
		1. reads MOF's
		2. charges on
		   invoices
		3. work slips in
		   books
			1. distributes

C. Very recently, French, Italian, Mexican, Slavic, Spanish, and German approval plans have been set up. Receiving, reviewing, and processing routines are approximately the same as those for English-language titles. For coverage, and reviewers, see the approval-plan file at the chief bibliographer's desk. This file also explains the details of each of these new approval plans.

A.8. "ORDER PROCEDURES": SUMMARY FOR NON-ORDER PERSONNEL (FACULTY, DEPARTMENTAL SECRETARIES, NONTECHNICAL-SERVICES LIBRARIANS)

The "Order Procedures" statements which follow constitute a short *pamphlet, complete in itself, constructed in self-defense to explain—to faculty library representatives, to their departmental secretaries who often mistype and botch request forms/cards, and to nontechnical-services librarians (I am sorry to say)—the ins and outs of some basic, simplified acquisitions procedures, requirements, and facts of life in one particular institution. Every library should, however, have at hand some kind of similar exposition to be given to all potential requestors and to their secretaries or assistants who type requests. A copy of some kind of order procedures summary in an Acquisitions manual is, as well, a useful refresher for all staff. Any such pamphlet must, of course, be adapted to each, particular institution and its programs, procedures, and goals.*

**ORDER PROCEDURES FOR BOOKS AND PERIODICALS:
FOR THE GENERAL LIBRARY SYSTEM AND DEPARTMENTAL
COLLECTIONS**

The Acquisitions Department
September, _____

ORDER PROCEDURES: TABLE OF CONTENTS

ORDER PROCEDURES FOR BOOKS AND PERIODICALS

1. FUNDS, DEFINITION OF

Funds for the purchase of library materials for the main library and its branches are allocated annually by the Library in conjunction with the Faculty Library Committee. The university administration also makes available annually to each department "supplies and expenses" (S&E) funds, "equipment and facilities" (E&F) funds, and "research grant" funds, which may be used for the purchase of books and serials (periodicals) for departmental collections. Requisitions for the purchase of library materials on either library or departmental funds must be submitted *typewritten on library request cards* to the Acquisitions department of the university library. The Acquisitions department will supply these request cards to anyone who needs them.

A. Library Funds

The funds listed below are available for the purchase of books and serials (periodicals) for the main library and its branches. *The abbreviation of each fund,* given within the parentheses below, *should be typed in the fund space* on each card submitted.

(1) Library: General (Lib:Gen)

Used for the purchase of library materials of general interest and for books that would be useful to several fields in the humanities, social sciences, and biological and physical sciences. This fund should *not* be used for the purchase of materials which fall within a particular Arts and Sciences discipline.

(2) Library: Agriculture (Lib:Ag)

Used for the purchase of library materials in all fields of agriculture and related sciences—for example, domestic economy, food sciences and technology, marketing, etc. This fund should *not* be used for the purchase of materials which fall within a particular Arts and Sciences discipline.

(3) Library: Engineering (Lib: Eng)

Used for the purchase of library materials for departments in the School of Engineering.

(4) Library: Veterinary Medicine (Lib:Vet Med)

Used for the purchase of library materials for departments in the School of Veterinary Medicine.

(5) Arts and Sciences Allocations (A&S: Anthropology, A&S: Botany, A&S: History, etc.)

a. Used for the purchase of library materials for disciplines represented by departments in the College of Arts and Sciences. The purchase of books on an A&S fund *must* be approved by the library representative of the department whose fund will pay for those books. For example, A&S: History purchases are approved by the library representative of the History department when he initials the "Authorized" space on the request card.

b. Referrals of suggested purchases that involve funding problems are handled by the Acquisitions department. Since Arts and Sciences funds are limited, it is *not advisable* for any one department to suggest very many purchases that would have to be funded by other departments in unrelated disciplines.

(6) Current Periodicals (C.P.)

Used for the maintenance and placement of subscriptions for periodicals (serials) for the main library and its branches.

(7) Serials and Sets: Humanities (S&S:Hum)

Used for the purchase of extensive backfiles and expensive sets in the humanities and social sciences for the main library and its branches. Sets consisting of more than *four* volumes and costing more than *$150.00* may be considered for purchase from this fund. Backfiles of serials which cost more than *$300.00* may also be considered for purchase from the "S&S: Hum" fund. In rare instances, an extremely expensive monograph may be purchased from this fund.

(8) Serials and Sets: Science (S&S:Sci)

Used for the purchase of extensive backfiles and expensive sets in science and agriculture for the main library and its branches. See "S&S: Humanities," above, for the kinds of sets and periodicals (and their cost) that are often purchased from this fund.

B. Departmental Funds

All departmental purchases must be approved *only* by the chairman of the department or by his formally designated representative. The following types of funds are normally available to departments for the purchase of library materials for departmental collections:

(1) Departmental Blanket Funds

Used for the purchase of titles for departmental collections. Such funds are drawn from a department's equipment and facilities (E&F) or supplies and expenses (S&E) accounts.

a. In some cases, books (and periodicals) purchased on a departmental blanket fund may be shelved in the main library or its branches. These books, however, are *cataloged and become* the property of the main library. Ownership of such books *cannot* later be transferred back to a department.

b. Titles purchased on E&F accounts may be cataloged by arrangement with the library. S&E-funded titles are not cataloged.

c. The following is an example of how the blanket fund should be listed in the fund space of a request card:

Chemistry: E&F 0782

(2) Departmental Non-Blanket Funds (Direct Charges)

Used for the purchase of library materials for departments that *seldom* purchase books or serials. These departments use their E&F and S&E funds to purchase non-book materials and do not, therefore, have a blanket order fund with the library.

a. Since these departments do not have a blanket fund number for the purchase of books through the library, they must use the *entire* funding code in listing a purchase fund on a request card.

b. The following is an example of how a departmental non-blanket fund should be listed in the fund space of a request:

Dean of Ag: 2-300200-18800-3 (Dir. Charge)

(3) Research Grants (Direct Charges)

Used for the purchase of library materials for a research project. Funds for these purchases are received from such sources as the National Institute of Health, Atomic Energy Commission, U.S. Public Health Service, National Endowment for the Humanities, etc.

a. Research Grants are not given blanket numbers by the library (since they are by nature, temporary sources of funds), and are handled as direct charges. Materials purchased from such funds are not cataloged.

b. The following is an example of how the fund of a research grant should be listed in the fund space of a request card:

Food Sci. & Tech.: NIH3-220148-21620-2 (Dir. Charge)

2. ORDERING BOOKS AND SERIALS (PERIODICALS)

A. Books

(1) Library and A&S Accounts

a. *Order Information*

The request card should have the author's full name with the *last name first*; title of the book; place of publication, publisher, and date of publication; statement of the edition wanted if *other than* the first; number of volumes if the title has more than one volume (do not record a "1" for a one-volume book); number of copies (if more than one is wanted); price or price estimate of book; and series information if book is one in a series.

It is *exceedingly important* that the author's name, the title of the book, and the place, publisher, and date of publication be given whenever possible and as accurately as possible, since error or omission of these points of information can cause considerable delay in ordering.

SECRETARIES PLEASE NOTE

1. Request cards *must* be *typewritten.*
2. Do *not* type above line at top of card. This space should be reserved for "Rush," "Rush To Order," and "Soon" notations (see "Priority System," d., below).
3. Dealer's name and address should not appear in "Place," "Publisher," or "Date" spaces on request card. If given, dealer's address should appear in "Secondhand Dealer" space.

4. "Destination" should be indicated only if the material is to be sent to a location other than the usual one for books purchased from your funds.
5. Order only *one* book on each request card (you can order a set with several volumes in it or a series with several titles in it on one card). The point here is *not to order several separate books on a single card.*

b. Fund Information

As noted previously, the proper fund should be listed. Each department's library representative must authorize all purchases from the funds that the department controls. No authorization is needed for those few recommendations for purchases to be made from funds other than a department's own.

c. Cataloging Information

All books purchased from the library and A&S accounts are cataloged into the main library or its branches. If a multiple copy is desired, the card should be marked as an "AC" (added copy) in the space provided on the request card. If the book requested for purchase is known to be an added volume to a set or series which is cataloged already as a set or series, the card should be marked "AV" (added volume) in the space provided on the request card.

d. Priority System

The Acquisitions department has the following priority system:

1. *Rush.* This is the highest priority and is to be used *only very occasionally.* (See the sample order cards in part 3 of this "Order Procedures: Summary" for position of all indications of priority on request cards.) "Rush" priority is to be used in those few instances when need is unusually urgent—that is, titles needed at once for current research, or reserve books that a faculty member has delayed in ordering. As you know, reserve books should be ordered with the note "soon," *two to three months in advance* of the course in which they will be used.
2. *Rush to Order.* This is the second-highest priority. The book is rushed through the Acquisitions department, but is given regular priority in the Cataloging department. This priority is used chiefly for books to be ordered at pre-publication discount rates.
3. *Soon.* This priority exists for those requests that rate higher in need for processing than regular requests, but not so high as to warrant rush handling. Such requests are usually included in the Acquisition department's next biweekly production group. *Reserve books* are normally in this priority, are to be ordered *two to three months before a course,* and are submitted to Circulation, *not* to Acquisitions.
4. *Regular.* This term simply describes the vast majority of requests which are routinely handled by the Acquisitons department. Please *note* that "regular" *does not appear* on a request card, unlike indications for "rush," "rush to order," or "soon." Almost all request cards submitted to Acquisitions *must* fall into this "regular" category; otherwise the system of priorities spelled out above would be meaningless.

(2) Departmental and Research Grant Funds

a. *Order Information*

See 2.A.(1).a., above.

b. *Fund Information*

See 1.B., above.

c. *Cataloging Information*

See 1.B., above. Books purchased from departmental E&F funds may be cataloged by agreement with the Acquisitions department. S&E and research-grant purchases are not cataloged. If an E&F-funded book is *not* to be cataloged, please *be sure* to check, the "DNC" space on the request card.

(3) Dealers' Catalogs, O.P. Titles, Photocopy Orders.

a. *Dealers' Catalogs*

1. These are catalogs of out-or-print materials, in contrast to *publishers' catalogs* which list in-print books. It is imperative that such out-of-print dealers' catalogs be marked for selections and forwarded to the Acquisitions department *within one or two days of receipt.* Catalogs should not be slowed down to have cards typed.

2. *Do not* indicate a dealer for in-print books selected from *publishers' catalogs,* since Acquisitions has its own vendors for these in-print titles. However, if such an in-print title is selected from an advertising flyer or a brochure, it is helpful to Acquisitions if this advertisement is sent along with the typed request card to Acquisitions.

3. All departments are urged to mark dealers' catalogs *selectively.* A maximum of twenty-five o.p. titles can usually be checked the same day as received by Acquisitions.

b. *O.P. Titles*

Out-of-print books are searched for (given to a special dealer who will hunt for them) if a requestor so desires. It should be remembered, however, that the searching process is uncertain and can be expensive. Also, when a title is searched for, the procedure places an encumbrance against library, A&S, or departmental funds, as the case may be, for an indefinite period of time.

c. Photocopy Orders

To acquire a photocopy of out-of-print titles is *difficult, if not impossible,* unless these appear in the University Microfilms catalog, *Books on Demand.* Anyone desiring the library to order photocopy of o.p. titles *must* first consult with the chief bibliographer in Acquisitions.

(4) Approval Plans

The Acquisitions Department has approval plans, which are as follows:

a. *Humanities and Social Sciences*

Provides books published by *all American university presses*; those *British university presses* that distribute their books through the American market (Oxford, Cambridge, London School of Economics, etc.); and a number of American trade publishers. You can assume, in fact, that any book of *academic* value published by the American trade will arrive on this approval plan. Acquisitions *will provide* an up-to-date printed list of considerable length upon request.

1. This plan was initiated July,____. These books are supplied automatically and charged to the proper library and A&S funds. Library representatives and subject specialists review these items.
2. Unless need is *especially urgent,* request cards should *not* be submitted for items that will arrive by approval plan.

b. Physical and Biological Sciences

Provides advanced texts, dictionaries, laboratory manuals, treatises, and similar publications of an *advanced nature*—that is, senior level and above. This plan was initiated at the same time as the humanities plan, and all statements about that plan apply to the sciences plan, except that the sciences plan includes *all American trade* publishers.

(5) U.S. Government Documents

a. Academic departments are authorized to make direct purchases by means of "U.S. Supt. of Documents" coupons for documents costing up to $4.00. A department makes requests for free federal documents directly to the appropriate governmental agency, *not* to Acquisitions.

b. Coupons may be requested and purchased from the Documents department on the standard request card.

c. Documents costing more than $4.00 are purchased for a department by the documents librarian. Requests are submitted on the standard request card, with the usual required information supplied. Since the general library is *both* a state and U.S. documents depository, any department requesting such documents for the library *should check first* with the documents librarian.

B. Serials (Periodicals)

Current subscriptions and orders for backfiles of serials—whether for the main library, its branches, or individual departmental collections—must be placed with the Acquisitions department. Request cards or lists should be submitted to the serials librarian. Serials are paid for by the library or departmental funds (discussed in part 1.A-B. of this "Order Procedures: Summary").

(1) Current Periodicals (C.P.)

The C.P. fund is intended for the purchase of subscriptions to current serials which will be shelved in the main library or one of its branches. Single requests should be submitted on the standard request card. If several subscriptions are being recommended, a typewritten list—*alphabetically arranged* by serial title—should be submitted, since this facilitates acquisitions procedures.

(2) Serials and Sets

Funds so designated are intended for the purchase of backfiles of serials and of sets (as explained in part 1.a. (7)-(8), above). A request for a single backfile of a serial or for a single set should be submitted on a request card; requests for a number of such titles should be submitted on typed, alphabetized lists.

(3) E&F, S&E, Research Grant Orders

Current subscriptions, backfiles, and single, unbound issues of serials may be purchased from equipment and facilities funds, supplies and expenses funds, and research grant funds.

(4) Reprints of Articles

Reprints of articles from journals are never purchased through the library. Each department should order these directly from the periodical's publishing offices.

3. SAMPLE ORDER CARDS: BOOKS AND SERIALS (LIBRARY FUNDS AND DEPARTMENTAL FUNDS)

A. Books

(1) Library Funds
a. Arts and Sciences (A&S): "Regular," Non-Priority Order

__ UNV __ NYP __ OP ORDER NO.				Call No.	
Date ordered	Author (last name first) or periodical title **Borning, Bernard C**				
Dealer	Title **The political** and social thought of **Charles A. Beard**				
L.C. Card No.	Series				
__ AC __ AV __ DNC Destination	Place **N.Y.**		Publisher **A. Knopf**	Date of Pub. **1972**	
	Edition	No. Vols.	No. Copies	List Price **$ 6.75**	Estimate
Reserve Books Course _____	Secondhand Dealer			Catalog No.	Item No.
Semester					
	Fund (see Procedure Manual) **A&S:Philosophy**			Recommended By **John James** Authorized By	

b. Arts and Sciences: RUSH

Two added copies are wanted to be placed on reserve for a course. *Be sure* to record the library call number *and* to send such requests for reserve books through the Circulation department, *not* Acquisitions.

__ UNV __ NYP __ OP ORDER NO.	RUSH			Call No.
Date ordered	Author (last name first) or periodical title			E189.2 B84
	Bowden, Peter J			
Dealer	Title			
	The wool trade in Tudor and Stuart England			
L.C. Card No.	Series			
X AC __ AV __ DNC Destination	Place N.Y.	Publisher St. Martin's press		Date of Pub. 1972
	Edition	No. Vols.	No. Copies 2	List Price $ 8.00/ea
Reserve Books Course _____ Semester	Secondhand Dealer			Catalog No. / Item No.
	Fund (see Procedure Manual) A&S: History	Reserve Course Hist. 105	Recommended By J.R. Orn Authorized By *a c .*	

Estimate: $ 16.00

c. Library Agriculture (Lib:Ag): SOON

Note that only the first author's name appears in the author space, although the book is by two authors, both of whose names appear after the title. The request is for the second edition of an English title, with price converted to dollars and cents.

__ UNV __ NYP __ OP ORDER NO.	SOON			Call No.
Date ordered	Author (last name first) or periodical title			
	Self, Peter			
Dealer	Title			
	The state and the farmer, by P. Self and Herbert J. Storing			
L.C. Card No.	Series			
__ AC __ AV __ DNC Destination	Place London	Publisher Allen & Unwin Ltd.		Date of Pub. 1972
	Edition 2nd	No. Vols.	No. Copies	List Price 30/-
Reserve Books Course _____ Semester	Secondhand Dealer			Catalog No. / Item No.
	Fund (see Procedure Manual) Lib: Ag		Recommended By A. Martin Authorized By *A.M.*	

Estimate: $ 4.50

d. Library: General (Lib:Gen): SEARCH
The requestor wants this out-of-print title searched for.

__ UNV __ NYP **X** OP ORDER NO.	SEARCH				Call No.	
Date ordered	Author (last name first) or periodical title Palmer, Henrietta Raymer					
Dealer	Title List of English editions and translations of Greek and Latin classics printed before					
L.C. Card No.	1641					
	Series					
	Place London		Publisher Blades, East & Blades		Date of Pub. 1911	
__ AC __ AV __ DNC Destination	Edition	No. Vols.	No. Copies	List Price	Estimate $ 10.00	
Reserve Books Course _____	Secondhand Dealer				Catalog No.	Item No.
Semester						
	Fund (see Procedure Manual) Lib:Gen			Recommended By M. Warren		
				Authorized By *a. C.*		

(2) Department Funds
a. Order for a Book Which Is Not to be Cataloged (DNC)

__ UNV __ NYP __ OP ORDER NO.					Call No.	
Date ordered	Author (last name first) or periodical title Altick, Richard Daniel, 1915-					
Dealer	Title The art of literary research					
L.C. Card No.	Series					
	Place N.Y.		Publisher Norton		Date of Pub. 1973	
__ AC __ AV **X** DNC Destination	Edition	No. Vols.	No. Copies	List Price $ 3.95	Estimate	
Reserve Books Course _____	Secondhand Dealer				Catalog No.	Item No.
Semester						
	Fund (see Procedure Manual) English E&F 0907			Recommended By B. Weems		
				Authorized By *B. W.*		

b. Order for a Book to Be Cataloged

If this order were for another copy of a book already cataloged and shelved in the department, the AC space would be checked and the Library call number typed in, as in (1) b., above.

__ UNV __ NYP __ OP ORDER NO.	Call No.
	Author (last name first) or periodical title Lamerton, L. F ed.
Date ordered	
Dealer	Title Cell proliferation
L.C. Card No.	Series
__ AC __ AV __ DNC Destination	Place: Philadelphia Publisher: F. A. Davis Date of Pub.: 1973
	Edition No. Vols. No. Copies List Price: $ 7.95 Estimate
Reserve Books Course _____	
Semester	Secondhand Dealer Catalog No. Item No.
	Fund (see Procedure Manual) Zoology E&F 0992 Recommended By: S. Amaral Authorized By

c. Order for a Single Monograph (Book) from a Monographic Series.

Note that both the title of the series and the number of the requested book in the series is given in the "Series" space. The book is to be cataloged.

__ UNV __ NYP __ OP ORDER NO.	Call No.
Date ordered	Author (last name first) or periodical title American Society for Testing and Materials
Dealer	Title Symposium on soil dynamics
L.C. Card No.	Series (ASTM special technical publ. # 305)
__ AC __ AV __ DNC Destination	Place: Philadelphia Publisher: The Society Date of Pub.: 1972
	Edition No. Vols. No. Copies List Price: $ 4.50 Estimate
Reserve Books Course _____	
Semester	Secondhand Dealer Catalog No. Item No.
	Fund (see Procedure Manual) Ag. Eng. E&F 0207 Recommended By: C. Beech Authorized By C. B

d. Order for a 2-Volume Set on a Direct Charge, Special Fund

__ UNV __ NYP __ OP ORDER NO.	Call No.
Date ordered	**Author (last name first) or periodical title** Hochster, R M
Dealer	**Title** Metabolic inhibitors; by R.M. Hochster and J.H. Quastel
L.C. Card No.	Series

	Place N.Y.	Publisher Academic Press	Date of Pub. 1974

__ AC __ AV **X**DNC
Destination

Edition	No. Vols. 2	No. Copies	List Price $ 46.00	Estimate

Reserve Books
Course _____
Semester

Secondhand Dealer	Catalog No.	Item No.

Fund (see Procedure Manual) Food sci. & Tech. Grain Prod. 3-440348-46822-3 ⌈DIR.CHG.⌉	Recommended By A. Tanner Authorized By *T.C.*

e. Order for a 3-Volume Set
This set, which is to be cataloged, is a new reprint of an earlier edition.

__ UNV __ NYP __ OP ORDER NO.	Call No.
Date ordered	**Author (last name first) or periodical title** Bower, Frederick Orpen
Dealer	**Title** The Ferns
L.C. Card No.	⌈reprint of 1923-8 edition⌉ Series

__ AC __ AV __ DNC
Destination

	Place N.Y.	Publisher Stechert-Hafner	Date of Pub. 1973

Edition rept	No. Vols. 3	No. Copies	List Price $ 32.50	Estimate

Reserve Books
Course _____
Semester

Secondhand Dealer	Catalog No.	Item No.

Fund (see Procedure Manual) Botany E&F 0881	Recommended By E.M. Gisford Authorized By *R. W.*

f. Order for Three Additional Volumes (AV) to Complete Departmental Holdings of a Cataloged Set

__ UNV __ NYP __ OP ORDER NO.				Call No. QP601 C66
Date ordered	Author (last name first) or periodical title Colowick, Sidney P			
Dealer	Title Methods in enzymology, Vols. 5, 6, and 7 [ONLY]			
L.C. Card No.	Series			
__ AC X̶AV __ DNC Destination	Place N.Y.	Publisher Academic		Date of Pub. 1972-74
	Edition	No. Vols.	No. Copies	List Price Estimate $ 90.00
Reserve Books Course _____ Semester	Secondhand Dealer			Catalog No.	Item No.
	Fund (see Procedure Manual) Food Sci. & Tech E&F 0442			Recommended By W. Duncan Authorized By E MͨD.

B. Serials

(1) Department Fund: Order for a Current Subscription not to be cataloged (DNC)

__ UNV __ NYP __ OP ORDER NO.				Call No.
Date ordered	Author (last name first) or periodical title American Chemical Society			
Dealer	Title Journal [November 1972 and continuation this is in addition to our present subscription]			
L.C. Card No.	Series			
__ AC __ AV X̶DNC Destination	Place Washington D.C.	Publisher Chemical Society		Date of Pub. 2/month
	Edition	No. Vols.	No. Copies	List Price $ 30.00 Estimate
Reserve Books Course _____ Semester	Secondhand Dealer Serial			Catalog No.	Item No.
	Fund (see Procedure Manual) Chemistry S&E 0890			Recommended By J. Jones Authorized By A. J.

(2) Library Fund: Order for a Current Subscription (C.P.) for a Serial to be Cataloged

__ UNV __ NYP __ OP ORDER NO.				Call No.
Date ordered	Author (last name first) or periodical title **Philological review**			
Dealer	Title **v.1 and future vols. as issued**			
L.C. Card No.	Series			
__ AC __ AV __ DNC Destination	Place **N.Y.**	Publisher **Academic Press**		Date of Pub. **Irreg.**
	Edition	No. Vols.	No. Copies	List Price **$ 12.00/vol.**	Estimate
Reserve Books Course _____ Semester	Secondhand Dealer **Serial**			Catalog No.	Item No.
	Fund (see Procedure Manual) **C.P.**		Recommended By **J. Johnson** Authorized By *J. P.*	

4. ACQUISITIONS DEPARTMENT ORGANIZATION CHART

It is important that this chart be kept simple and clear; have current names *(possibly the phone numbers) of key personnel; and spell out what questions particular staff members can answer, and their duties.*

This chart is constructed to tell you who does what in Acquisitions and who can answer particular questions or help with particular problems.

ACQUISITIONS DEPARTMENT: ORGANIZATION CHART

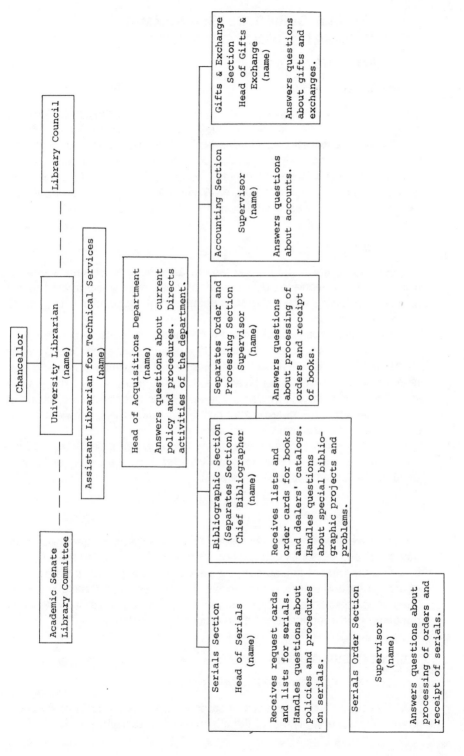

A.9. SERIALS, SERIES, SETS: A SUMMARY FOR SEPARATES BIBLIOGRAPHERS

A. DEFINITIONS OF TERMS

1. SERIALS

A serial is a publication issued *in successive parts* at more or less regular intervals, and *intended to be continued indefinitely* into the future. Serials include such publications as periodicals, annuals, yearbooks, scholarly journals, little magazines, symposia, congresses, proceedings and transactions of societies, newspapers, etc. Typical serial titles would be *Saturday Evening Post; New Yorker; Vogue; Who's Who in . . .; Advances in . . .; Year's Work in . . .; First Symposium on . . .;* and so forth.

2. SERIES

A series is a serial publication issued as a number of separate works which can stand alone (as books/monographs), are usually related to one another in subject, and are issued in some sort of succession with a collective title.

A. Series *are* serials, since they are planned to be continued indefinitely.

B. There are two types of these monographs-in-series (monographic series) publications: what we can *arbitrarily* call academic series and publishers' series. Academic series are issued by some kind of scholarly sponsoring body and almost always *numbered.* Publishers' series are issued by commercial firms and *may or may not be numbered* (such series can, of course, be highly academic in content).

We do not often put *unnumbered* monographs in series in the Kardex (since they are very difficult to keep track of), and we simply order such unnumbered monographs as separates.

3. SETS

A set is a number of volumes related to one another in subject *or* a collection of various works by one author—these volumes related by subject or by being the work of one author being issued by one publisher in some kind of sequential and standardized format. A set differs from a serial (including the monographic series) in that it is not intended to be continued indefinitely, but completed sooner or later in several or more volumes.

B. PROCESSING DEFINITIONS

1. TO ANALYZE (TO MAKE ANALYTICS)

A. To analyze is to make a set of cards for the added entries of a work for which the main entry is that of the title of a series as a whole (see "To Cata-

log in Series," below). Analytics make it possible to approach such a mono-
graph-in-series through author, title, and subject of the monograph as well
as through the main—the title—entry.

B. Series analytics require time and cataloging expertise and are less
commonly constructed today than in former years.

2. TO CATALOG AS A SEPARATE ("CAT SEP")

This procedure means that the *main entry* for each work in a series will be
the author's name, not the series title, and that the monograph will have its
own individual call number (LC classification). Such monographs are referred to as "Cat Seps."

3. TO CATALOG IN SERIES

To catalog in series means that each work in the series will have the series
title as the main entry and one call number for all titles issued in the series.
To provide a user with an author, title, and subject approach, such a series
would have to be "analyzed" (as in B.1., above).

C. BIBLIOGRAPHIC AND ORDER PROCEDURE

1. SERIALS

As you know, the Serials section is responsible for almost all of the work
done on serial publications, from current subscriptions to backfiles. As a
rule of thumb, a title main entry is often, although not always, a tip-off to a
serial publication. Since it is not always possible to tell whether or not a
work is intended to be continued indefinitely (publications of symposia are
one example), a single work of this indeterminate nature may occasionally
be ordered by the Separates section with the notation "examine for standing order."

2. SERIES

A. The Serials section handles the ordering and processing of subscriptions for current monographs in series and backfiles of such titles. *Single
monographs* of such series (if required to fill in gaps, for example) are ordered
by Separates. If a title of a monographic series that is on subscription (standing order) is processed through Separates, the bibliographic checker *must*
stamp "Separate: Copy of Order to Serials" in the "Secondhand Dealer"
space on the request card.

B. Any title that is part of a monographic series received on subscription
(standing order) will fit into one of the following categories: AC, AV, DNC,
Repl., or Split Series (part of the titles in a series cataloged as separates,
with author of each monograph as main entry; part of the titles in the series

cataloged with the *series title* as the main entry under one call number for these titles).

(1) All bibliographers *must* understand these terms, as well as those explained previously in this section of the manual (see also "Definitions of Terms," Section A.3.).

(2) The Split Series, which is found often in MCC entries, is proof positive of the practice of not doing the analytics in the present days that were a common practice in days past (see "Processing Definitions," above).

C. There is nothing else peculiar to the purchase of titles/monographs in series. But it should be obvious that the careful recording of series notes in the "Series" space on the request card, and of the holdings for titles in a series already in the library, are of great importance in dealing with monographic series. (See also Section A.4.C. for some examples of monographic-series entries in the MCC.)

3. SETS

Sets that seem to be planned to be issued over a period greater than *three* years are ordered by Serials so that a Kardex record control of them can be kept until they are completed. If there is doubt about length of planned publication, the set is usually ordered in Separates with the penciled notation in the "Destination" space on the request card of "Examine for transfer to serials." Very large sets with an extended time planned for publication (or published in many volumes over a number of years in the past) are referred to as "monumental sets."

4. KARDEX CONTROL

As you know, we subscribe to large numbers of serials, particularly in a great variety of scientific disciplines; and many of these serials are located in special and departmental collections, cataloged and uncataloged. We are very proud of our Kardex Control and the personnel (2½ FTE) who maintain it. They will answer any questions, help you with any problems, and give you any orientation you may need at the Kardex work station. All Acquisitions personnel are expected to take advantage of this Kardex expertise.

A.10. FUNDING

As with the Checking Manual in general—and this entire guide, for that matter—this section assumes an overall "book budget" (budget for monographs and serials, properly phrased) allocated between the main library system, which includes several different subjects and several kinds of materials to be purchased, and some of the various departments in Arts and

*Sciences. This assumption enables the reader to get an idea about a more
diversified method of funding than is found either in cases where the library
or the academic departments have complete, or almost complete, control
over the budget for monographs and serials.*

Bibliographers please *note* that the "Order Procedures" pamphlet (Section A.8.) included in this Checking Manual contains pretty much all of the
funding detail with which the bibliographer needs to be familiar in the course
of handling most requests. The funding information below may further clarify
some subjects and remains, thus, a section of the Checking Manual.

A. FUNDING INFORMATION

The materials purchased by Acquisitions are paid for from three different
types of funds: library, departmental, and research grants.

1. LIBRARY FUNDS

A. Library funds are used for books and periodicals (monographs and
serials) destined for the main library collections or one of its branches. Almost all are cataloged. The librarians "control" the first seven allocations on
the list of *"Library Accounts,"* (covered in part C of this section). The faculty
of Arts and Sciences controls the remaining allocations listed thereafter.
By "control" is meant authorization to purchase materials from the budget.

B. Should a faculty member wish to purchase a book from the "Library:
General" fund, a librarian must authorize same. Should the library wish to
purchase a book on any of the A&S budgets, the departmental library representative responsible for the budget involved must authorize the request.

C. Two of the library funds are designated as "Serials and Sets" (S&S:Humanities; S&S:Science). These two allocations are intended for the acquisitions of backfiles of serials, large sets, and, on occasion, expensive monographs.

(1) Serials Backfiles

Backfiles of serials priced at more than $300.00 are considered for purchase on the Serials and Sets account, humanities or science as the case
may be.

(2) Large Sets

Any set of four volumes or more and priced at $150.00 or more is given
consideration for purchase from the S&S account. Any very expensive set,
regardless of the number of volumes, is given similar consideration. Sets of
fewer than four volumes, and appropriate to an A&S subject area, are referred to the proper department for authorization.

(3) Expensive Monographs

Even though it would normally be purchased from an A&S account, any
monograph which costs more than $100.00 is considered by the chief

bibliographer for purchase from the S&S budget. Several factors influence such a decision: amount of funds in the A&S account; amount of funds in the S&S account; curricular or research need for the requested title; and intuition.

2. DEPARTMENTAL FUNDS

A. Funding Code

Throughout our university system, the funds for each department are kept by a numbering system called the funding code, which indicates the name of a department, the source of the money, the name of the campus or location, and the final use of the funds.

(1) This code is composed of the following elements: campus location; name of department; source of fund (general university funds, research grants, etc.); and physical nature of materials purchased (Equipment and Facilities [E&F] describes inventoried items, such as cataloged books; Supplies and Expenses [S&E] describes non-inventoried items, such as *un-cataloged* books).

(2) A typical code would be written as

                   3-404024-1880-2

which translates as

          "Library location—Biology Dept.—General Funds—S&E"

B. Blanket Number

Each campus accounting office assigns most departments a "blanket number," a simplified code reference to the funding-code number—i.e., "Biology: S&E 0620," rather than the string of numbers in (2), above. The chief bibliographer, the bibliographic checker doing departmentals, and the Order section have a listing of departmental funds and codes for catalog or DNC information. *Please remember* that E&F blankets may or may not be cataloged (although usually cataloged), but that S&E blankets are *not* cataloged. However, such fund blankets must appear on all requests for books.

C. Direct Charge

Direct-charge funds do not have blanket numbers, and must be given in their entirety in the fund space on requests for books—for example, "FS&T NIH 176 2-330238-11620 (Dir. Charge)." Such charges are for books that are DNC and shelved in the departments ordering them.

3. RESEARCH GRANTS

Books purchased from research-grant funds have these characteristics: full code fund for grant must be written out; titles are *uncataloged*; and titles so purchased are shelved in the department purchasing them.

B. FUNDING INFORMATION AS APPLIED TO DESTINATION AND CATALOGING TREATMENT

Type of Fund	Destination	Cataloging
A. Library (See Library Accounts following for listing of Library funds)	Main Library and Branches Depts within Library: Reference Acq. & Cat.	Yes Yes No
B. Departmental (See A.2.B., above, for lists of funds)	Departments	E&F: yes, usually (see A.2.B., above) S&E: no
C. Research Grants (Fund lists kept by Departments)	Departments	No, always

C. LIBRARY ACCOUNTS

The funds listed below are called "library accounts" because they are intended for the purchase of materials destined to be cataloged into the main library or one of its branches. As indicated in B., above, some few books purchased from these funds for special-reference use by Acquisitions and Cataloging are DNC, so that patrons at the MCC will not be confused and try to find such titles on the shelves of the Main Library.

Library Accounts Controlled by Library

Library: Agriculture	S&S:Humanities
Library:General	S&S:Science
Library:Engineering	Current Periodicals (C.P.)
Library:Veterinary Med.	

Library Accounts Controlled by A&S Faculty

A&S:Anthropology	A&S:History
A&S:Art	A&S:Mathematics
A&S:Bacteriology	A&S:Military Science
A&S:Botany	A&S:Music
. . .	. . .

D. [SAMPLE] FUND MEMORANDUM, 1 MAY _____

To: Acquisitions Department Personnel
From: Chief Bibliographer

Subject: Fund Names 19_____/19_____ (latest fiscal year)

The following names and abbreviations for new funds and sub-allocations have been decided upon for the new fiscal year. On request cards, please use the abbreviations given below for material to be paid for from these funds and sub-allocations.

Health Sciences: New Funds Divided as Follows:

Health Sciences: Veterinary Medicine	HS:Vet
Health Sciences: Medicine	HS:Med
Health Sciences: Serials & Sets: Veterinary Medicine	HS:SS:Vet
. . .	
Health Sciences: Current Periodicals: Medicine	HS:CP:Med

Library General: Several New Allocations Now under this Fund

Library General	Lib:Gen
Library General: Documents	L Gen: Doc
Library General: Map Collection	L Gen: Map
Library General: Microforms	L Gen: Mic
Library General: Replacements of Missing Material	L Gen: Repl
. . .	
Library General: History of Science	L Gen: Hist Sci
Library General: Medieval & Renaissance	L Gen:M&R
. . .	

A.11. DEALERS

In an operation which supposes an informed and intelligent staff, there is no reason that bibliographic checkers cannot in most instances assign dealers for the acquisitions of monographs. But any manual, however the responsibility for selecting appropriate dealers is assigned, should have lists of dealers for the ready reference of both professionals and clericals.

A. DOMESTIC DEALERS

Checkers are to use first priority dealers only; where second and third priorities (choices) of dealers are listed, these are guides to replacing canceled searches and for suggesting options to the chief bibliographer for the further pursuit of elusive titles.

1. IN-PRINT TITLES

A. Trade

Humanities	_____
	(name of dealer)
Social Sciences	_____
Physical Sciences	_____
Biological Sciences	_____

B. Non-Trade

(1) Directly to publishing or issuing body if address becomes available in the course of routine checking.

(2) _____ if address does not become available in the
(name of dealer)
course of routine checking.

C. Quotes

Domestic Quotes go directly to publisher of title; if publisher is not known, quote goes to our regular trade dealers.

D. Music

(1) Scores   _____
(name of dealer)

(2) Records   _____

2. OUT-OF-PRINT TITLES

For O.P. Titles, use _____ for second search
(name of dealer)
where no second dealer is specified. Use _____ for third, last-resort searches.

American Literature

(1) _____
(name of dealer)

(2) _____

Art

(1) _____

(2) _____

Chinese

(1) _____

Cinema

(1) _____

.   .   .

B. FOREIGN DEALERS

1. IN-PRINT TITLES AND QUOTES
Africa
(1) All Nations except Union of So. Africa _____
                                             (name of dealer)

(2) Union of So. Africa _____

Australia and New Zealand _____
                          (name of dealer)

Austria

(1) _____

(2) _____
.   .   .

2. OUT-OF-PRINT TITLES: QUOTES AND SEARCHES

For O.P. Titles, Use _____ for second search
                     (name of dealer)
where no second dealer is specified. Use _____ for
third, last-resort searches.
Africa
(1) All Nations except Union of So. Africa   _____
(2) Union of So. Africa _____
Australia and New Zealand _____
Austria _____
Canada_____

.   .   .

A.12. MONETARY EXCHANGE RATES

All manuals should have some such listing, which must be kept current by typed or penciled revisions. Percentages can be rounded off—for example, U.S. $ .1770 equals 20– equals 1/5 equals 5 into the amount of this foreign currency for any title listed to give U.S. dollar equivalent.

Foreign Exchange Rates _____
                                                    (Date Penciled In)

Country	Unit	Symbol or Abbreviation	Equivalent in U.S. Dollars (Penciled In)
Argentina	Peso	Arg. $	_____
Austria	Schilling	S or DM Ost.	_____
Australia	Dollar	A $	_____
Belgium	Franc	F	_____
Brazil	Cruzeiro	Cr. $	_____
Canada	Dollar	Can. $	_____
Czechoslovakia	Koruna	Kcz	_____
Denmark	Kroner	D.Kr.	_____
Finland	Markka	MK	_____
France	Franc	F	_____
Germany	Deutsche Mark	DM	_____
Hong Kong	Dollar	HK $	_____

. . .

A. 13. LIBRARY REPRESENTATIVES, AND OTHER USEFUL NAMES

A. LIBRARY REPRESENTATIVES

Discipline	Name	Phone #
Anthropology		
Botany		
Entomology		
Foreign Languages		
Classics		
French		

. . .

Political Science
Pomology

. . .

B. OTHER USEFUL NAMES

Name	Position	Phone #

. . .

II.3

HOW TO ORGANIZE AN *ORDER MANUAL*: AN OUTLINE OF SOME PROCEDURES AND PROBLEMS

A.

  The chief bibliographer (head of Acquisitions, head of Separates, etc.) and his bibliographic checkers (bibliographers, bibliographic searchers, bibliographic assistants, etc.) work primarily with request cards, as well as with, on occasion, LC proof slips, work slips for approval-plan titles, antiquarian catalogs, and so forth (as discussed at length in the *Checking Manual,* II.2.). When the checking (searching, precataloging) procedures have been completed as described in II.2., the polished, finished request cards for titles to be bought are given to the Order librarian, who will in turn assign them by dealer groupings to clerical assistants, who will then type the bibliographical and order information from the front of each request card onto a multiple order form—the ever-present MOF. The MOF's, which run in numbered sequence for records control, are presumably typed neatly and correctly, and are then returned to the order librarian to be proofread by the staff at that work station and sent out as orders for monographs or serials.

It is important that both order and typing personnel be sufficiently trained in bibliographic checking procedures to catch errors or omissions on request cards (which should ideally come without errors from the bibliographic-checking work station). The order librarian and Order section personnel are, thus, largely concerned with the MOF and its parts, just as bibliographic searchers are largely concerned with request cards.

MOF's vary a great deal in printed format and number of slips (parts) per individual MOF, according to the bibliographic and order routines and record-keeping needs of individual libraries. There is, thus, no standard MOF, just as there is no standard set of order routines. All that can be suggested here are kinds of routines. Similarly, the samples of a possible MOF format and its parts, given below, can only provide an idea about the possible form and function of the MOF. It should be added that, as a fact of life for Order section personnel, the MOF slips that are pulled apart from each form and distributed upon *ordering* a particular title must be retrieved again in the *receiving* process. No doubt machines will one day entirely replace these manual and repetitive tasks, in a time devoutly to be wished for. But no matter what the methods and devices employed, order procedures must be logical and adhered to carefully and consistently.

The order librarian should be able at any time to tell an inquirer several things: (1) *when* a particular title was ordered (if it has not been ordered at all, the head of Acquisitions or the chief bibliographer will then be on the firing line); (2) *what* the status of any order is at any given time; (3) *when* an ordered title might be expected to arrive; (4) *when* (how soon) a title will be processed to Cataloging after arrival; (5) *when* (on what specific date) a title has passed from the Order section to Cataloging; and (6) *where* any title in the receiving process is *located,* in the event that it should be necessary to lay hands on it to expedite its processing.

B. (SUGGESTED) TABLE OF CONTENTS: ORDER MANUAL

1. The Request Card and MOF Slips (C., below)
2. Ordering Separates (C., D.1., below)
   a. Standard Order Procedures for Library Materials
   b. Other Order Procedures
      (1) Quotes
      (2) Searches
      (3) Reserves (from Antiquarian Catalogs)
      (4) Special Materials (records, educational kits, etc.)
3. Receiving Separates (D.2-3., below; C. basic as well)
   a. Arranging Books for Checking In
   b. Pulling Request Cards and MOF Slips
   c. Checking Invoices against Shipments
   d. Checking Books against Request Cards
   e. Handling MOF Slips
   f. Arranging MOF Work Slips and Completed Books
   g. Handling Incomplete Orders/Shipments
   h. Completing and Sending Trucks to Cataloging
   i. Dispersing and Filing Invoices, Slips, Etc.
4. Receiving Separates: Special Routines
   a. Cat Seps (monographs in series cataloged separately; see II.2.A. 9.B.1-3., above)
   b. Approval Plan Books (see II.2.A.7., above)
   c. Gifts (see II.4., below)
   d. Maps, Microforms, Etc.
   e. Music
   f. Rare Books
5. Credit "Memos" (Memoranda)
6. Bill Letters
7. Statistics
8. Returns of Duplicate and Faulty Material
9. Cancellations
10. Claims and Reports
11. Periodic Reviews of Searches and Quotes
12. Miscellaneous

C. THE REQUEST CARD AND MOF SLIPS

1. THE REQUEST CARD

(See II.2.A.3., above, for a *detailed* discussion of the *front* and the *back* of the request card.)

A sample *front* of a request card is given below. The MOF sample slips which follow it (in C.2.) are taken from this sample front, as they would be in actual practice in order procedures. The bibliographic-checking corps is responsible for all bibliographical and order information supplied on the request card *except* the *order number* and the *date of order*, which are supplied for the request card and the MOF by the Order section department personnel when the MOF is typed from the request card. (See II.2.A.8., above, for various examples of request cards.)

The request card is filed in the O.O. file after the MOF is typed from it, and is the control in the O.O. file. It is retrieved and sent to Cataloging as a bibliographical record of precataloging (verification), along with the book it describes when that book is sent from Acquisitions to the Catalog department.

__ UNV __ NYP __ OP				Call No.
ORDER NO. 5697854-NY				
Date ordered 5/21/77	Author (last name first) or periodical title Schlesinger, Arthur Meir, 1886-			
Dealer Bertram	Title The American as a reformer			
L.C. Card No.	Series (John Randolph Haynes ... Amer. problems)			
__ AC __ AV __ DNC Destination	Place Cambridge	Publisher Harvard UP		Date of Pub. 1950
Reserve Books Course _____	Edition	No. Vols.	No. Copies	List Price $ 2.50	Estimate
Semester	Secondhand Dealer Bertram			Catalog No. 127	Item No. 3275
	Fund (see Procedure Manual) A&S:History			Recommended By Smith	
				Authorized By *T. G.*	

2. MOF SLIPS

The explanations of the use of the *seven* slips of the sample MOF follow. Some institutions would require fewer similar slips; perhaps some would require more.

a. FUND SLIP (PINK)

(1) Note that MOF slips are color coded to aid filing and distribution of slips to proper locations; some slips are of thicker paper than others because they will get heavier wear (the MCC; public catalog slip, for example).

The bookkeeper (or machine) will use the information from this fund slip to encumber funds as books are ordered but not yet formally received. As you know by now, encumbered funds must be considered as monies spent, although the titles ordered have not yet arrived and been formally processed and paid for.

(2) When the title arrives, the Order section records on this slip the date of its invoice *and* the actual cost to the penny as listed on this invoice *and* the date the title has been received in the Order section. When the bookkeeping/accounting personnel *formally* pay the invoice, which they will normally batch with several others, the date of this last, formal payment is recorded in the "Bill Date" space; *and* the money paid for this particular title is subtracted from the amount of funds encumbered in a particular account (A&S: History) and now considered as funds formally spent and no longer available to that account (see II.7. for a number of illustrations of encumbrances, formal expenditures, etc.).

ORDER NO.	FUND		
5697854-NY			
DATE OF ORDER			
5-21-77			
DEALER	Schlesinger, Arthur Meir, 1886-		
Bertram			
NO. VOLS. | NO. COPIES	The American as a reformer.		
	Camb., Harvard UP, 1950		
	(John Randolph Haynes ... Amer.		
FUND	problems, 1950)		
A&S:History			
	$2.50		
DESTINATION	Cat.127, item 3275	INVOICE DATE	
RECOMMENDED BY		COST	
Smith			
DATE RECEIVED	BILL DATE		

B. PUBLIC CATALOG SLIP (PC, MCC SLIP; LIGHT BROWN)

Some libraries—as a rule those utilizing solid routines and giving *superior service* to patrons—file such a slip in the MCC for the information of users. Obviously, filing such a slip requires adequate staff time, plus a willingness to undergo and be responsible for answering questions about why a title ordered at such and such a time has not yet been processed onto the library's shelves. This kind of order-information slip is removed from the MCC at the time the Cataloging department files the permanent main-entry card into the MCC for the particular ordered title that has now been received, cataloged, and shelved.

ORDER NO. 5697854-NY	PUB. CAT	
DATE OF ORDER 5-21-77		
DEALER Bertram	Schlesinger, Arthur Meir, 1886- The American as a reformer. Camb., Harvard UP, 1950	
NO. VOLS. | NO. COPIES	(John Randolph Haynes … Amer.	
FUND A&S:History	problems, 1950) $2.50	
DESTINATION	Cat.127, item 3275	
RECOMMENDED BY Smith	**ORDERED**	

C. PURCHASE ORDER SLIP (WHITE)

This slip is sent to the dealer and is his formal authorization to supply the title required. Purchase Order slips also contain further instructions on the back; so both the front *and* the back of this sample slip are shown below.

(1) Front of P.O. Slip

ORDER NO.	PURCHASE ORDER	
5 6 9 7 8 5 4 - N Y		
DATE OF ORDER		
5 - 2 1 - 7 7		
DEALER	Schlesinger, Arthur Meir, 1886-	
Bertram	The American as a reformer.	

PURCHASE ORDER

Schlesinger, Arthur Meir, 1886-

The American as a reformer.
Camb., Harvard UP, 1950
(John Randolph Haynes … Amer.
problems, 1950)

$2.50
Cat. 127, item 3275

NO. VOLS.	NO. COPIES

INVOICES IN QUADRUPLICATE
FOLLOW INSTRUCTIONS ON BACK
ORDER AUTHORIZED BY:

SHIP TO: ACQUISITIONS DEPARTMENT
The Library
The University
Greenwood, Conn. 06880

(2) Back of P.O. Slip

INSTRUCTIONS

1. <u>All</u> orders to be invoiced in quadruplicate

2. All invoices, correspondence, mailing-labels, etc., must give our order number.

3. When publication does not agree with your description with regard to author, title, edition, imprint, etc., we reserve the right to return.

4. Report before sending if your price is considerably higher than our estimate.

5. Unless item is received within 3 months for domestic orders, 6 months for foreign orders; or we are advised of a specific date to expect delivery; order will be considered cancelled. If available later, please <u>offer</u> again.

D. NOTIFICATION SLIP (GREEN)

(1) This slip is sent to an academic department *when* an ordered title has been processed, cards filed for it in the MCC, and the title placed *on the shelf* ready for use. The slip goes to the requestor of the particular title. Since academic departments can use these slips to keep track of expenditures of their funds, some one in the department should be responsible for keeping a central file of such slips.

(2) The notification slip is another mark of a properly functioning library. It should be kept with the temporary-catalog slip (e., below). The notification slip is sent to the requestor by Circulation as soon as the Catalog department files its permanent cards for the title in the MCC, removes the on-order slip (the PC slip, b., above) from the MCC, and so informs Circulation of this fact.

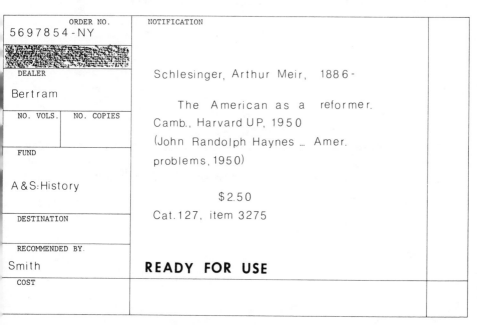

ORDER NO. 5697854-NY	NOTIFICATION	
DEALER Bertram	Schlesinger, Arthur Meir, 1886-	
NO. VOLS. | NO. COPIES	The American as a reformer. Camb., Harvard UP, 1950 (John Randolph Haynes … Amer.	
FUND A&S:History	problems, 1950)	
DESTINATION	$2.50 Cat. 127, item 3275	
RECOMMENDED BY. Smith	**READY FOR USE**	
COST		

E. TEMPORARY CATALOG SLIP (GOLD)

The availability of such a slip is, again, the mark of a very well run library. The temporary-catalog slip and the notification slip (d., above) are filed together in Circulation, and enable personnel there to answer questions about titles listed in the MCC as on order, but not yet cataloged, without having to go to the MCC for information. Also, the presence of only the gold temporary-catalog slip in the Circulation file shows that the green notification slip has indeed been sent to a requestor *and* gives backup when notification slips go astray in the mail, are lost or misplaced by requestors, and so forth.

ORDER NO.		TEMP. CAT.
5697854-NY		
5-21-77		
Bertram	Schlesinger, Arthur Meir, 1886-	
	The American as a reformer.	
	Camb., Harvard UP, 1950	
	(John Randolph Haynes ... Amer.	
	problems, 1950)	
A&S:History		
	$2.50	
	Cat.127, item 3275	
Smith		

F. INCOMPLETE CLAIM SLIP (YELLOW)

This slip is for use as a record in the O.O. file when *only part* of a set ordered has been received. Information pertinent to what has been received is written into the "Vols. & Date Received" space at the bottom of the slip. A notation about the date when the Order section sent a follow-up letter of inquiry about the missing volumes is also helpful.

ORDER NO.	INCOMPLETE CLAIM	
5697854-NY		
DATE OF ORDER		
5-21-77		
DEALER	Schlesinger, Arthur Meir, 1886-	
Bertram	The American as a reformer.	
NO. VOLS. / **NO. COPIES**	Camb., Harvard UP, 1950	
4	(John Randolph Haynes ... Amer.	
FUND	problems, 1950)	
A&S:History		
	$2.50	
DESTINATION	Cat.127, item 3275	
RECOMMENDED BY		
Smith		
VOLS. & DATE RECEIVED	*Vols. 1-2 only, received on Invoice # ——— of July 15, ——— Letter of Inquiry sent July 17, I.*	

G. ORDER RECORD SLIP (BLUE)

This slip is filed in *numerical order* in Acquisitions, *with* date of receipt of title and all invoice information written in, as the piece is received and the bill received and sent on for payment. If necessary, cost of item is corrected from the invoice (see also, Fund Slip, a., above).

ORDER NO.	ORDER RECORD	
5697854-NY		
DATE OF ORDER 5-21-77		
DEALER Bertram	Schlesinger, Arthur Meir, 1886-	
NO. VOLS. | NO. COPIES	The American as a reformer. Camb., Harvard UP, 1950	
FUND A&S:History	(John Randolph Haynes … Amer. problems, 1950) $2.50	
DESTINATION	Cat. 127, item 3275	
RECOMMENDED BY Smith		COST
DATE RECEIVED	BILL DATE	

D. ORDERING AND RECEIVING ROUTINES: SUMMARY

1. If you look again at the MOF sample slips above, and think about their functions, you can visualize a general picture of an order librarian's work. In *ordering,* verified and completed (polished) request cards are received from the chief bibliographer, typed on MOF's, and the MOF's are pulled apart and distributed.

However, *none* of this distribution begins *until* the purchase-order slip has been batched with others, by the names of dealers to whom they will go, and sent out in the mail. *Then,* we have the following procedures: the request card itself goes into the O.O file, with the order number and order date having been typed on it; the incomplete claim slip is clipped to the request card in the case of orders for multi-volume sets and the possible need for this slip in the event of volumes missing from such orders; the fund slip is sent to the bookkeeper (person or machine) for funds to be en-cumbered in the appropriate account; the public-catalog slip is picked up by Cataloging and filed into the MCC; the notification slip and temporary catalog slip go to Circulation; and the order record slip is filed numerically in a separate file in Acquisitions. These routing functions are largely clerical, but require careful overseeing to keep them running smoothly and correctly.

Since the request card and all but one of the MOF slips (the order record slip) are filed alphabetically by main entry in their various locations (the fund slip is filed alphabetically within its individual fund in Bookkeeping), it would be hard to overstate the importance of correct bibliographical routines to establish main entries correctly *before* any distribution and filing begins.

2. I am not attempting to describe all Order section intricacies here; but we know also that *receiving* routines, like those of ordering outlined above, involve a number of additional activities. For example, the books that arrive in the mailroom daily must be placed on book trucks in proper invoice order and, along with their invoice, wheeled into the Order section. Here, the books must be checked against the invoice to be sure that all of the shipment is correct; and invoice prices for particular titles must be checked against those on the request card and the order-record slip, and corrected on these forms if necessary (such a procedure involving retrieval of the request card, which will go to Cataloging, and the making of notations on slips in the order-record-slip file. With a title in hand, Order section personnel must check it against the request card to be sure that what has been received is what was ordered, or an acceptable version thereof. If books and invoice match and there are no bibliographical discrepancies, invoices are sent on their way to Bookkeeping to be paid; and books, *accompanied* by the request card with its bibliographical record, are delivered to Cataloging (some MOF's also have a "catalog" work slip for use in that department).

3. So far so good with *receiving.* But *what if* all books in a shipment do not match the invoice for the shipment (books listed on the invoice are missing; books not on the invoice are in the shipment)? And there are other problems that can and do arise with rather unpleasant frequency, and can be summarized by a few more questions: *what if* a particular title proves to be an unwanted duplicate at some stage of the game? a particular book arrives in damaged, unacceptable condition? part of a set is missing? the invoiced price of a title differs greatly from that indicated or estimated on the request card? a book falls within the various definitions that may make it "rare"? invoices arrive unaccompanied by shipments of books? books arrive unaccompanied by an invoice, etc.?

I do not propose to grapple with such problems or answer such questions here; for we would then have yet another book, perhaps even longer than the Checking Manual, on our hands.[12] But I wish to point out that each such hitch in the system demands some kind of a corrective routine, many of which can be dealt with by the use of forms and form letters constructed to deal with particular and repetitive situations (some of these forms are given in II.9.). It is, in fact, to answer such questions in the real world of a working day that the chief bibliographer, order librarian, head of Acquisitions, and anyone else appropriate will commonly be found gathered in session at sunset to deal with such troublesome items that may have arisen in the hours before.

4. In the Order section, there are additionally such obvious activities as supervision of personnel; recommendations for promotions, raises, terminations; keeping statistics; preparing work studies to justify present staff or ask for more; and so forth. But I think that I have suggested enough, and supplied sufficient illustration, in this outline of order routines to indicate what they are, how they work, and what an order manual should have in it to explain and control such routines.

II.4

HOW TO HANDLE
GIFTS AND EXCHANGES (G&E)

A. GENERAL REMARKS

Any library recognizes that gifts can constitute a unique and valuable means of developing holdings. It will, therefore, welcome or solicit gift materials which are in keeping with the research goals and acquisitions programs of the library in particular and the university in general.[13]

However, gifts can present problems, some of them complex, at every level of the library's operation—involving collection development aims and academic goals, administrative time, staff time, public relations, and, above all, budget. Such terms as "gift" and "donation" imply something free, costing nothing. But any "gift" that ties up staff time and physical space is *not free,* not without cost to the receiver of that gift; and the *immediate cost* and the *ultimate cost* in *personnel time* and *space* of any gift must be weighed against the value of the gift in direct relation to the academic aims of the library and the university. Dealing with gift materials requires, thus, educated and sufficient personnel and *written* policies and routines which should be uniformly followed.

The natures of donors, donations, and donees—if you prefer, givers, gifts, and givees—produce a complex interplay of factor and circumstance with which most academic and research institutions have never entirely come to grips. Some potential or actual donors are bibliophiles or specialists in fields of great academic research value. But many donors are well aware of the uniquely American tax write-off for gifts to nonprofit institutions, and give solely for such monetary benefits to themselves—that is, many givers are motivated not only by their personal and emotional evaluations of what they are giving, but as well by the specific monetary evaluations which might be placed on their gift by others (among these, the income tax appraiser).

It is, thus, very important that right *at the point of* a gift offering, its true, overall value to the donee be carefully considered. It appears inherent in human nature to act in haste and repent at leisure. Numbers of administrators in various institutions have so erred and have stuck themselves, those who follow after, and their institution with one kind or other of perpetual white elephant.

In a correctly administered institution, there will be a *detailed written gifts policy,* with which all librarians and library and university administrators are familiar, and to which all such parties adhere. Informed and firm-minded library personnel should implement this written policy. After all, any gift that will be used seldom or never in one particular institution is, at best, worthless to that institution and, at worst, very costly to maintain—although that *same gift* might have been of great and lasting value in advancing the academic aims and goals of another institution. Large gifts unaccompanied by *open-ended* supporting funds should be looked at *very closely,* with cost of housing and servicing weighed into the far future. A realistic comprehension of the library's present and future needs is essential, in such instances, to correct evaluation.

Donees grab unsuitable gifts from several generally indefensible motivations: (1) the hope that a wealthy donor may later be persuaded to give either money or materials of more academic utility; (2) the desire of those in an institution with very little to have something; (3) the persistence of an individual strong in an administrative structure who has been smitten by the nature of a particular gift; (4) a penetrating voice from Professor X for a gift somehow related to his own obscure specialty; (5) the all-too-common faculty practice of attempting to discard personal copies of outdated texts, paperbacks, etc., into the library for a tax write-off; and so forth. Any of these motivations can exert a knee-buckling force that has placed good books and collections in the wrong places and not-so-good books and collections in many places across the United States.

Any satisfactory G&E operation will spell out *both* gifts policy and the responsibilities and procedures of the G&E librarian. The gifts policy, below, should be in *one separate written statement* for the information of both the university community and the public. The G&E librarian's responsibilities, etc. C., below), should be written out in *another separate document* for library use, so that the G&E librarian's responsibilities and procedures are understood by all other library personnel. Gifts policies and procedures vary, of course, from institution to institution, but should be understood and followed within each.

B. GIFTS POLICY

1. The library's gifts policy follows the usual principles for book selection and collection development—namely, the aim of bringing into the Library the greatest possible wealth of materials relevant to the teaching and research functions of the University.

2. The library endorses an active program of gifts solicitation *based upon* a detailed evaluation of any book or collection in relation to academic programs under way or projected.

3. The library as a rule makes no formal commitments concerning the housing or final disposition of gifts. Gifts will receive the same treatment as that given comparable materials being considered for or processed into the library's holdings. Gifts with restrictive conditions attached are not usually accepted.

4. As stated in 3., above, a donor understands how his gifts will be handled. If there appears to be any problem about agreement to this stated procedure, any final resolution must be given in writing. Appropriate letters and/or forms will acknowledge all donations.

5. The library cannot legally make its own appraisals for purposes of tax deduction. If such an evaluation is necessary, the library may suggest a competent appraiser. The cost of appraisal rests in most cases with the donor. For tax deduction purposes, the donor must write a *formal and specific* letter about his gift: its content, the date of donation, etc. The gifts librarian will respond formally in writing.

6. If a gift is refused, the library may suggest alternative solutions or locations for the placement of materials.

7. No gift will be accepted by the library or the university before the gifts librarian has been informed and has had time to consult with library subject specialists.

8. Gifts of funds for general library use or for particular collections and memorials are always welcome. Funds so contributed will be used in accordance with usual library procedures for collection development.

C. G&E LIBRARIAN: RESPONSIBILITIES AND PROCEDURES

1. LOCATION OF OPERATION

The G&E activities of any library almost necessarily fall within the administrative lines of the Acquisitions Department.[14] Here, the G&E librarian will work directly under the head of Acquisitions and will as well be in a location to work across administrative lines for advice from subject bibliographers and the chief bibliographer and within the structure of regular acquisitions routines to process his materials.

The G&E operation is physically in the pattern flow of the mailroom operation, which it can use to receive titles to be processed and to move unwanted titles out of the library. It is vital that G&E have sufficient storage space, coordinated with the storage space of other sections of Acquisitions, since any active gifts program will inevitably from time to time produce more titles than can be processed on a regular day-to-day basis.

2. RESPONSIBILITIES AND PROCEDURES

A. LIAISON

Perhaps the basic responsibility of the G&E librarian is to evaluate the potential of gifts in relation to the collection-development policies of his institution. As a rule, such evaluation will require the opinions of various subject-specialist and special-collections librarians. Even if it is clear to the G&E librarian that a gift is unsuited to the library, he will want confirming evidence for his point of view and suggestions about where a rejected donor might try next. Also, the academic worth of many offerings will exceed the range of any one librarian's expertise, and consultation will be essential in such instances. With all evidence in and summarized in writing, if necessary, the G&E librarian will have executed his liaison work.

Gifts containing titles destined for Special Collections are normally handled by that staff, although the G&E librarian should be apprised about such gifts because he may have to supply some of the muscle for pickup and delivery. Also, titles culled from potential special-collections donations often come to the G&E librarian for processing into stack holdings. He is, however, free from the liaison, public relations, and bibliographical activities usually associated with such gifts.

B. PUBLIC RELATIONS

Public relations for the G&E librarian may be defined largely as suggesting alternative actions to potential donors whom he has refused (he will have good public relations as a rule with donors whose materials he accepts to their satisfaction). Here, liaison is again important; for other librarians, especially those in Special Collections, may have sound ideas about appropriate institutions or book dealers whom a refused donor might contact.

Polite forms acknowledging small gifts and letters of appreciation for larger gifts are obviously an important public-relations function of the G&E librarian. Another less obvious but very important contribution toward the good will of donors is logistical (see also "logistics," below)—namely, the prompt, polite, and neat pickup of gift items. Failures of library representatives to show up to take gifts at agreed-upon times and sloppy, not to say brutal, pickups of materials from the residences of donors create more ill will than a host of posh receptions can ever redeem.

C. LOGISTICS

Moving physical objects in space and time is an important part of G&E routine. Getting the proper librarians and other necessary personnel to a donor's residence and out again is not, however, necessarily so simple as it sounds. Further, as noted before, gifts must be picked up and delivered to appropriate library areas in some kind of orderly fashion, and arranged logically on receiving-area shelving for review by subject specialists and for processing thereafter. Processing in turn requires refining materials into several categories: books for general library collections, for Special Collections consideration, for possible sale to or credit allowances from various dealers, for student book sales, and for discarding. Also an integral part of G&E logistics are routines of gifts acknowledgment; record keeping for titles accepted and processed, or otherwise dispersed; and production/ work records.

D. PROCESSING

Gift books added to the library must be verified by the G&E section, using the routines described in the library's "Checking Manual."[15] Gift books are in hand, of course, and do not have to be ordered; but request cards and MOF's must be typed out to provide bibliographical and order-record control for titles which the library was decided to process.[16] The main thrusts of verification and order-record procedures are to find a bibliographic record of a title in LC, NUC, OCLC, or other sources to facilitate professional procedures in the Catalog department; to file MOF slips for records of gift titles so that books received by gift will not be purchased as unwanted duplicates; and to inform users of the MCC that any particular gift title is in process for the library's collections.

This processing activity presupposes G&E personnel are as well trained as those in the other sections of Acquisitions. It is a truism that a sufficient and trained G&E staff is vital if large acquisitions of gifts are to be kept under control.

E. EXCHANGES, TRADES, DISCARDS

(1) *Exchanges* is descriptive of the practice whereby one large research institution exchanges its scholarly publications (almost always serials— journals and monographs in series—but occasionally individual monographs) for the scholarly publications of another research institution on a free, roughly even-Steven basis. Such exchanges require, however, considerable logistical activity. Also, if staff time is counted as cost—and it certainly ought to be—any kind of a cost study will show exchanges to be an expensive method for acquiring "free" materials. For these and other reasons, exchanges are perhaps not so popular as they once were; at any rate, they form only a small portion of the work duties of most G&E librarians, though the "gifts and exchanges" terminology persists.[17]

(2) *Trades* is simply a jargon term to describe books and serials which a bookseller or dealer is willing to take from a library and, in return, pay cash for or give credit against future purchases. "Trades" books can come from gifts as unnecessary duplicates or may be titles "weeded" from the library's

collections. The trading procedure can be, however, very tricky, with librarians constantly over- or under-evaluating the books which they wish to trade, and with interested dealers constantly under-evaluating such books (the librarian's evaluation often being from a genuine ignorance of pricing itself and of dealer cost and profit margins; the dealer's evaluation being from every businessman's desire to make money). The G&E librarian must take it as a rule of thumb, to be used with some tact and discretion, that no dealer will overpay for a book if he knows his business.

In the matter of "trades," the G&E librarian can only consult his own knowledge, that of library subject specialists in the kinds of books to be traded (certainly including librarians from Special Collections), and, perhaps, that of knowledgeable dealers known from previous transactions to be disinterested enough to give fair judgment. Since a good deal of money can be involved, more than one opinion is certainly indicated in the process of judging the reasonable worth of trade items. On the other hand, to be overly precise and finicky can be very costly in personnel time and is a hazard to be avoided.

(3) Deciding what titles to destroy as *discards*—rather than consider as materials for trades, student-faculty book sales, and so forth—can also be a tricky and time-consuming problem. As a generalization, G&E librarians tend to be overly conservative in discarding and waste a good deal of money in staff time by fiddling with worthless titles, procrastinating about disposing of them. A student-faculty book sale, with prices being progressively reduced to almost nothing, can be helpful with the problem of discards. Some such sales have been held with great success; and any books left unsold after such a method has been pursued can certainly be defined as true discard material.

D. QUALIFICATIONS OF THE G&E LIBRARIAN

There has been, and continues to be, an unfortunate inclination on the part of some library and technical-services administrators to throw neophytes, or experienced professionals momentarily at loose ends, into G&E slots. But I think the reader can now see that the position of G&E librarian is really not an ideal place for any greenhorn and is certainly not a position for the ill-trained or the weak-kneed. To use G&E either as a training ground or a depot for professional or clerical personnel is to ask for and get a great deal of trouble. G&E professionalism requires common sense; an ability to work with a variety of librarians, donors, book dealers, faculty, and clerical staff; an aptitude for writing tactful letters and keeping records; a knowledge of bibliographical procedure; and a capacity for making and executing decisions.

Finally, a particular point should be clarified: it should *not* normally be an important function of the G&E librarian to discover and solicit donors; and neither his work nor his advancement should be weighed against his public-relations proclivities in this particular area. All universities pay a number of persons a great deal of money to perform PR work; and within the library itself, the director, his staff, and the staff of Special Collecitons will lead the charge actively enough. The G&E librarian who performs his duties competently will—as I think should now be clear—have quite enough to do without being expected to hazard the murky and treacherous currents of PR solicitations.

II.5

HOW TO SET UP
OR WORK WITHIN A
BIBLIOGRAPHIC DEPARTMENT

I think that to begin a discussion of a Bibliographic department, some history, accompanied by an inevitable degree of definition, is necessary. Then we can concern ourselves with the *function* of such a department; the *surveying,* the studying, of the present state of a particular collection in a particular subject; the *current* and *retrospective* work of collection development in relation to a survey (see I.5., where current and retrospective titles are defined and dealt with in some detail); and the human *interrelationships* of the bibliographer's various responsibilities. As any reader is probably aware, bibliographers and Bibliographic departments *as devices for acquisitions* are historically a recent concept in the development of academic and research libraries—a recent concept, in fact, in professional librarianship as we know it today. Please note that I am *not* aiming here at defining either "bibliography" or "bibliographer" in the traditional, classical sense of such terms. Anyone interested in the subject of this chapter should, however, be familiar with the work of McKerrow, Padwick, Bowers, and Gaskell.

A.

Historically, and until a not-very-distant past, academic and research libraries were built almost entirely by a combination of time and chance. Gifts came by no established plan or rationale (for the subject of gifts, see II.4.); more importantly, the faculty, always arriving and always passing on, assisted acquisitions only insofar as each specialist could demand or wheedle particular materials directly related to his particular interests. Such a course of events has produced curious combinations of amazing strengths and weaknesses in almost every research library in the United States and elsewhere. When it began to occur to those in our profession who think about such things that the acquisitions of library materials should have some relation to overall student and faculty needs in the present and to plans for academic development in the future, librarians began to get into collection development in an organized way and to assume responsibilities for acquisitions and collection development previously delegated, chiefly by default, to academic faculties.

This new idea of librarians working in faculty preserves has had various degrees of success in various institutions. In some, the faculty still controls and spends all acquisitions funds, just as it did in the bad old days; in some, the pot of money is divided between faculty and library selectors; and in some, the library controls and spends all acquisitions funds. When the faculty entirely controls acquisitions of materials, there is no Bibliographic department. Where acquisitions activities are divided between library and faculty, we would not expect a full-fledged Bibliographic department; but, depending upon the size of the slice of the monetary pie retained by the library, there might be an occasional bibliographer or two working in some selected disciplines. Where a large research library controls most or all acquisitions funds and the budget is adequate for both materials and personnel, there may be a Bibliographic department of some substance.

A Bibliographic department, with its proper complement of Bibliographers, exists, however, only where an institution's administration has faced up to the fact that in-depth collection development is full-time work which cannot be performed adequately by acquisitions or reference librarians handling it on a part-time basis. Many administrators are not, however, willing to foot the bill for a Bibliographic department; and a number of these attempt to get two jobs done for the price of one by using Reference subject specialists as selectors. Since I have discussed this particular approach to collection development previously in this text (I.5.A.1.), I need not consider it further here.

I have also discussed the Bibliographic department as a selection device earlier in this text (I.5.A.1.), and will do so further in the discussion which follows. However, anyone seriously interested in the subject of this chapter should *at this point* read two articles which are most helpful for an understanding of the subject in hand: Robert Haro's "The Bibliographer in the Academic Library" and Helen Tuttle's "An Acquisitionist Looks at Mr. Haro's Bibliographer," which appear in *Library Resources & Technical Services*, 13, no. 2 (1969), 163-174. Unlike many professional writings, these two statements retain contemporary value. Haro's article claims perhaps too much performance for his bibliographer, and Tuttle's seems overly devoted to a traditionalist point of view; but both expositions are of importance for an understanding of the bibliographer in the library.

B.

The *function* of a Bibliographic department (Collection Development department, Book Selection department, etc.) is to build collections by the acquisition of *current* and *retrospective* monographs, serials, and other materials relevant to the present and projected teaching and research needs of the institution. This function presupposes a staff trained in the basic procedures of bibliographic checking (described at length in II.2.A.5.), of order work (II.3.), and of gifts (II.4.). The bibliographer is a part of the Bibliographic department and, to view the matter impersonally, one of the tools of that department's functions.

A bibliographer should have one or more subject specialties (sometimes called "area" specialties) and a good general ("generalist") understanding of the interrelationships of the various subjects within his disciplines—the arts, the humanities, the sciences, and so forth. He should certainly have one foreign language well in hand and have at least what is called "title-page" competency in several others (bookmen call this touch of, say, classical Latin, "title-page Latin"—thus, "title-page" German, Russian, and so on). It almost goes without saying that a bibliographer should understand the current and retrospective national bibliographies of the language areas and nations related to his discipline(s). And he should also possess a solid knowledge of the book trade, an understanding of current trade publications and catalogs and current trade publishers, a familiarity with serials concerned with bibliographical and antiquarian matters (*Book Collector, Antiquarian Bookman, Bulletin of Bibliography*, etc.), and a fairly thorough grasp of the specialities of relevant antiquarian dealers and the catalogs they issue. A bibliographer must also understand pricing practices in the reprint and the out-of-print trade, and be well informed about all major, and most minor, reprint and microform publishers and their present and planned projects.

Such an enumeration of qualifications may seem modest; but competent bibliographers are not, in fact, always easy to find. For this reason, some bibliographic departments are on occasion willing to accept and train promising novices who possess a degree of background in books and languages (see II.11., for further commentary on the book trade).

C.

A bibliographer is, as we now know, a *collection developer; and, as such,* he will be concerned with both the *current* and *retrospective* titles necessary to the teaching and research programs of his particular institution. He must therefore, as soon as he is on the job, begin to survey/evaluate the collection(s) for which he is responsible while *at the same time* initiating a *system* for the current acquisitions of academic titles within his particular area(s) of responsibility. Thereafter, he will begin his retrospective work. I *stress* the importance of a bibliographer's immediate initiation of a system of current acquisitions because it is an all-too-often-neglected truism that the missed in-print title of today becomes the costly out-of-print desideratum of tomorrow.

With the fact clearly in mind that a bibliographer's survey/evaluation of any collection is contemporaneous with his procedures for acquiring the new titles in his disciplines as they come out, I would like to look at some of his activities in the following order, which is dictated primarily from the aim here of getting a prospective bibliographer oriented (what to do and how): (1) an approach to a collection survey/evaluation; (2) a specific sample of how such a survey might be written up; (3) a consideration of the acquisitions of current titles; and (4) a consideration of the acquisitions of retrospective, chiefly o.p. or antiquarian, titles (see I.5. and II.11., where such terms as "in-print," "out-of-print," "current," "retrospective," antiquarian," "reprint," etc. are dealt with).

1.

As a first move toward his collection surveys, a bibliographer will want to poke around in the stacks to get a general idea about present holdings (here, I will take *English literature* for an arbitrary sampling of books in our native tongue), just as he will wish to begin to survey library holdings in the various bibliographical resources with which he will be working from day to day. Very probably, the institution requiring his services will possess most of the national, trade, and author bibliographies for his work in English literature. Ideally, his institution will also contain some kind of bibliographical center, formed to facilitate work in acquisitions, reference, and special collections. An experienced bibliographer will also bring with him his own well-thumbed and well-marked bibliographical and reference guides. Any bibliographer will acquire more and more such guides as time goes by.

Reading the shelves in the stacks for English literature, or any other discipline, is pleasant. However, such shelf reading by no means gives a clear picture of total holdings, since any collection in active use will be in large part checked out or in active use by students and faculty. Thus, a survey of the *shelflist* (located in the cataloging area of every Technical Services division and arranged alphabetically by LC classification and not by main entry) will provide a much better, theoretically complete, picture of a library's holdings. Here, a bibliographer must assume that most titles appearing in the shelflist (or in the MCC for that matter) are in fact in the control and possession of the library—at the bindery with a record of so being, checked out, or in process to or from the library's shelves—not stolen, misplaced, or permanently out of hand in some arcane location. Thus, a bibliographer's assumption of shelflist accuracy calls for a strong heart and a very positive power of thinking, especially if he is working in an open-stack library and/or an urban or other location patronized by users with sticky fingers. In times past, libraries pursued semiannual or annual inventories; now, very few if any libraries have the staff for thorough inventory, and detailed information about the actual physical whereabouts of particular titles is often difficult to come by.

Whatever the case may be, if a bibliographer in English literature reads his shelflist PR's, he will get an idea about the scope and depth of what he surveys. He should annotate both his specialized bibliographical guides and his *LC Classification Schedule* as he reads through the shelflist, to note particular strengths and weaknesses as he goes along. He will also keep some kind of title count for the PR holdings in the shelflist, so that he can write a "collection survey" report somewhat resembling the sample that follows.

2.

As Aristotle recommends, any narrative should have a beginning, a middle, and an end; and the *collection survey* following this logical advice would have three sequential components: (a) an introduction, (b) relevant statistics, and (c) a concluding commentary on various periods, genres, and authors. The skeleton sample of an English literature survey, below, will suggest how to proceed. Any discipline, be it viticulture and enology to plasma physics, lends itself to such methodology.

SURVEY OF THE ENGLISH LITERATURE COLLECTION AT _____
A. *Introduction*
This survey of the holdings in English literature in the university library was begun in mid-June and completed at the end of August. The purpose of the survey is to determine the strengths and weaknesses of the collection in those genres and periods relevant to the needs of the students and faculty of the department of English. The survey evaluates both quantitatively and qualitatively. Included in both the statistics and the commentary are the titles of *bound* serials; however, since serials are expensive and represent particular problems, especially those of filling in backfiles, comments about them here are limited to their relation to the strengths and weaknesses of monographic holdings. . . .
B. *Statistics*
PR 1509-1799 (Anglo-Saxon Literature, individual authors and works) Title Count: 522
PR 1800-2165 (Anglo-Norman Period, individual authors and works) Title Count: 1843
PR 2199-2405 (Renaissance Prose and Poetry [1500-1640], individual authors) Title Count: . . .
PR 2411-3198 (Drama [1500-1640], individual authors) Title Count: . . .
PR 3291-3784 (1640-1770/1800, individual authors)[18] Title Count: . . .
. . .

C. *Commentary* (Individual Analyses of the Various PR Subdivisions)
Here, a bibliographer would provide a series of statements, a couple of which follow, about the various PR subdivisions. Then, if he were in top form, he would conclude with a paragraph or two summarizing all of his findings and future activities to be related to them.

PR 1509-1799 ANGLO-SAXON LITERATURE

This collection is generally strong in facsimile texts, edited texts, and critical studies of particular authors in the period. Definitive textual editions are, however, spotty; and a number of these, some of which have been reprinted and a few of which are currently still in print, will be ordered. Serial representation is weak, and a number of important backfiles are missing. After in-depth consultation with period specialists in the English Department— namely, Professors _____, _____, and _____—a program with _(dealer)_ and _(dealer)___ is under way to obtain these backfiles. Current serial requirements are being reviewed in collaboration with Professor _____, the English department's library representative.

. . .

PR 3291-3784 (1640-1770/1800, INDIVIDUAL AUTHORS)

The genres of critical prose, prose fiction, drama, and poetry are generally strong from ca. 1700 to 1800 (prose fiction really from ca. 1750 on); but critical works related to Restoration dramatists, and holdings of particular individual plays and of collections of plays, are deplorably weak. The poets are, however, surprisingly well represented. Prose fiction to 1750 is, on the other hand, almost nonexistent in our collections; and this genre-period, like the Restoration drama, will receive as much priority as budget, availability of newly edited individual titles and collections or reprints of same, and time permit. Since the university administration has decided to provide the money to sponsor a journal in this period, it becomes a high priority in my work to develop our holdings in the field. Professors _____ and _____ and I will work closely in this endeavor.

. . .

3.

The process of collection surveying will take some time, as I hope the brief illustrations above indicate, especially since careful notes *must be taken at the time of the survey,* and pertinent bibliographies and other selection tools must be *marked* as appropriate. As his surveys are under way, a bibliographer must at the same time not neglect the other requirements of his work and must begin to bring into play his resources for current and retrospective collection development.

For *current collection development,* if we take an English-language humanities bibliographer as a convenient example—continuing for illustrative purposes to stay with the English-American native tongue—we would find him dealing certainly with some classical, all English and American literatures, some philosophical and theological titles, and with relevant scholarly historical and bibliographical studies. Whatever the range set for him by his Bibliographic department, his basic tool will be the BNB for Britain and the BPR for the United States. Because the BNB appears weekly and is classed by subject, it is particularly useful for scanning recent publications in particular subject areas. The monthly BPR is a primary tool as well, since it is also classed and very useful for subject survey. Of course, our sample bibliographer would back up these national listings by perusing appropriate review organs, such as TLS, the *New York Times Book Review,* and so forth. Not all of the titles falling within a bibliographer's discipline(s) will be reviewed in current publications; but, with some experience, he will be able to judge rather accurately those titles useful for upper-division, graduate, and postdoctoral researches (textbooks *excluded*). Of course, if a bibliographer were located in, say, Canada or Australia or institutions emphasizing the literatures of these countries, he would rely as well upon such publications for current titles as *Canadiana* and *Australian National Bibliography.*

It should be emphasized here that even a beginning collection developer can, given sufficient time, piece together the national and trade bibliographies and listings necessary for current collection development in almost any language area. The essential guide here is a bibliographer's Sheehy (*Guide to Reference Books*; the ninth edition of which, 1976, largely replaces what many of us have always referred to as Winchell—the basic volume and its three supplements), which basic tool is not sufficiently known by some librarians and most academics.

A bibliographer will also keep an eye out for new reprints in his areas of responsibility. Strictly speaking, reprints in various formats, codex or microform, are important aids to retrospective collection development as well. But any bibliographer must remember that reprints—just like new, hot-off-the-press publications—go out of print, and thus become o.p. items. New reprints should, therefore, be surveyed and ordered as they appear— treated in other words like new titles. Reprints are noted again in this chapter, as a part of retrospective as well as current collection development resources (see also I.5. and II.11.).

Approval plans (sometimes rather confusingly called standing-order plans) will be discussed in some detail in the chapter following this one, and are also most important instruments for current collection development. Once approval plans have been set up, they presumably provide a comprehensive coverage for new titles published in designated subject and language areas. If such plans are operative for an English-language bibliographer, it will be his duty to monitor titles coming in on approval: accepting most, rejecting some, checking the range of titles arriving against his notations in his national BNB or BPR, and ordering any worthwhile volumes overlooked by the approval-plan jobber. If approval plans are not operative in his institution, a bibliographer can use Chapter II.6. as a guide to set up such plans.

Faculty input and book review sources are, as noted before, backups for the selection of current new publications and reprints. If all goes well, however, new titles should be already on order, actually in process within the library, or already on the library's shelves by the time a faculty member requests them, since faculty requests are usually received far after the fact of actual publication. Still, faculty can always be used by a bibliographer as a resource to measure his own efficiency in acquiring current material. Faculty assistance will in reality probably be more useful in retrospective development, if faculty can be motivated to work in this area.

Book review resources in the academic arena of the scholarly journal are usually so late in appearing that they are generally useless if current collection development is to be carried on with any degree of efficiency. However, such a publication as *TLS* can be useful in monitoring approval plans for quality, since it surveys the current English languages in some detail. In creative writing—a most difficult field for selection in any language area—the *New York Times Review of Books* can be helpful occasionally, as can a number of other review organs concerned with telling readers something about contemporary fiction, poetry, and drama. But it is well to keep in mind that bibliographers chiefly inhabit research institutions, and are usually little concerned with the bestsellers or potential bestsellers puffed by ads and expensive promotional programs and sketchily reviewed in commercial trade publications. In such a difficult field as, say, contemporary poetry, any bibliographer who finds it necessary to attempt to come to grips with the avant-garde is far better off talking with a bookseller who specializes in such materials, reading new titles himself, or talking with the poets of various schools of activity, than in relying on establishment review organs that tend to run years behind the current scene or to be oriented toward certain coteries (see also II.11.A.).

Some departments of the humanities are anxious to collect all of the titles, and sometimes all of the editions, by particular authors, and the biography, critical studies, and so forth related to these particular authors. For example, a number of English departments (to mention, for illustrative purposes only, one group of the many that could be cited) have prepared lists of authors particularly related to their current teaching, and wish to pursue the acquisitions of titles by and about these selected authors at a total, blanket level. These lists can be most helpful to the bibliographer for both current and retrospective work. Similarly, classics, philosophy, history, and other departments often have certain subjects, periods, and authors in which they are especially interested. And lists of these also provide useful guides for current work as new editions appear, as well as being helpful in retrospective collection work (see II.2.A.6.B. for examples of some specialized collecting policies).

The principles for placing subscriptions for new serial titles are the same as those for the selection of current monographs; but there is an added consideration of great importance—namely, *cost*. Given the escalating costs of serials subscriptions in the present and foreseeable future, I do not believe that any bibliographer should order any new serial title—from little magazines to highly academic monographs in series—without consulting several responsible faculty members in the department of the discipline treated by the serial. To save time, I would go to these faculty with a group of serial titles to consider for subscription, rather than try to crank such titles one by one through the academic machinery. I emphasize that such consideration should be set up by formal appointment and, further, that a bibliographer remember that he is far more responsible for considerations of present and ultimate cost than is a busy academic.

It may be somewhat evident by now that current collection development will keep an English-language humanities bibliographer busy for at least part of his working day. Other bibliographers will, of course, be doing similar work in the social sciences, the biological and physical sciences, various selected language areas, and so forth; this fact means as well that several selectors will be using BNB and BPR as major tools for current selection, and that efficient logistics call for a sufficient number of copies of these publications to be on hand.

4.

With current collection development in hand and with surveys of his collections completed, a bibliographer can begin to give a good deal of his attention to the vital, and enjoyable, task of *retrospective collection development.* Some of his bibliographical weapons in this arena of action will be national and trade bibliographies; library catalogs, listing the holdings of particular institutions; reprint catalogs; books-in-print listings to distinguish in-print from o.p. titles (U.S., BIP; Britain, BBIP; etc.); antiquarian catalogs and other listings (including the many catalogs and listings of backfiles of o.p. serials issued by specialists in these materials); and author and subject bibliographies.

All disciplines, humanistic or scientific, have guides to most of the retrospective tools useful to a bibliographer (bibliographies of bibliographies, research and reference guides, etc.). For example, if we work retrospectively in our own American and English literatures, we would find useful handbooks in Donald F. Bond, *A Reference Guide to English Studies* (1962); Clarence Gohdes, *Bibliographical Guide to the Study of the Literature of the U.S.A.* (1963); F.W. Bateson, *A Guide to English Literature* (1968); and Richard Altick and Andrew Wright, *Selective Bibliography for the Study of English and American Literature* (1975). The *New Cambridge Bibliography of English Literature* (NCBEL) is now out (4 vols., 1969-1974) and is a basic tool in the field, as is Robert Spiller, et. al., *Literary History of the United States: Bibliography* (1974). The *Bibliography of American Literature* (BAL), an incomparable resource developed by the late Jacob Blanck, is in progress and is definitive for the American authors which it treats (1955- ; 6 vols., through Parsons, as of late 1977).

I need only observe that new subject and author bibliographies, bibliographies of bibliographies, biographies, bio-bibliographies, and so forth (not to mention reprints of o.p. basic tools or revisions of older guides) appear constantly. From where I write just at this moment, I can see an interesting sequence of excellent bibliographical resources: T.H. Howard-Hill, *Bibliography of British Literary Bibliographies* (1969); Elgin Mellown, *A*

Descriptive Catalogue of the Bibliographies of 20th Century British Writers (1972); and Margaret Patterson, *Literary Research Guide* (1976). And on my desk is Sheehy's *Guide to Reference Books* (1976), the essential replacement for the last edition of Winchell and its three supplements. Sheehy was eagerly awaited by all of us, no matter what our areas of interest and expertise; and I must confess to reading its preliminary explanations about changes and arrangements with some interest. Both the *English Catalogue* and the Shaw-Kelly-Roorbach-*U.S. Catalog*-CBI sequences are important resources for nineteenth-century and later monographic publications in English. Any bibliographer will have his older and newer bibliographic resources in hand, annotated of course, and will use them in his own particular way to cover his disciplines and areas of responsibility.[19]

Library catalogs may or may not be national bibliographies (many are very close to so being); but surely the LC-NUC sequences, with which the reader is now familiar, and the various author and subject spin-offs from these (pre-1956 imprints, fictional titles, etc.) are of primary importance; the BMGC (the British Museum has now, for me somewhat unhappily, come to be called the British Library) and the hosts of catalogs derived, and often expanded, from it are also or primary importance; and the same observations hold for the BN catalogs and a number of others as well (enumerated in Sheehy). The subject of the sales catalogs of the libraries of noted collectors is one, perhaps, a little advanced for our consideration here; but any prospective bibliographer can find ranges of these in the Special Collections area of his institution, and should at least look through Edward Lazare's classic "Index" to the seven volumes for the Streeter Sale of Americana, and the seven volumes themselves, to get an idea about the bibliographical importance of such resources.

The reprint trade that makes available many of the monographs and serials cited in retrospective bibliographies and the entire subject of *reprints* have been tousled time and time again in panels, symposia, professional articles, and other vehicles for the expression of opinion. Any antiquarian bookman and many librarians will give you chapter and verse on numerous instances of what they view as overpriced reprints. A bibliographer, however, must weigh need against the cost of a reprinted title, and that cost against the availability of a given title through non-reprint channels *and* the cost in time to acquire a reprinted title in its earlier o.p. edition(s). For example, no bibliographer could live long enough, let alone have sufficient funds, to acquire the literary materials contained in such reprint projects as those covering three centuries of British and American drama, and American fiction to 1900. It is somewhat depressing, moreover, to hear a bookseller rail at the cost of the reprint of a particular title, but then have to admit that not only does he not have that title on hand as an o.p. item, but he has not seen it for years.

It is, of course, true that many titles, both monographs and serials, can be purchased more cheaply in original than in reprinted format. But condition must be remembered as an important consideration when any title is available in both o.p. and reprinted form. The *cost of binding originals,* especially backfiles of sets and serials, must always be viewed as a critical element in price evaluations. On the other hand, I well recall buying a long run of *Gentleman's Magazine* (1731-1856) in superb condition in fine leather bindings for very much less than the price of the reprinted run, and a number of sets in mint condition of definitive collected works by American and English authors at prices well below those for reprints of exactly the same collected editions (see I.5. and II.11. for more about reprints). On this matter, thus, we are not talking about an acquisitions subject that has any one, fixed guideline for any particular case.

Having achieved a comprehensive grasp of the reprints and reprinters in his subject areas, a bibliographer next turns to the subject of the *antiquarian* and *o.p.* resources available to him. He will work into these with his various, personally annotated, author and subject bibliographies and guides and with any departmental lists of authors and subjects to be collected always in mind. Seemingly o.p. titles should almost always be checked against in-print tools, since some original printings are kept available for remarkably long periods of time, and many in-print tools list the reprinted as well as the newly issued titles. "O.P." is a somewhat more déclassé descriptive term than "antiquarian"; but the latter does not necessarily designate a dealer in, as the layman puts it, "really old books." After all, many important antiquarian booksellers specialize or deal extensively in twentieth-century out-of-print titles, some of which bring very high prices indeed.

A bibliographer should make it a point, as he does in seeking out reprinters and their catalogs, to *write personally* to the antiquarian and/or o.p. dealers in his subjects and to solicit catalogs and lists. If a bibliographer is seriously interested in the offerings in the catalogs of particular dealers, he should request "advance" mailings of these catalogs, airmail at the least. He should, after a period of demonstrating his abilities and good faith, begin to be offered special lists and, sometimes, groups of three-by-five-inch slips by dealers who are willing to provide such a service for offering their antiquarian/o.p. holdings. The advantage of such offerings is that a bibliographer knows that his time, and that of his staff, will not be wasted, since in such cases he is working with sources of pretty much one-hundred-percent-guaranteed acquisition. Because of the large sums of money involved in such transactions, almost any dealer specializing in serials backfiles will answer inquiries promptly and will prepare special lists of his holdings for whatever subjects in which a library might be interested.

D.

The human relationships in play between the bibliographer and the other librarians, booksellers, and faculty with whom he works also demand some time. The bibliographer should, first, make it a point to understand, and try within reason to accommodate himself to, the personalities of the subject specialists and special collections librarians with whom he will have to work closely. He should also understand the duties of such librarians and the demands of the professional routines within the departments/areas in which they work. That the bibliographer must cultivate booksellers is, as we know, of great importance. And it almost goes without saying that the better the bibliographer comprehends the nature and expertise of each academic faculty member in the areas for which he is responsible, the better his work will go.

As we have followed routines in the varieties of acquisitions, I may have overemphasized the role of the faculty as a bull in the china shop of orderly, logical collection development. I should, thus, say here that no bibliographer (in point of fact, no librarian) can afford to be unaware of potential faculty utility in assuring that important current and retrospective monographic and serial titles do not somehow get lost in the shuffle of the complexities of collection-development work. Pointing out shortcomings in library collections can sometimes be a useful faculty specialty. Moreover, common sense dictates that a bibliographer must always realize that a scholar working in particular fields—teaching, researching, and publishing in them—will as a rule have a deeper and more particular grasp of the materials with which he works than will any bibliographer other than one whose work is luxuriously specialized in scope. What I am, in short, attempting to emphasize is that by legwork, expenditure of time, and application of diplomatic liaison efforts with his faculty, a bibliographer may be able to extract uniquely valuable suggestions and assistance for his programs. I am here, as previously, using the term "bibliographer" as approximately synonymous with that of "collection developer," and not with any qualitative distinctions or comparisons in mind between him and "a bibliographer" or "a textual critic," although a bibliographer as we have been discussing him may very well be both within particular areas of his expertise.

Once upon a long time ago, I became enmeshed in the French Revolution for an academic paper I was attempting to commit. Someone suggested that I should consult "the man" in the History department for advice in my project. Off the top of his head and in a most kindly manner, he gave me author, title, and date of publication for some seventeen scholarly works that, in his opinion, constituted a kind of basic starter set for initial explorations in the period; and I was on my way. In the past twenty or so years, I have seen other similarly impressive displays of scholarly fire power. Few bibliographers, as we have defined their functions, can or should expect to have such insights and recalls within the wide subject areas for which they are responsible. Any bibliographer must, however, be expected to exercise the patience, firmness, and constructive guidance that can bring such faculty resources fully into play.

The assistance of booksellers is also vital to a bibliographer. And I think it worth noting that many booksellers understand librarians remarkably well and are quick to discover ignorant arrogance and disinterest. Conversely, booksellers are at times surprisingly positive about supplying information to remedy a bibliographer's admitted lack of knowledge. Some booksellers are most interesting people; some are not. Many of the best are, however, willing to take a great deal of time to work with collection-development programs. All booksellers are, of course, in business to make money. But there are and always will be libraries and collections everywhere that owe a great deal to booksellers who have provided advice and assistance far above and beyond the call of monetary compulsion. A bibliographer should, then, cultivate solid booksellers and use them; if a bibliographer does not have friends, or at least good acquaintances, in the book trade, something is seriously wrong.

E.

We may conclude by pointing out that the time during which a bibliographer is learning his collections and developing current and retrospective approaches to strengthen them, he is working with a variety of professional and clerical fellows, faculty, and booksellers; reading appropriate journals and other bibliographical resources in his areas of competence; and monitoring all of the budgets for which he has the responsibility of neither overspending nor underspending. Any bibliographer must also prepare a number of statements relevant to his professional duties (in addition to his written collection surveys): journals read, faculty contacted in liaison work, national bibliographies used as current and retrospective collection-development controls, approval plans monitored, and reports of progress about the development of the various collections with which he is working.

A bibliographer may also be expected to take courses in special languages or subjects. He may on occasion be asked to teach bibliographical courses in his disciplines. Whatever else he may do (and I exclude social and domestic activities), I think the reader can see that his days will be full enough to occupy most of his time. Question: are these duties almost necessarily full time, or are they better left to the attentions of part-time Reference subject specialists? To whoever has followed this exposition thus far, I hope the answer is obvious.

If I may, I would now suggest a project for a reader to work out—namely, to select a subject and/or language area, to list the reference and bibliographical tools relevant to it and the methodology with which they might be applied, and to compile a statement of the various responsibilities and activities of the bibliographer working within this selected subject and/or language area. Not all of the details of this project may be immediately obvious, but it can now be attempted. Good luck.

II.6

HOW TO CONSTRUCT
APPROVAL PLANS

A.

Before getting into the details of approval plans, we must first straighten out terminology and define purpose. As the title of this chapter indicates, I believe the use of the simple terminology of "approval plan" is best. But these plans can also be denominated as "blanket-approval," "blanket-order," "standing-order," etc. However, the usage of "standing-order" can be somewhat confusing, since the same terminology is used in Technical Services to describe sets being issued in volumes over a period of time for which an order for all volumes to be issued has been placed with some dealer, *or* used to refer to agreements with any one of a number of university presses, research institutions, and such for a copy of every monograph issued by that particular press. Some librarians still persist in referring to "subscriptions" as "standing-orders." Let us, then, stay with the term "approval plan," which indicates that duplicates, within reason, and inappropriate materials delivered by a dealer/jobber responsible for the plan can be returned for credit against future invoices.

The twin purposes of the approval plan are often described as identical with those of data-processing systems: to achieve *economy* and to render better *service*. Since experienced acquisitions personnel are adept at juggling figures, they seem sometimes to be able to "prove" the economy of approval plans in their institution. Some of this so-called proof is valid; some is not. As a matter of fact, to promote and institute either machine programs or approval plans on the basis of saving money seems to me to be a very dubious procedure, and one conducive to a mean frame of the administrative mind when it discovers that the savings assured are not forthcoming.

The services rendered by successful approval plans seem, on the other hand, to be demonstrable. Certainly, *if* a reliable jobber/dealer can deliver exactly the right titles covering exactly the right subjects in exactly the language areas desired, and *if* he can do it with facility, an approval plan will be of great service. After all, individual selection time for current imprints will have been eliminated in large part; and saved as well will be the time required for typing, distributing, filing, mailing, and retrieving necessary for ordering and receiving routines (see II.3.). Moreover, a successful plan will often have delivered new titles to the library by the time initial announcements in flyers and brochures have appeared to announce these titles; and they will certainly be on the library shelves long before reviews appear in the academic journals.

The *if* noted above is, however, a big one. For example, since the *Economics of Approval Plans: Proceedings of the Third International Seminar . . . 1971* (Westport, Conn.: Greenwood Press, 1972) was edited by Spyers-Duran and Gore, one of the largest United States approval-plan companies represented in the seminar has gone bankrupt. The efforts of competitors to assume the functions of the defunct have not been invariably successful. I would say that any librarian or student interested in the subject in hand should read *Economics . . .* through, but view it more as a study in methodology and theory than as an instrument for proving the general worth of approval plans. Further, not all institutions need approval plans; others require only a limited number.

My own point of view finds two difficulties with approval plans: first, I have seen the now-fashionable "profiles" of approval plans that were not clear to me and, I suspect, not clear to the company offering them;[20] second, no matter what routines are used by an approval-plan dealer, at some point a successful plan requires that a good bookman get into the act. The attributes of an excellent memory, wide education, knowledge of the academic book field (pricing, discounting, the ins and outs of reprints, etc.), common sense, ability to act swiftly and surely, and the capacity to work with quantities of trivial and often dull detail are not commonly found in mere mankind. For some reason, European approval-plan jobbers seem to discover more such personnel than appear to be available in the United States.

B.

Given the above comments, and remembering that for the sake of discussion we assume the existence of dealers capable of handling approval plans, let us now look at a *selling job* to persuade an institution to adopt such plans. This statement perhaps overly accentuates the positive. However, if a potential acquisitions librarian or bibliographer ever has to attempt to persuade some less-than-knowledgeable administrator to accept the idea of approval plans, he should be able to adapt some of the following presentation to his own particular needs. The argument which follows is for the library of a relatively small research institution with fewer disciplines than would be found in a larger library of a similar nature (see also II.2.A.7., in the Checking Manual, where approval plans are explained).

APPROVAL PLANS

I. Introduction

Almost all research libraries active in acquisitions have found it necessary to set up approval plans for books published in the U.S., Latin America, Western Europe, and other countries or language areas of particular interest to the student body and faculty.[21] These plans, which are defined in nature and scope by the needs of each particular institution, have been necessitated by the ever-increasing numbers of contemporary publications which have made it almost impossible for any library to order these multitudes of titles on an individual basis. Since unsatisfactory titles can be returned, these comprehensive plans do not obviate the principles of selection. Furthermore, the library has an opportunity to review what titles are to come and what others are required before the volumes actually arrive. Whenever national bibliographies or national trade tools of the countries concerned are available, these are used as controls. For example, BPR is the control for a domestic approval plan, *Livres du Mois* for a French, *Deutsche Bibliographie* for a German, etc.

Such approval plans, it should be noted, free professors and bibliographers or subject specialists for the task of working chiefly to acquire important retrospective titles lacking in the research collections. The plans which follow are based in part upon those in operation in various large research libraries in the U.S. Figures are for fiscal year 197__ and are based upon various statements of actual cost and some informed estimates. The plans presented for consideration attempt to meet some of the requirements of our main library. Materials to be acquired would be specified as upper-division or graduate-level and would *exclude* textbooks. Pamphlets, publications in spiral bindings, laboratory manuals, and such would also be excluded.

II. Approval Plan: U.S. Imprints

1. Material to be supplied will fall into the following broad categories:
a. Humanities and Social Sciences
b. Physical and Biological Sciences

2. All material supplied would be of an advanced nature, junior or senior level or above.

3. BPR is to be the control. The selected dealer will stamp titles he will be providing as "sending" or "sent," as the case may be, and will airmail each marked copy of BPR to the library where bibliographers, subject specialists, and faculty may examine it, note any additional titles desired, and, if necessary, may eliminate titles not desired.

4. Humanities and Social Sciences

a. Material from all American publishers (excluding vanity presses) as well as from those British firms distributing their books through the American trade should be included. Publications of non-trade as well as those of trade publishers should be considered. In the selection of non-university-press publications, "quality" should be a primary consideration.

b. The specific disciplines to be included in the humanities and social sciences follow. If a discipline is not noted, it is not to be acquired.

(1)	Anthropology	$1300.00*
(2)	Art	1720.00
(3)	Classics	540.00
(4)	Drama and Speech	400.00
(5)	Economics	3000.00
(6)	Education	500.00
(7)	English (including creative writing and criticism, but excluding avant-garde)	8000.00
(8)	Foreign Languages and Literature	
	French	350.00
	German	130.00
	Spanish	100.00
	Italian	100.00
	Russian	50.00
(9)	Geography	500.00
(10)	History	5000.00
(11)	Philosophy	760.00
(12)	Philology (classics, French, German, Spanish, etc.)	400.00
(13)	Political Science (including Government and International Relations)	3400.00
(14)	Sociology	1300.00
(15)	Theology	500.00
(16)	Interdisciplinary Titles	3000.00

c. Items costing more than $100.00 should not be sent automatically. Slips should be sent instead; and we will inform the dealer if the item is desired.

d. The estimated total expenditure for the humanities and the social sciences (based on the figures given above, plus an estimate for expenditures with other non-university press publishers not listed in the starred note, below) is $40,000.00.

*The figures which follow are for all university-press publications and for such publishers as the following, which do, in fact, comprise a good portion of all trade publishers in the U.S.: Aldine, Bollingen, Columbia Teacher's College and Hispanic Institute, Council of State Governments, Economic Growth Center at Yale, Folklore Associates, Harvard Grad. School of Business, HRAF Press, Huntington, Met. Museum, Museum of Modern Art, New York Graphic Society, Phaidon, Praeger. . . .

5. *Physical and Biological Sciences*

a. This program would include material from *all* American publishers as well as from British firms distributing their titles through the American trade.

b. The specific disciplines to be included in the physical and biological sciences follow. If a discipline is not noted, it is not to be acquired. For example, engineering, mathematics, and medical titles are excluded.

(1)	Bacteriology	$200.00
(2)	Biology, Biochemistry, Biophysics (including Space Science)	500.00
(3)	Botany	700.00
(4)	Chemistry (Physical)	3600.00
(5)	Geology	1000.00
(6)	History of Science	200.00
(7)	Physics	3800.00
(8)	Psychology	1000.00
(9)	Technology (including scholarly books on General Science and scientific methodology)	300.00
(10)	Zoology (including Embryology and Comparative Anatomy)	1400.00

c. Allowing for price increases, the estimated annual cost for the physical and biological sciences would total $14,000.00.

6. The total cost for monographs in the humanities, social sciences, and sciences would be about $54,000.00. This sum would assure a generally comprehensive acquisition of current imprints required by the majority of our students and faculty. This plan should be initiated immediately—i.e., in fiscal year 197____, and additional appropriations budgeted at once for the following fiscal year.

III. *Approval Plan: British Imprints*

1. This plan would be similar to that described above for U.S. imprints. Such publishers as Oxford, Cambridge, etc., would be specifically included or excluded, dependent upon our decision to handle them through our U.S. or British agent.

2. Approximately $16,000.00 annually would be required to cover the same subjects in the humanities, social sciences, and sciences. This cost statement *excludes* contemporary British literature, which would require probably no less than $3,000.00 annually to acquire such titles comprehensively.

3. Control would be BNB.

IV. *Approval Plan: French Imprints*

1. By examining approval-plan costs for comprehensive coverage of French imprints at other comparable institutions, and from in-depth corres-

pondence and conversation with _____ in Paris—a specialist in approval-plan imprints in French and a close, personal acquaintance of long standing—I think an estimate of $10,000.00 for the humanities and social sciences would be reasonable for scholarly, critical, and literary publications. Scientific publications would estimate at $5,000.00 per annum.*

2. The control would be *Livres du Mois.* [22]

V. *Approval Plan: German Imprints*

Tailored to the library's present and projected needs, such a plan would probably entail an estimated expenditure annually of $15,000.00. The control would be *Deutsche Bibliographie.*

VI. *Approval Plan: Spanish Imprints***

A plan for Spanish imprints could probably be set up with _____ for about $4,000.00 per annum. The control would be *Libros Nuevos.*

VII. *Approval Plan: Russian Imprints*

According to our studies and consultations with local specialists, of whom we are fortunate to have a number around, a plan designed to fulfill the library's present requirements would estimate at $3,500.00 a year. The control would be *Novye Knigi.*

VIII. *Cost Summaries*

Estimated annual costs follow for the approval plans outlined above. The plan for U.S. imprints should be put into effect as soon as we can set it up with _____ .

1. U.S. Imprints	$54,000.00
2. British	19,000.00
3. French	15,000.00
4. German	15,000.00
5. Spanish	4,000.00
6. Russian	3,500.00
TOTAL:	$110,500.00

IX. *Conclusion*

That approval plans are the only way in which to cope with contemporary publications seems generally self-evident. Almost every major research library has instituted such plans because of some or all of the following reasons:

*I call the administration's attention to the fact that I have on file at my desk all figures and all correspondences relevant to my statements about U.S. and foreign approval plans.

**Approval plans related to Latin-American imprints are at present being studied in relation to present and planned programs at the University and the responses of the various dealers in various South American countries with whom we are currently holding dialogs.

1. The dealer/jobber assumes the time-consuming task of gathering materials and marking the control bibliography.

2. Within a particular framework, the dealer must detail what is to be sent *and* must send whatever else the library may request.

3. The dealer accepts a certain number of returns; the library usually has to pay for duplicates ordered outside approval-plan routines.

4. With book in hand, the librarian can select more wisely than he can when working from a description in a trade or national bibliography.

5. With material at hand, bibliographic checking is minimized and pre-cataloging by LC or OCLC resources becomes largely a clerical task.

6. Approval plans free faculty, bibliographers, and subject specialists for retrospective collection development.

7. Dealers with whom libraries have approval plans are usually very helpful about answering difficult bibliographical inquiries, handling orders for troublesome non-trade publications, and searching for desired o.p. items.

8. Finally, the approval-plan approach to library development is the only one that will enable our retrospective collection development to take place simultaneously with our assured acquisitions of current materials.[23]

C.

Lest the simplified outlines for approval plans above be deceptive about the possible ranges of such plans, I include, below, an abbreviated sample of an approval-plan list for a large research library. I omit book dealers and allocations; but any library with approval plans should have some such control list for ready reference and for faculty information. It would probably be worth a reader's while to check with some knowledgeable acquisitions librarian in a large department to find out something about possible dealers in possible subject/language areas—remembering of course that dealers used will vary from library to library.

(NAME OF LIBRARY): LIST OF APPROVAL PLANS

Country or Area	Dealer	Allocation	Bibliography	Order Number
Australia	. . .	. . .	*Australian National Bibliography*	NY 345-001
Austria			*Oesterreichische Bibliographie*	NY 345-002
Canada	. . .	. . .	*Canadiana*	NY 345-003
China (mainland)			None	. . .

Denmark	*Dansk Bogfortegnelse*
Estonia	None
Finland	*Finnish Bibliography*
France	*Bibliographie Officielle* and *Bulletin Critique du Livre Français*
Germany	*Deutsche Bibliographie*
Greece	None
Ireland	None
Italy	*Libri e Reviste d'Italia*

. . .

Nations (dealers, allocations, controls, order numbers) omitted from the very abbreviated sample above would include Japan, Korea, Czechoslovakia, Hungary, Israel, all of Latin America, Lithuania, Luxembourg, Netherlands, New Zealand, Norway, Philippines, Poland, Portugal, Roumania, South Africa, other African nations, Spain, Sweden, Switzerland, U.S., U.S.S.R., Yugoslavia, etc.

Such a sample as that above shows, at least, how an overall framework of approval-plan control should look. Some nations obviously provide more challenges in the acquisitions of their publications than others. An acquisitions librarian will have to exercise varieties of approaches in working in such areas as, for instance, Africa, the Near and Far East, and Latin America. And however he decides to deal with them, he must set up clear methodologies and controls and be able to evaluate these, whenever he may be called upon to do so, in writing supported by solid statistics.

D.

Now, let us look at (1) an arrangement for a simple approval plan for music and (2) a comprehensive, detailed approval plan for German-language titles. The procedures for getting the German-language plan into operation are given in some detail to serve the reader as a guide, which he may modify as necessary, for setting up almost any kind of approval plan. It is exceedingly important that the logistics for any approval plan *be spelled out* and *clearly understood* by *both* a dealer and an Acquisitions department *before* the plan goes into effect. An approval plan that commences in a confused manner may be not only difficult or impossible to readjust, but conducive to painful psychological and professional consequences.

1. MUSIC

This approval plan for music is set forth in the letter which follows—that is, in only one basic document. The German-language plan which follows it, contains a number of documents which should be looked at closely.

May 197__

Dear Mr. (Name of Selected Music Dealer):

Professor Smith and I have had a followup discussion subsequent to his visit with you a few weeks ago. We in the Library are most amenable to the idea of having you as our approval-plan agent in the discipline of Music. For your consideration, we offer the following ground rules, which, if I understand Professor Smith correctly, you have in principle agreed to:

1. *Frequency of Shipping*

Material should be sent on a regular, once-a-month basis. We would prefer receiving this material during the last week of the month, so that we may call in the library representative (at present, Professor Smith) for the department of Music on the first week of each month.

2. *Invoicing*

Because we use invoice workslips in our approval-plan procedures, each title must have a separate invoice. Each invoice should be in quintuplicate.

3. *Returns*

Materials which duplicate our holdings, and those considered inappropriate for our collection, may be returned. Three years of experience with various approval plans demonstrate that our percentage of return is very low. All material will be returned unmarked and in the same condition as received. You must, however, allow at least a month for receipt of returned items.

4. *Languages*

Materials should represent scholarly studies in English, French, German, Italian, Latin, and Spanish.

5. *Specification of Coverage*

a. History of Music

Include scholarly works only and *exclude* popularized or elementary texts. Include both general histories and more specialized titles concerned with particular periods, places, groups of composers and schools, instruments, form of composition, etc.

b. Biography

Include scholarly and definitive biographies of composers of serious music. Also include the autobiographies, letters, literary works, and facsimiles of musical manuscripts of such composers.

c. Theory and Aesthetics

Include studies and editions of theorists up to ca. 1900 only.

d. Musicology

Include scholarly works dealing with the entire range of musicology, with particular attention to those focused on historical musicology.

e. Bibliography

Definitive bibliography related to any of the subjects cited above is of particular interest to us.

f. Festschriften

If scholarly, these are always acceptable.

g. Reports of Congresses

National and international reports of scholarly societies, symposia, congresses, etc. are to be included.

6. *Specification of Exclusion*

a. Date of Publication

All materials are to be of recent date. No antiquarian or retrospectively published materials are to be sent, although you are welcome to offer these for our consideration.

b. Music Scores

c. Ethnomusicology

d. Music Education

e. Memoirs, Biography, Autobiography

No materials in these fields should be supplied for recent or living performers, critics, conductors, etc.

f. Textbooks

g. Peripheral Material

Please exclude all such materials. As a guideline, do not send material which the Library of Congress would not include in class "M." Choreography and ballet are examples of this type of material.

7. *Purchase Order Number*

Upon the implementation of this plan, a single music-approval-plan purchase-order number will be assigned to you. Actually—and please *note* this—I have reserved NY 444-001 for you. *All invoices* for materials you supply on approval *must* bear this number. This arrangement is essential for our statistical controls.

8. *Starting Date for the Music Approval Plan*

Should the foregoing guidelines meet with your approval, and I understand that they will, your plan should be implemented 1 August 197__. The first shipment would be sent to arrive by the last week of August—God and the U.S. mails willing.

9. *Budget Allocation*

A tentative allocation of $5,500.00 for the fiscal year 1 August 197__ to 31 July 197__ has been agreed upon by the library here. Please advise us any time during this fiscal period if this sum seems likely to prove to be inadequate to meet our commitment with you.

Would you call me by telephone and give me a verbal commitment as soon as you receive this statement. I am sending you this original and two copies. Will you return one carbon signed by you, plus a formal letter of agreement. If you wish to add anything to the preceding statements, restrictions, etc., please do so on the signed carbon and your formal letter, after we have talked by telephone. The director of the _____ libraries has, by the way, approved all statements above.

As soon as I hear from you, I will cancel the plan with _____, started by my predecessor. Hence, I will appreciate your prompt response to my formalized statements, since I wish to give _____ gentlemanly notice.

I, like Professor Smith and his Department, look forward to your next visit with us. The Music Department *always*, of course, looks forward to your lists and advance catalogs of antiquarian offerings.

Most Cordially,

Dr. _____
Chief Bibliographer

2. GERMAN LANGUAGE

A.

May 20, 197__

Dear Mr._____:

Enclosed with this statement of our approval-plan agreement are our purchase-order agreement *and* various attachments spelling out logistical details relevant to our plan to have you supply new academic publications in German-language areas from August 197__ onward. Kindly examine all statements and enclosures and let us hear promptly if you have any questions. Since we discussed this German-language plan extensively during your last visit with us, I trust that the statements which follow will be to your satisfaction.

This agreement for German-language materials—which is understood to include titles published in the German Federal Republic, East Germany, and East and West Berlin—authorizes you to select new publications issued, on a title-by-title basis within the guidelines specified below. For this plan, we have initially allocated $15,000.00 for the period 1 August 197__ through 31 July 197__.

This $15,000.00 should not be exceeded without our written authorization. If it appears to you at some point, however, that this sum will not be sufficient, please inform us immediately, so that we may consider increasing the allotment.

The basic provisions of the approval plan which we wish to set up with you are as follows:

1. *Publications to Be Selected and Supplied*

Beginning with materials issued from 1 August 197_____, you are to select and send, without further authorization, all solid academic publications produced in the German-language areas specified. For purposes of definition, you are to begin with publications listed from the first August 197__ issue of *Deutsche Bibliographie*.

From time to time, we will advise you concerning your selections. *Attachment A* lists the subjects which comprise our interests. Please notice that your selections will not be limited to works having Germanic subjects as a focus. For example, in the discipline of "Economics," we would expect you to select not only those works dealing with Economics in Germany, but also those titles published in Germany which deal with the economics of other nations, language areas, and so forth.

2. Publications Not to Be Supplied

Attachment B spells out the subjects and types of publications which the library does not wish supplied.

3. Use of "Deutsche Bibliographie"

As part of the approval-plan operation with you, we should like you to provide us with marked copies of Deutsche Bibliographie, and by means of these advise us of the publications you have selected and will be sending to us. The procedure for your marking of these bibliographies is spelled out in Attachment C.

Once a bibliography has been checked, it should be airmailed to us with the following designation:

> The Approval-Plan Librarian
> Acquisitions Department
> The Library
>
> . . .

The Deutsche Bibliographie should be sent to us immediately after you have reviewed it, and indicated in it should be the selections you have made. However, a number of books will be published before they are listed in this control bibliography; if they are appropriate to our approval plan with you, we ask that you send them to us immediately without waiting for their appearance in DB. The procedure for this is spelled out in Attachment D.

4. Publications to Be Selected by the Library

Upon receipt of the airmailed copy of the Deutsche Bibliographie, we will re-view it immediately and advise you of any additional selections by means of an air-mailed form letter which will specify the number and date of the DB in which these titles appear and their specific item number.

5. Shipping, Invoicing, and Payment

Attachment E spells out the subject of invoice arrangement (distinguishing between your selections and those of the library); Attachment E also spells out invoice requirements.

Shipments should be made at least twice monthly, with all packages labelled as "1 of 5," "3 of 5," and so on, as we agreed. We have decided that you should not bind monographs in paper covers; we will handle binding here.

Cordially,

Dr. _____
Chief Bibliographer

Enclosures: Attachments A-E

Purchase Order Agreement

TG/tc

B.

May 22, 197__

Dear Mr._____:

As of this date, the *Purchase Order Agreement* authorizes you to select and send to the _____ Library new publications produced in the German-language areas spelled out in my letter of May 20, 197__, with which this letter is enclosed. The publications you are to send are further described in 1. and 2.a., below. You are to send these without further request from the Library. It is understood that the publications supplied under this Purchase Order Agreement will not be priced higher than the trade price which is current at the time of shipment to the Library. We will, of course, adjust monetary fluctuations here to the current value of the market. The total cost of these approval-plan titles cannot exceed $15,000.00 without the Library's *written* consent.

Your Purchase Order Number for *all* approval-plan titles is NY 555-555; and as you know, it *must* appear on all invoices and all of the MOF (multiple-order-form) work slips which you have agreed to supply for each individual title.

1. *Publications to Be Supplied in One Copy*

One (1) copy of each newly published monograph of importance. *Attachment A* lists the subjects in which the Library is interested.

2. *Serial Publications*

a. One sample issue of each serial (periodical) title issued within the areas defined is to be supplied. The library subject specialists will examine such titles, and the library will send to you a separate subscription order for desired titles.

b. Please do *not* use the approval-plan purchase order number for any subscription so placed.

3. *General Conditions for This Approval-Plan Agreement*

Unless otherwise agreed upon, all normal transportation charges and insurance charges to assure the safety of materials in transit will be paid by the Library, except in cases where imperfect material has been shipped. It is understood that the Library can *not* be responsible for loss or damage to materials in transit. No change in this approval-plan arrangement is valid without the written consent of the library. Sixty days' notice can terminate this plan—by formal written notice from either the Library or the approval-plan dealer _____.

Cordially,

Dr._____
Chief Bibliographer

TG/tc

C.

Attachment A: SUBJECT GUIDE FOR APPROVAL-PLAN TITLES

1. Bibliography and Library Science. History of books and bookmaking. Book trade. Book publishing and relevant statistics. Copyright. Libraries. Information storage and retrieval. Book collecting. Bibliographies (*excluding* law, medicine, agricultural techniques).

2. Economics. Commerce. Economic theory. Finance. Money and banking. Labor. Transportation. Communication. Insurance and taxation. *Exclude* all legal publications on this subject.

3. Education. History of education (including histories of individual colleges and universities). Theory and practice of education. School administration. Sociological aspects of educational procedures. Education and religion. Teacher training.

4. Fine Arts. Architecture. City and regional planning. Sculpture and related plastic arts. Caricatures. Pictorial humor and satire. Industrial Art. Techniques of print making, etching, lithography, painting, etc. Catalogs of exhibitions.

5. Geography. Anthropology. Folklore. Voyages and travel. Dance. Ethnology.

6. History. Archeology. Biography. Historical criticism. Any publications relevant to resource material.

7. Language and literature. Philology and linguistics. History of literature. Literary texts. Critical works. Critical apparatuses (concordances, indexes, etc.). Social and historical critiques. Literary works: prose fiction, descriptive and critical prose, the drama, poetry, etc.

8. Military (and Naval) Sciences. History and logistics of these are of interest.

9. Political Science. Theory of state and local governance. Emigration and immigration. National and international relations. Particular problems in administration, diplomacy, and colonialism. National government, elections, and political parties.

10. Religion (*excluding* devotional literature). Theology (*excluding* doctrinal theology). Philosophy.

11. Sciences. Mathematics. Astronomy. Meteorology. Physics. Chemistry. Geology. Biology. Botany. Zoology. Physiology. Any space sciences. Any energy sciences (see also Technology).

12. Sociology. Social psychology. Social welfare. Social history and reform. Socialism. Communism (see Political Science). Social customs and usages.

13. Technology. *All* engineering sciences. Building construction. Chemical, metallurgical, photographic, data-processing techniques.

D.

Attachment B: PUBLICATIONS NOT TO BE SUPPLIED
   1. Law
   2. Medicine
   3. Agriculture
   4. Juvenilia and Children's Books
   5. Antiquarian materials, including manuscripts
   6. Maps
   7. Reprints
   8. Expensive Publications (in excess of $100.00)
   9. Maps
   10. Government Publications (Documents)
   11. Textbooks
***12. Music (this is very *important*; we have another plan in arrangement
to cover this subject entirely)
   13. Instructional Texts: Laboratory manuals, etc.
   14. Theses and Dissertations

E.

Attachment C: INSTRUCTIONS FOR MARKING
APPROVAL-PLAN BIBLIOGRAPHIES

To assure our correctly interpreting the selections and comments of approval-plan dealers, we detail below our instructions for marking bibliographies. The symbols listed below are to be used to indicate your action on the individual items in the control bibliography. They are to be placed in the margin *immediately beside* the item annotated. *Do not* underline any titles. Please *do not* use any symbols other than those shown below. Your careful compliance with these instructions is greatly appreciated.

✔ This symbol will indicate titles you have aleady sent or intend to send on the approval plan.

☆ This symbol will indicate that the title cannot be supplied under the terms of our approval-plan agreement, but is one which you believe we may wish to purchase.

CONT This abbreviation/symbol will indicate that a title is one which you have already supplied or intend to supply on a subscription (continuation) for a serial title (Such titles must have previously been formally ordered from you).

REP/UNREV/EXT These abbreviations/symbols will indicate respectively that the title is a reprint (REP), or an unrevised edition of an older publication (UNREV), or an extract (EXT), and that for these reasons these titles are not appropriate to the approval plan.

SAMPLE This term will indicate, for a new serial title, that you are supplying a single sample issue as specified in 2.a., above, of the Purchase Order Agreement.

F.

Attachment D: SELECTING AND BILLING PUBLICATIONS IN ADVANCE OF THEIR LISTING IN A CONTROL BIBLIOGRAPHY

1. Publications selected for us under the approval plan should be sent to us immediately upon their availability and should not be held until the publication is listed in the control bibliography.

2. The proper procedures to be observed are as follows:

(a) Select and send immediately publications conforming to the provisions of the approval-plan agreement.

(b) Indicate such selections on an invoice as "Items not yet listed in national bibliography," whenever appropriate.

(c) Type on each MOF the following information: author, title, place of publication, publisher, and date of publication. Each typed MOF should be inserted in each title and should be shipped with it.

3. Approval-plan material should be identified on the overall invoice as follows:

*National Bibliography #*_____

   (a) Dealer selections

   (b) Library selections

Items not yet listed in National Bibliography

   (a) Dealer selections

Please alphabetize the entries within each grouping.

G.

Attachment E: INVOICE AND SHIPPING INSTRUCTIONS

Please note that these instructions do not apply to invoices for the library's subscriptions (continuations). Special instructions for subscription invoices are sent on request and are already in the hands of most of our dealers.

A. *Invoicing*

In order that the library may pay promptly for materials sent and that the return be avoided of improperly prepared invoices, the following instructions should be carefully observed:

1. Invoices should be typewritten and prepared in *triplicate,* with an original and two (2) copies made out to The Approval Plan Librarian, Acquisitions Department, The Library. . . .

2. Each invoice should specify the library's approval-plan purchase order number. Please *do not* invoice non-approval plan titles with approval titles.

3. An invoice should list and identify as completely as possible *each* publication for which payment is claimed. The price of each publication should be indicated.

4. Invoices should be itemized and totaled in the currency in which a title is originally offered (bibliography, trade catalog, list, etc.). Invoices originating outside the U.S. will be paid in U.S. currency at the rate of exchange prevailing at the time of payment. If payment is desired in currency other than that of the U.S., the invoice should carry a statement to this effect.

5. Invoices listing charges in excess of $50.00 for prepaid freight or express must be accompanied by a receipt from the shipping agency. Postage charges may be listed without sending a receipt.

6. The original and both copies of the Invoice (for *non-subscription material*) should be enclosed with the material for which the Invoice was prepared.

B. *Shipping Instructions*

Address mail and ocean freight shipments as follows:
    The Approval-Plan Librarian
    Acquisitions Department
    The Library
    . . .

C. *Payment*

To insure prompt payment, detailed instructions for the preparation of Invoices are given in this *Attachment E.* and in *Attachment D., above.*

E. PROCESSING, AND RECORDING STATISTICS

When approval-plan books arrive, they must obviously be processed through Acquisitions, moving from the mailroom to the assigned shelves in Acquisitions—then, to be reviewed by library or faculty subject specialists; to have funds assigned to them (i.e., undergo the process which determines which library or department funds should properly pay for a particular title);

to be verified (searched or precataloged in LC, in other bibliographies, in such machine resources as OCLC, etc.); to be entered statistically in a title count of approval-plan books; and to be recorded by MOF slips in fund-record files, in the O.O. file, and in the MCC (so that duplicates will not be ordered by mistake in Acquisitions and so that library patrons will know that a given title is in process). One sketch of a method of such processing is given in the approval-plan section of the Checking Manual (II.2.A.7.); and a reader might now wish to review this sketch. He should try to put himself in the position of an approval-plan librarian/assistant and be able to have clearly in mind his responsibilities and sequences of activities. It is especially important, I think, for whoever heads an approval-plan operation to keep careful control of whatever weekly or monthly national bibliographies are used as controls for particular plans, and to make sure that these bibliographies are always on hand for the use of subject specialists and faculty reviewing approval-plan titles.

The approval-plan librarian must also—in addition to handling shelving, invoicing, verifying, and so on—keep statistics: there must be a daily title count, and titles processed must be accounted into the records of the funds that pay for them. This kind of statistical record is essential in order that there be a month-by-month, and finally an annual, count of approval-plan titles processed and of the amount of monies spent on any particular approval plan and on the various academic disciplines within the plan. This annual accounting is vital, since a library must know how much money an approval plan has taken out of its various budgets in a given year and how much money the plan can be projected to remove from these budgets in subsequent years.

In sections 1-4, below, there follow four tables (four "Summary Sheets") which represent *four kinds* of annual breakdowns for approval-plan expenditures for acquisitions of monographs in a medium-sized U.S. research library—say, one with holdings of from 750,000 to 1,000,000 volumes. Tables 1-3 (Summary Sheets 1-3) are *approximate* representations of one year's approval-plan expenditures for domestic (U.S.) monographs in the humanities, social sciences, and sciences. Table 4 (Summary Sheet 4) represents a *projected* approval-plan budget for the fiscal year following the fiscal year summarized by Tables 1-3, and is based on the figures recorded in Tables 1-3.

Such "summary sheets" as in these four tables illustrate the kind of monetary record keeping which any technical-services or university administrator would expect from his Acquisitions department. Summary sheets like these are absolutely necessary to record both the numbers of books received on approval and the costs of present approval plans, and to project the costs of such approval plans into the coming year(s). The *forms* of these tables can serve as a guide for setting up statistical controls for any kind of an approval plan—small or large, domestic or foreign.

1.

When we look closely at Table 1 (Summary Sheet 1), we can discover several things about the institution in which our sample library is located. It is certainly in the University of California system, since it gets some books from the U.C. press in conjunction with other approval-plan titles. Its expenditures for agriculture are large, so this field is obviously basic to the institution. On the other hand, it has a good many Arts and Sciences disciplines. Since "aggie" schools do not as a rule develop *from* liberal arts institutions, but on occasion *into* them, we would expect a program of collection development expanding in a demonstrable and perhaps interesting manner. A reading of expenditures in the physical and natural sciences certainly indicates a large school of engineering and a variety of research facilities, probably in one way or another related largely to different aspects of agricultural studies and research. The Acquisitions department in this institution has established approval plans prior to the year for which it gives statistics, since it is able to give figures for percentages of unit-cost-increase, an important consideration in anticipating increased approval-plan costs for the next year.

From the figures in Table 1(B), we can further discover that the library itself controls the funds for agriculture, engineering, veterinary medicine, and some "general" funds to back up the Arts and Sciences departments. We may guess that these A&S departments either control their own funds entirely (the library having, so to speak, farmed out some of its collection-development responsibility in these disciplines) or the departments have somehow been delegated the power to monitor closely expenditures of A&S allocations. For example, we note that Lib: Gen funds have been used in three of the four approval plans to purchase a relatively large number of titles, and would guess that Acquisitions picked up the tab for a number of titles it thought should be in a research library but may have felt that A&S departments might balk at as titles from their own funds.

TABLE 1

Summary Sheet 1: Approval Plan 1976/1977

(A) OVERALL EXPENDITURES

	No. Titles	*No. Vols.*	*% of Total AP Cost*	*Total Cost*	*Unit Cost Per Title*	*% of Unit Cost Increase*
1. U.S. Hum. & Soc. Sci. (Order No. NY 100)	1,731	1,767	44.50	$19,896	$11.48	14.90
2. U.S. Physical Sci. (Order No. NY 101)	770	805	43.50	19,458	25.26	15.51
3. U.S. Life Sci. (Order No. NY 102)	223	237	11.40	5,117	22.94	19.31
4. U.C. Press Publs. (Order No. NY 103)	33	33	.60	236	7.16	11.17
TOTALS	2,757	2,842	%100.0	$44,707	$16.70	%15.22

TABLE 1 (continued)

(B) QUANTITY OF TITLES RECEIVED, IN DESCENDING ORDER*

1. *U.S. Humanities & Social Sciences*	Number Received		3. *U.S. Life Sciences*	Number Received
Lib: Gen	494		Lib: Agr	118
A&S: History	234		Lib: Vet Med	47
A&S: English	226		A&S: Zoology	17
A&S: Political Science	184		Lib: Gen	12
A&S: Economics	104		A&S: Botany	10
A&S Sociology	88		A&S: Bacteriology	7
A&S Anthropology	59			
A&S Education	56		4. *U.C. Press Publications*	
A&S Philosophy	51			
A&S Psychology	39		Lib: Gen	9
A&S Psychology	39		Lib: Agr	7
Lib: Agr	36		A&S: Political Science	6
			A&S: English	3
2. *U.S. Physical Sciences*			A&S: History	3
Lib: Engr	225			
A&S: Mathematics	121			
Lib: Agr	117			
A&S: Chemistry	109			
A&S: Physics	93			
Lib: Gen	52			

---

*Major areas of expenditures only; see Tables 2 and 3 for completer statistical breakdowns.

2.

Table 2 (Summary Sheet 2), below, breaks down A&S approval-plan costs more comprehensively than Table 1 (Summary Sheet 1), and uses a different methodology to approach the statistics it contains.

TABLE 2

Summary Sheet 2: Approval Plan Expenditures on General Library Accounts 1976/1977

VOLS.	FUND NAMES	TOTALS SPENT	HUM. & SOC. SCI.	PHYSICAL SCI.	LIFE SCI.	U.C. PRESS PUBLS.
294	Lib: Agr	6,397.10	656.20	3,215.86	2,490.06	34.98
584	Lib: Gen	7,250.78	5,591.98	1,382.10	215.90	60.90
230	Lib: Engr	5,782.14	—	5,708.20	73.94	—
60	Lib: Vet Med	1,588.38	—	246.80	1,341.58	—
	Serials & Sets					
	S&S: Hum	—	—	—	—	—
	S&S: Sci	—	—	—	—	—
59	A&S: Anthro.	793.86	793.86	—	—	—
31	A&S: Art	601.66	601.66	—	—	—
9	A&S: Bact.	160.10	4.06	14.98	141.06	—
13	A&S: Botany	222.58	8.00	18.72	195.86	—
120	A&S: Chemistry	3,147.22	—	3,100.72	46.50	—
29	A&S: Drama	290.56	282.76	—	—	7.80
109	A&S: Econ.	1,292.64	1,232.20	42.64	—	17.80
59	A&S: Educ.	445.44	406.14	7.48	31.82	—
234	A&S: English	2,308.98	2,297.28	—	—	11.70
	A&S: For. Lang.					
22	Classics	297.70	297.70	—	—	—
9	French	90.68	90.68	—	—	—
6	German	90.60	90.60	—	—	—
4	Oriental	73.32	73.32	—	—	—
6	Russian	52.82	44.42	8.40	—	—
7	Spanish	96.60	96.60	—	—	—
18	A&S: Geog.	222.84	198.92	23.92	—	
22	A&S: Geology	579.74	13.52	566.22	—	—
237	A&S: History	2,727.12	2,702.44	—	—	23.64
131	A&S: Math.	2,402.96	63.40	2,339.56	—	—
7	A&S: Mil. Sci.	69.66	69.66	—	—	—
18	A&S: Music	190.20	190.20	—	—	—
51	A&S: Phil.	520.94	520.94	—	—	—
3	A&S: Phys. Ed.	77.70	22.48	—	55.22	—
101	A&S: Physics	2,412.16	—	2,399.40	—	12.76
191	A&S: Pol. Sci.	2,193.28	2,133.42	—	—	59.86
47	A&S: Psych.	557.18	435.86	43.88	77.44	—
92	A&S: Soc.	1,028.68	978.68	28.08	15.92	6.00
29	A&S: Zoology	644.00	—	211.68	432.32	—
	TOTALS	44,609.62	19,896.98	19,358.64	5,117.62	235.44

3.

Table 3 (Summary Sheet 3) approaches approval-plan statistics by a title
and volume count.

TABLE 3.

**Summary Sheet 3: Approval Plan Titles and Volumes
Acquisitions on General Library Accounts, 1976/1977**

FUND NAMES	TOTALS		HUM. & SOC. SCI.		PHYSICAL SCI.		LIFE SCI.		U.C. PRESS PUBLS.	
	T	V	T	V	T	V	T	V	T	V
Lib: Agr	278	294	36	36	117	125	118	128	7	7
Lib: Gen	567	584	494	510	52	53	12	12	9	9
Lib: Engr	226	230			225	229	1	1		
Lib: Vet Med	56	60			9	9	47	51		
Serials & Sets										
Humanities										
Sciences										
A&S: Anthro.	59	59	59	59						
A&S: Art	27	31	27	31						
A&S: Bact.	9	9	1	1	1	1	7	7		
A&S: Botany	12	13	1	1	1	1	10	11		
A&S: Chemistry	111	120			109	118	2	2		
A&S: Drama	29	29	28	28					1	1
A&S: Econ.	109	109	104	104	3	3			2	2
A&S: Educ.	59	59	56	56	1	1	2	2		
A&S: English	229	234	226	231					3	3
A&S: For. Lang.										
Classics	22	22	22	22						
French	9	9	9	9						
German	6	6	6	6						
Oriental	4	4	4	4						
Russian	6	6	5	5	1	1				
Spanish	7	7	7	7						
A&S: Geography	18	18	17	17	1	1				
A&S: Geology	22	22	2	2	20	20				
A&S: History	237	237	234	234					3	3
A&S: Math.	125	131	4	4	121	127				
A&S: Mil. Sci.	7	7	7	7						
A&S: Music	18	18	18	18						
A&S: Phil.	51	51	51	51						
A&S: Phys. Ed.	3	3	2	2			1	1		
A&S: Physics	94	101			93	100			1	1
A&S: Pol. Sci.	190	191	184	185					6	6
A&S: Psychology	47	47	39	39	3	3	5	5		
A&S: Sociology	92	92	88	88	2	2	1	1	1	1
A&S: Zoology	28	29			11	11	17	18		
TOTALS	2,757	2,832	1,731	1,757	770	805	223	237	33	33

4.

The Arts and Sciences departmental breakdown (Table 4, below), which is based on Tables 2 and 3, above, shows the process of estimating approval-plan expenditures and correcting these estimates where necessary for a subsequent year. Some of the allowances for the current fiscal year were under the mark, and some were over. The parentheses in the table indicate *minus figures* for estimates exceeded. Funds for disciplines under-allocated have been increased, and funds for disciplines over-allocated have been decreased. Such figures are, as the reader now knows, annual summaries based on daily and monthly cumulations of the record keeping which is a vital part of Acquisitions. Remember, we are dealing only with U.S. imprints.

TABLE 4.

Summary Sheet 4: Approval Plan Suballocation for A&S:
(Next) Fiscal Year, 1977/1978

DEPARTMENT	1976/1977 SUBALLOC.	SPENT	BALANCE	SUGGESTED FOR (NEXT YEAR) 1977/1978
Anthropology	1,000.	793.86	206.14	900.
Art	1,000.	601.66	398.34	700.
Bacteriology	200.	160.10	39.90	300.
Botany	200.	222.58	(22.58)	400.
Chemistry	4,000.	3,147.22	852.78	3,600.
Drama	400.	290.56	109.44	400.
Economics	2,000.	1,292.64	707.36	1,600.
Education	400.	445.44	(45.44)	450.
English	3,000.	2,308.98	691.02	3,000.
For. Lang.				
Classics.	000.	297.70	(297.70)	300.
French	400.	90.68	309.32	100.
German	100.	90.60	9.40	100.
Oriental	100.	73.32	26.68	100.
Russian	100.	52.82	47.18	100.
Spanish	100.	96.60	3.40	100.
Geography	100.	222.84	(122.84)	300.
Geology	1,000.	579.74	420.26	700.
History	3,000.	2,727.12	272.88	3,000.
Mathematics	1,600.	2,502.96	(906.96)	3,000.
Mil. Sci.	000.	69.66	(69.66)	100.
Music	300.	190.20	109.80	300.
Philosophy	600.	520.94	79.06	600.
Phys. Ed.	50.	77.70	(27.70)	100.
Physics	5,500.	2,412.16	3,087.84	3,000.
Pol. Sci.	3,000.	2,193.28	806.72	2,500.
Psychology	600.	557.18	42.82	700.
Sociology	1,000.	1,028.68	(28.68)	1,300.
Zoology	1,000.	644.00	356.00	800.
TOTALS	30,750.00	23,691.22	7,058.78	28,550.00

F.

We may conclude, I think, that an understanding of approval-plan procedures is important to any acquisitions librarian, whether or not he works in depth with such plans. To understand these procedures is to understand some of the important techniques of acquisitions. And while it is true that the financial crunch of the present, which promises to extend into the foreseeable future, means that the days of the grandly sweeping acquisitions of all appropriate titles in given areas may be over, there is nothing to prevent the continuation of more limited, more closely defined approval plans— provided, of course, that satisfactory dealers can be found to handle them.

At any rate, if a library has any budget at all, it must acquire research materials, whether by approval plans, by the use of a corps of bibliographers, or by the part-time attentions of reference subject specialists. Now, in the course of this text, we have looked at all of these techniques of acquisitions in some detail. As has been noted before, some libraries may use a combination of all three of these techniques to acquire selected titles; and a reader now has sufficient information at hand to enable him to understand the interrelationships of such a combination.

II.7

HOW TO RECORD AND USE
STATISTICS: LIBRARY
ACCOUNTS, WORK STUDIES,
ANNUAL REPORTS

This somewhat pretentious heading simply describes the evident fact that all competent acquisitions librarians must keep track of their funds; must keep records of requests and orders processed out and titles and volumes processed through the Acquisitions department by purchase, gift, or exchange; and must have reasonably solid figures as guides to expectations of the amount of work that can be done by any given number of professional and clerical staff. There are, of course, many different ways to work with figures, and no one can say absolutely that any one method or group of methods is necessarily better than any other. An acquisitions librarian must always keep in mind, however, that he must account for money spent upon his operations during any given fiscal year; must be able to project monies necessary to acquire and process materials for the next year(s); must satisfactorily justify present staff size, or appeal for more staffing assistance (see also, II.10.); and must, sometimes on rather short notice, supply his superiors with valid, preferably impressive, figures and facts for an annual report, which explains and justifies present activities and may suggest new procedures for the future and the amount of money necessary to implement them.

A. LIBRARY ACCOUNTS

Almost all records of expenditures in Acquisitions are now produced by machine and can be printed out on just about any required time schedule. But monthly fund record reports during most of a fiscal year, and weekly reports toward the end of that year (when remaining monies must be spent out and deficits adjusted) represent a normal expectation for frequency of such records. In Sections 1-3, below, the three tables of records of expend-

itures are sample reduplications of machine printouts: the first table represents a page showing about half of a relatively simple overall review of annual expenditures for a medium-sized research library of about 1,000,000
volumes; the second and third tables present only a single, selected page
from larger, more complex institutions with varieties of special funds and
endowments to back up the annual budget appropriated by the university
for purchases of library materials. These three examples aim at illustrating
some of the kinds of statistical record keeping we would expect to find in an
effectively run Acquisitions department.

Fund records are kept to prevent *gross overspending* and *underspending*.
As we have noted previously, an acquisitions librarian should *at the least*
spend all of his annual budget. As a rule of thumb, he will aim at *overspending* by about 25 percent, certainly by no less than 10 percent. Such percentages must *always include* encumbered funds.

TABLE 1.

General Library Accounts: _____
			(date)		
FUND NAMES	1. INITIAL SUM ALLOC.	2. BALANCES	3. SEARCH* TITLES	4. APPROVAL PLAN RESERVE	5. FREE BAL.
Lib: Agr	$31,000	$2,022	$386	$580	$1,056
Lib: Gen	60,000	6,030	750	3,040	2,240
Lib: Engr	16,000	1,480	200	(1,186)	74
Lib: Vet Med	6,400	918	160	(520)	238
S&S Humanities	85,000	(4,628)	1,062	460	(5,230)
S&S Economics	14,000	1,836	—	—	1,836
S&S Oriental Lang.	5,000	(240)	—	—	(240)
S&S Russian	11,000	80	—	—	80
S&S Science	57,000	7,262	712	143	6,693
Current Periodicals	195,000	6,704	2,436	—	4,268
A&S Anthropology	11,400	(650)	143	(47)	(840)
A&S Art	10,400	(350)	130	(436)	(916)
A&S Bacteriology	3,000	970	80	92	798
A&S Botany	6,400	(84)	80	(250)	(414)
A&S Chemistry	9,000	584	106	118	596
A&S Drama	10,000	(548)	126	(99)	(773)
A&S Economics	10,200	1,665	132	(372)	1,161
A&S Education	5,800	782	72	28	738

. . .

*Search Titles calculated at ½ total search encumbrances

1.

Table 1, the account record for the main or general library of a medium-sized research library, is for very near the end of the fiscal year, as a reader can tell from the "Free Balances" (column 5, which represents the amount in column 2 minus amounts in columns 3 and 4); figures within parentheses indicate accounts overspent. The "Balances" (column 2)—which give a truer picture of expenditures than that provided by "Free Balances"—would include monies paid out for books received *and* monies encumbered for books ordered but not yet received or paid for. The "Search" estimates (column 3) are for o.p. titles currently on search with various dealers. Amounts set aside for the "Approval-Plan Reserve" (column 4) have been recorded separately. Accounts with overspent allocations—those within parentheses—will have to be readjusted in the fiscal planning for the next budgetary year.

2.

Table 2, the account record for the main or general library of a larger research library (2,000,000 or more volumes), might indicate a fiscal mid-year point of some kind, as the "% Spent" column indicates. The sample is *only* of one part of one of the many printed-out pages that such a library requires to record various kinds of fund accounts from the library budget allocated by the university and from donors and grants. Special donor funds are probably from endowments that can cumulate from year to year. Such donor funds should be monitored; but it is the funds from the library budget and from grants for fixed periods that must be watched closely and used up by the end of the library's fiscal year or by the terminal date of the grants. Fund names and figures are arbitrarily assigned for illustration.

TABLE 2.

General Library Accounts: _____
(date)

ACCOUNT # AND TITLE	CURRENT MONTH'S EXPEND-ITURE	AVERAGE MONTHLY EXPEND-ITURE	TOTAL FUNDS	TOTAL EXPEND-ITURE	BAL-ANCE	% SPENT
NFD 321 Johnson Fund	148	727	5,534	4,361	1,173	79
651 Oral History Resources	—	8	1,353	47	1,306	3
653 John Smith Fund	459	163	3,004	979	2,025	33
662 Rowell Book Fund	26	14	248	86	162	35
669 Willison	—	95	3,343	572	2,771	17
NFD SUMMARY	1,357	1,822	28,446	10,929	17,517	38

ACCOUNT # AND TITLE	CURRENT MONTH'S EXPEND-ITURE	AVERAGE MONTHY EXPEND-ITURE	TOTAL FUNDS	TOTAL EXPEND-ITURE	BAL-ANCE	% SPENT
NGA 022 Special A&S Grant	2,130	2,589	17,481	15,331	1,950	89
NGB 001 Slavic Languages	2,332	2,688	41,380	16,125	25,255	39
002 Romanic Languages	2,000	1,775	41,200	10,649	30,551	26
003 Germanic Languages	4,255	2,860	41,520	17,162	24,358	41
004 Latin American	1,703	2,330	37,487	13,981	23,506	37
005 African	712	1,139	12,730	6,836	5,894	54
006 East Asian	1,813	968	11,870	5,810	6,060	49
NGB SUMMARY	12,815	11,761	186,187	70,563	115,624	38
NGC 001 Special Collections	1,641	577	4,904	3,460	1,444	71
301 Morton	(85)	597	7,258	3,472	3,786	48
302 Rogers Rare Books	—	55	1,511	328	1,183	22
303 Smith	858	677	8,721	4,060	47	47
304 Donovan Family	—	30	640	181	459	28
NGC SUMMARY	2,414	1,917	26,601	11,501	15,100	43
NGD 001 Gov. Docs.	3,124	3,526	39,428	21,154	18,274	54

. . .

3.

The account record for the main or general library of a large research library (3,000,000 or more volumes) might look something like Table 3, our third simulated printout, which gives a clear picture of overall expenditures in various disciplines, forms of materials (documents, maps), and the separate libraries which the printout includes. The Table 3 sample is, like Tables 1 and 2, only one page of a number that would spell out the entire budgetary situation. Any large research library would also have printouts detailing expenditures with particular dealers and printouts enumerating expenditures for a host of special donor funds. Our sample library is probably a couple of months from the end of its fiscal year, as the minus amounts and relatively low amounts of money in the "Free Balances" column indicate. Certainly, no one would dispute the value of any data process that can provide such a clear survey of acquisitions expenditures at any given point in a fiscal year.

The figures given in Table 3 are expressed only in thousands of dollars. The "Free Balances" column shows what dollar amount would be left if all

TABLE 3.

Total Libraries Accounts: _____ (date)

UNIT SUMMARIES (CONT.)

No.	Name	Total Allocated	Prior Yr. Payment	Prior Yr. Encumbered	Available This Yr.	This Yr. Payment	This Yr. Encumbered	Free Balances	Dollar Balance
Central Collections									
200	English	73,000	12,000	4,000	57,000	42,000	14,000	1,000	15,000
201	Americana	95,000	6,000	1,000	88,000	83,000	8,000	−3,000	5,000
210	Spanish Port	38,000	5,000	4,000	29,000	19,000	12,000	−2,000	10,000
211	French Ital	41,000	10,000	2,000	29,000	16,000	8,000	5,000	13,000
220	Germanic	59,000	11,000	7,000	41,000	28,000	31,000	−18,000	13,000
221	Scandinavian	6,000	0,000	0,000	6,000	3,000	2,000	1,000	3,000
250	Africa Asia	21,000	2,000	0,000	19,000	5,000	3,000	11,000	14,000
TOTAL		333,000	46,000	18,000	269,000	196,000	78,000	−5,000	73,000
Special Collections									
230	Slavic	57,000	1,000	0,000	56,000	65,000	1,000	−10,000	−9,000
310	Greek	11,000	0,000	0,000	11,000	8,000	0,000	3,000	3,000
360	Hebrew	34,000	1,000	1,000	32,000	34,000	1,000	−3,000	−2,000
370	Mid East	19,000	0,000	1,000	18,000	18,000	1,000	−1,000	0,000
461	Doc & Micro	14,000	1,000	1,000	12,000	8,000	2,000	3,000	4,000
471	Map	5,000	1,000	0,000	4,000	6,000	0,000	−2,000	−2,000
TOTAL		140,000	4,000	3,000	133,000	139,000	5,000	−11,000	−6,000

TABLE 3. (continued)

Total Libraries Accounts: _____ (date)

UNIT SUMMARIES (CONT.)

No.	Name	Total Allocated	Prior Yr. Payment	Prior Yr. Encumbered	Available This Yr.	This Yr. Payment	This Yr. Encumbered	Free Balances	Dollar Balance
General									
110	Exchange	12,000	0,000	0,000	12,000	25,000	0,000	-13,000	-13,000
243	Serials	251,000	1,000	2,000	248,000	199,000	5,000	44,000	49,000
299	Reserves	32,000	2,000	2,000	28,000	18,000	1,000	9,000	10,000
345	Preservation	19,000	0,000	0,000	19,000	14,000	0,000	5,000	10,000
	TOTAL	314,000	3,000	4,000	307,000	256,000	6,000	45,000	51,000
TOTAL Main Library	798,000	76,000	23,000	699,000	611,000	98,000	-10,000	88,000	
Graduate Bus School									
	TOTAL	46,000	3,000	2,000	41,000	37,000	5,000	-1,000	4,000
Undergraduate Library									
	TOTAL	49,000	1,000	1,000	47,000	42,000	2,000	3,000	5,000
Sciences Library									
	TOTAL	52,000	1,000	1,000	50,000	33,000	4,000	13,000	17,000
Department Libraries									
	TOTAL	12,000	1,000	1,000	10,000	2,000	1,000	7,000	8,000
. . . .									

titles encumbered were to arrive and be paid for. The "Dollar Balance' column is roughly equivalent to the amount for books actually paid for by formal invoice, subtracted from the basic budget; but this column is also used to keep track of money freed by encumbered titles that were ordered but were not received, for one reason or another.

B. WORK STUDIES

In considering work done or work to be done in a particular year, we should remember that in an Acquisitions department there will generally be four chief work stations: Monographs (Separates, including sets), Serials, the Order department/section, and G&E. If there are approval plans, the staff handling them will form another work station. If there is a bibliographic corps, it will form still another work station. Whether there are four, five, or six such stations, each of them will be involved in keeping relevant statistics for such activities as titles verified; orders sent out; volumes received and processed; and monies expended or encumbered.[24]

All of these records of titles ordered and processed in the fiscal year, and of bills paid and funds encumbered from various work stations, will provide the factual, statistical input for the department's "annual report." These records will also provide guidelines for the staffing necessary to perform the work at these various stations. Such records also enable the acquisitions librarian to calculate how many FTE (full-time employees) will be required to order and process a given number of titles. Since both the book budget and the average cost of monographs in various academic disciplines are known quantities, the chief bibliographer (head of Separates) will be able to calculate (1) how many books must be bought to spend out the book (monographs and sets) budget and (2) how much staff will be needed to do the work of buying, receiving, and processing this necessary number of books.

It is important to remember, however, that if backlogs of books exist in G&E, special plans for verifying and processing these must be made. Also, if a backlog of requests (cards, slips, etc.) exists, special plans must as well be made for reducing it. Backlogs of requests at monographic and serial work stations and backlogs of various kinds of titles at the G&E work station are not uncommon, just as backlogs of titles received in Acquisitions but not processed to the Catalog department, and of titles processed through Acquisitions to the Catalog department but not yet cataloged, are unhappily far more common than a neophyte might suspect.

Now, for purposes of demonstration, let us simply select the Bibliographic Checking work station (the Separates, the Monographs work station) to see how we might determine how many FTE are required to prepare requests so that they can be ordered, and any given budget spent out. This demonstration *assumes* a reader's *thorough comprehension* of the *Checking* Manual (especially II.2.A.5.A.-B.)

1.

The place to begin a production study for the Bibliographic Checking work station is at the desk of the chief bibliographer, where at a fixed time he simply gives several of his checkers—who work a *four-hour,* half-time day—a certain number of request cards, and keeps a record of the time it takes them to run these cards through verification routines (described at length in the Checking Manual, II.2.A.5.A.-B.).[25] Of course, if LC proof slips are used for ordering titles, the main LC entry is automatically established by the proof slip entry; and the title ordered by this means has been automatically verified by the slip itself. Thus, relatively little checking time will be required for titles ordered from proof slips. Similarly, a title verified by a computer resource will require less time than one that must be put through a number of other bibliographical resources. "Departmental requests," to be purchased from non-library funds and placed in departmental libraries, are also less time consuming than are titles requested for the main library, since departmental requests do not require extensive time for verification (see II.2.A.6. and II.2.A.8. for discussions of such departmental requests). Two sample production studies, with a commentary by the chief bibliographer, follow.

BIBLIOGRAPHIC CHECKING PRODUCTION
Date:_____

The Chief Bibliographer is making a three-month study of production expectation for Bibliographic Checkers. A limited sampling this week gives the following results and conclusions:

a. Departmentals: DNC and Cataloged

Sampling: 25 cards, mostly in-print domestic.   Checker: MH

Task	*Time Required*
Alphabetize cards	2 minutes
Holdings in MCC, incl. transit time	43
Price verif., transit, recheck on holdings	31
Further holdings check	2
Revision (polishing), incl. Kardex and transit	29

TOTAL TIME REQUIRED FOR 25 CARDS	107 minutes
TIME REQUIRED PER CARD	4.2 minutes

Based on this sampling, expectation would be as follows:

Time available: 240 minutes
Coffee Break: 10
Misc. time off: 10

___

Time available: 220 minutes

Production Expectation: 220/4.2 = 52 cards per 4-hr. day

b. Regular Cards (A&S History)

Sampling: 67 cards, mostly domestic, in and   Checker: TG
out-of-print.

Task	Time Required
Alphabetize cards	5 minutes
Holdings in MCC, incl. transit time	90
Verification & BIP, incl. transit (59 cards)	413
Further holdings check	6
Revision, incl. Kardex and transit	60

TOTAL TIME REQUIRED FOR 67 CARDS   574 minutes
    (Lib Has: 8; Verif.: 59)

TIME REQUIRED PER CARD   8.5 minutes

c. Commentary: Chief Bibliographer

Based on b., above, a reasonable expectation would be as follows for a
four-hour day with "regular" cards:

Time available: 240 minutes
Coffee Break: 10
Misc. time off: 10

___

Time available   220 minutes
Production Expectation: 220/8.5 = 25 plus cards per 4-hr. day.
An average month of twenty-one working days would yield the following:
            21 x 25 = 525 cards per month.[26]
Let me add that we are all aware of many variables in a group of cards.
However, certain statements can be made. If the verification of any one
title takes more than 10 minutes, the checker is not dropping the card quickly
enough. If a holdings check takes more than 1.5 minutes per card, something
is wrong. Furthermore, all cards that look as though they are going to take
more than 10 minutes to verify should be returned to the chief bibliographer.

We still need to develop a system to short-circuit such cards. Please return these problem cards in a separate group.

Cards that appear to have insufficient information should *not* be checked, but should be returned to the chief bibliographer in a separate group. He will, as you know, return them to the sender with our ugly form note.

As always, comments and suggestions are encouraged. This study, which is also being made for the G&E bibliographic checkers, is not intended to turn our department into a factory. Rather, the study is to discover what procedures we can develop to make the job easier. Too, Checkers have a right to know production expectation. So far, I can only say two things: *do not* spend more than 10 minutes on a card; *aim for* 25 verified requests in a four-hour period.

2.

If a Bibliographic Checking work station agrees to take the achievable and fair figure of 20 verified request cards per one-half (.50) FTE (see footnote 26) as a base for "regular requests" for titles to be placed in the main library or its branches, we can then calculate 40 cards per 1.00 FTE checking $\times$ 21 8-hour days per month = 840 cards/month $\times$ 11 (months) = 9240 cards per FTE checking per working fiscal year. We can then set up a statistical sequence, such as the one which follows below, to calculate checking FTE required to spend X number of dollars *at* the Bibliographic Checking work station. We are, of course, concerned *only* with checking personnel, not with those involved in ordering and receiving procedures.

Similarly, if we take 50 request cards per .50 (½) FTE as a fair base for "departmental requests" (DNC and cataloged, as in 1.a., above), we can then calculate 100 cards per 1.00 FTE checking $\times$ 21 8-hour days per month = *2100 cards/month* $\times$ 11 (months) = 23,100 cards per FTE per working year. (See especially II.2.A.6.A., which explains why departmental requests generally fall outside the complexities of the holdings check and verification routines of "regular requests" for the main library or its branches.) Of course, if departments begin ordering heavily from antiquarian catalogs on their own non-library funds, adjustments will have to be made for staff for such time-consuming bibliographic checking routines.

The figures below are necessarily only approximate, and would have to be updated and increased in relation to contemporary book prices and other variables as time passes. But given the framework with which we are dealing here, the *process* of calculation will remain the same, and can be adjusted to procedures and costs as need be. The point is that any work station in Acquisitions *must* have time-cost studies in relation to figures for work production, cost of materials, and budget if it is to have any standards of performance and a proper and sufficient staff to back these standards up.

ACQUISITIONS DEPARTMENT BUDGET REQUEST FOR
STAFFING: 197__/197__

Bibliographic Checking Work Station

A. Funds

Library Books	$360,000
Library Sets (65% of 135,000; Serials	87,750
work station spends other 35% for monumental,	
continuing sets that must be recorded in Kardex)	
Departmental Books	52,000

TOTAL MONOGRAPHS FUND $499,750

B. Unit Price Per Title

Books	$12.00 per order
Sets	$36.00 per order

C. Requests To Be Checked and Orders To Be Placed

Library Books (360,000/12)	30,000 orders to be placed
Library Sets (87,750/36)	2,400 orders to be placed
Total number of orders to be placed	32,400
Total number of cards to be checked (rule of thumb: 50% of requests are already in the library)	64,800
Departmental Books (52,000/12) Nearly 100% of departmental orders are placed	4,333 orders to be placed

D. Production Expectation

Library Orders To Be placed	Library Orders Placed Per FTE	FTE Required
32,400	9,240	3.5

Departmental Orders To Be Placed	Departmental Orders Placed Per FTE	FTE Required
4,333	23,000	.25

E. Total FTE at Bibliographic Station

  (1) 3.75 FTE Checking
  (2) .50 FTE Checking/Checking Supervising
  (3) .50 FTE Professional Administration
              (½ Separates station; ½ Order station)
    Total   4.75 FTE

Similar studies can be made at the Serials, Approval Plan, Order, G&E, and, even, the Typing Pool stations. Every effort should be made to bring such studies into line with human realities and frailties. The fact that some particular bibliographic checker is a compulsive worker capable of almost abnormal productivity (such types, however, tend to burn out) should not mandate expectations that all checkers match his standards. Order department personnel, with the associated typing pool, may also be able for a period of months to order, receive, and process rather heroic numbers of titles. But to expect such performance month in and month out, year in and year out, is simply unrealistic and, in the final analysis, inhumane.

It is important as well to note that the Serials Acquisitions work station can not be judged by the same methods of production study applicable to the acquisitions of monographs. The placing of current subscriptions, the ordering and processing of serials backfiles (the last often requiring laborious collations and difficult binding decisions), and the proper control and maintenance of the Kardex records of subscriptions and serials holdings—all demand careful methods of decision making and control; and every serials title either represents large sums of money in the present for the acquisition of backfiles or large sums of monetary expenditure extending into the forseeable future for serials subscriptions.[27] However, as with that for monographs, serials staffing is determined by budget and the number of subscriptions placed and backfiles purchased necessary to spend out that budget.

3.

Simply by reversing the sequence of the methodology in 2., above, Acquisitions can tell how much money and FTE it will need in a fiscal year to buy any given number of in-print books. In other words, if a university decides that it wants to build from approximately 600,000 volumes to approximately 1,000,000 volumes in a period of approximately five years, Acquisitions can project roughly what it would cost in book and serial money and FTE salaries to achieve this goal. Gifts must be treated as imponderables outside the monetary lines, except for backlogs already in the library, which will require staff time for processing. And the price of collections which might become available, and the money that will be spent through antiquarian catalogs and lists, can only be surmised with some degree of accuracy; but monies should certainly be laid aside against these eventualities. Approval-plan expenditures must also be considered, but can be laid down with a considerable degree of certainty after the first year of operation.

I do not propose here to present a chart calculating the cost in purchase and salary money to produce this hypothetical growth of 400,000 volumes in five years; but a reader should now be able to make his own cost and staff projection for bibliographic checking if, say, 300,000 of these volumes are to be from monographic purchases. In fact, why not *now* construct such a projection, working with the figure of 300,000 monographic acquisitions and the unit-price-FTE figures in 2., above. Inquiries about salary levels for bibliographic checkers, chief bibliographers, and administrative staff assistance should also make possible a projection of X amount of money for salaries for X amount of work to be done.

C. ANNUAL REPORTS

The *Acquisitions annual report* is, as we have already noted, made up from the statistics and records of activities at the various work stations during the year. I am not here giving a complete sample of such an annual report, chiefly because almost any Acquisitions department will have a file of annual reports from past years which will guide anyone composing a new report. Further, any established Acquisitions department will have a standard approach (format, methodology, etc.) to annual reports, as indicated by those of past years, and will expect a new report to conform to this standard unless there is good reason for varying from it.

We can generalize, however, that most annual reports are a mix of exposition and statistics summarizing the year's work in Acquisitions. Some tend to be largely narrative; some tend to be heavily statistical. But I think that a judicious blend of narrative and statistics might provide an acceptable golden mean. It is important to remember that the director of libraries is going to cull the annual reports from the various public and technical services departments to write his own annual report, and will appreciate any adroit verbiage. He will also appreciate some kind of listing of specific titles of academic interest acquired during the year, since he will be able to use these to demonstrate his knowledge of books.

Let me, then, suggest what might constitute the four parts of the contents of an annual report, and then indicate possible subdivisions of these four parts. These four chief parts would generally be as follows: (1) a narrative exposition of the year's work in the department; (2) statistics which include comparisons with previous years and support the narrative; (3) statements about and listings of personnel; and (4) recommendations for the coming year.

1. THE YEAR'S WORK IN ACQUISITIONS (NARRATIVE)

a. The *En Bloc Purchase of Collections:* citing particular collections; describing their contents; and listing the authors, titles, and imprints for especially interesting volumes.

b. *Reprints* (monographs, sets. serials) as a resource for retrospective collection development: citing titles of particular interest.

c. A description and discussion of *Approval Plans* and of *Plans To Collect Special Authors* (literary, dramatic, etc.) *and Subjects* (for example, avant-garde literature).

d. *Microforms* as a resource for retrospective collection development: citing titles of particular interest.

e. *Gifts:* including a statement about any notable donations and citing titles of particular interest.

f. *Searching Procedures:* explaining that placing search requests for o.p. materials with antiquarian dealers or library-specialist-dealers in various countries is producing retrospective titles and citing some of these.

g. *Development of Relations with Antiquarian and Library-Specialist-Dealers* as a resource for finding collections and particular titles (this last activity is a valuable, interesting, and all-too-often neglected aspect of Acquisitions): citing dealers and projects and programs with them.

h. Etc.

2. STATISTICS

Statistics would be grouped under such activities and routines as funds expended; requests checked; separates ordered and received; serials orders placed; serials orders received; and G&E—for which skeletons of charts follow.

A. FUNDS EXPENDED

	Preceding Year	*Current Year*	*Change*	*% of Change*
Library Book Funds				
Separates				
Serials and Sets				
Current Periodicals				
TOTAL LIBRARY				
Department Book Funds				
Separates				
Current Periodicals				
TOTAL DEPARTMENT				
Funds, Other Sources				
TOTAL, OTHER SOURCES				
Special Grants				
TOTAL GRANTS				
TOTAL BOOK FUNDS				

Binding Funds
    Library
    Department
       TOTAL BINDING FUNDS

GRAND TOTAL FUNDS

B. REQUESTS CHECKED

	Preceding Year	Current Year	Change	% of Change
Separates Section				
G&E Section				
Serials Section				
Total Requests Checked				

C. SEPARATES ORDERED AND RECEIVED

	Preceding Year	Current Year	Change	% of Change

Orders Placed

    Separates
       Regular
       Rush

    Miscellaneous
       Microforms
       Music Scores
       Records
       Other

       TOTAL ORDERS PLACED

Cancellations

Pieces Received

    Separates
       New Titles
       Added Volumes
       Added Copies

    Miscellaneous
       Microforms

Music Scores
Records
Other

   TOTAL PIECES RECEIVED

D. SERIALS: ORDERS PLACED

	Preceding Year	*Current Year*	*Change*	*% of Change*
New Subscriptions				
Library				
Department				
TOTAL NEW SUBSCRIPTIONS				
Backfiles				
Library				
Department				
TOTAL BACKFILES				
Miscellaneous Pieces (individual issues, binding, fill-ins, etc.)				
Library				
Department				
TOTAL MISCELLANEOUS				
TOTAL ORDERS PLACED				

E. SERIALS ORDERS RECEIVED

	Preceding Year	*Current Year*	*Change*	*% of Change*
New Subscriptions				
New Titles				
Library				
Department				
TOTAL NEW TITLES				
Added Copies				
Library				
Department				
TOTAL ADDED COPIES				
TOTAL VOLUMES RECEIVED				

Backfiles

   Library
   Department
      TOTAL BACKFILES

E. SERIALS: ORDERS RECEIVED (Cont.)

	Preceding Year	Current Year	Change	% of Change

Added Copies/Added
  Volumes

   Library
   Department
      TOTAL AC/AV

Miscellaneous Pieces
  (individual issues,
  binding, fill-ins, etc.)

   Library
   Department
      TOTAL MISCELLANEOUS
      TOTAL NUMBER OF ORDERS RECEIVED
      TOTAL NUMBER OF VOLUMES RECEIVED

F. G&E

	Preceding Year	Current Year	Change	% of Change

Separates Received

  Books
   New Titles
   Added Volumes
   Added Copies

  Miscellaneous
   Music Scores
   Records
   Microforms
   Other
      TOTAL SEPARATES RECEIVED

Serials Received

New Titles
Added Copies/Volumes
    TOTAL SERIALS RECEIVED

     TOTAL NUMBER OF UNSOLICITED
     VOLUMES RECEIVED

Exchanges

    Separates Ordered
    Separates Received
    Serials Ordered
    Serials Received
     TOTAL NUMBER OF EXCHANGES
     TOTAL NUMBER OF TITLES RECEIVED
     TOTAL NUMBER OF VOLUMES RECEIVED

3. PERSONNEL

The traditional listing of positions and the names of personnel filling those positions in the Acquisition department's "annual report" is customarily preceded by a sometimes lengthy narrative, which is usually a mixture of lament for staff turnover and understaffing and praise for those who have held the thin red line.

    Head, Acquisitions Department (name[s] would follow here, and below)
    Assistant Head, Acquisitions Department (Chief Bibliographer, Head
      of Separates)
    G&E Librarian
    Serials Librarian
    Bibliographic Checking Section Supervisor
    Separates Order and Receiving Section Supervisor
    Serials Order and Receiving Unit Supervisor
    G&E Assistant
    Approval-Plan Assistant
    Bibliographic Checkers
    Separates Order and Receiving Assistants
    Kardex Assistants
    Typing/Secretarial Pool
    Serials Order and Receiving Assistants
    Students (part-time)

4. RECOMMENDATIONS FOR THE COMING YEAR

A. INTRODUCTION

B. BODY OF STATEMENT

(1) Expansion of approval plans, or contemplated changes therein.

(2) Restatement of necessity for travel plans for acquisitions personnel in order for them to develop dealer relations, implement discovery and purchase of collections, etc.

(3) Liaison programs to produce closer working relations among Acquisitions, faculty, subject specialists, and other librarians involved in collection development.

(4) Review of G&E policies.

(5) Discussion and suggested resolutions of problems that have arisen in the past year.

(6) Etc.

C. CONCLUSION

In addition to a conclusion, there might be appendices dealing with special activities—for example, purchases from special funds, if these had been substantial.

D.

We have now looked at some of the approaches to record-keeping and the use of statistics. These vital devices of control are admittedly not nearly so interesting as the ins and outs of current and retrospective collection development, but are absolutely essential if acquisitions work flows and budget monitoring are to escape utter chaos. And I can assure the reader that if affairs ever get truly out of hand in an Acquisitions department—and a lack of proper statistical control is a major sign of such a situation—it is, to mix a figure of speech, extremely difficult ever to get Humpty Dumpty back together again.

II.8

HOW TO DESCRIBE
CLERICAL POSITIONS,
WITH A NOTE ABOUT SALARIES

The definition or description of clerical positions is not a particularly attractive task; but it is an essential professional duty which must (1) differentiate expected levels of performance from employee to employee and (2) enable clericals performing higher-level work to move into positions salaried at a level commensurate with the work which these positions demand. Whenever a clerical, like a professional, is put forth as a candidate for a higher position, his supervisor will have to justify the advance with a *job description* spelling out the duties for the position to be held, or will at least have to demonstrate that the candidate fulfills the requirements outlined in a proper job description.

Many libraries, although not all, have their own personnel positions described separately from those of personnel in the university as a whole, simply because a good deal of library work—certainly all in Technical Services, except perhaps for such things as labeling and some typing—demands more training and application than does general clerical work. Also, high clerical rank in a university as a whole tends to be based directly, often solely, on administrative or supervisory capacity, whereas in the performance of techniques in Acquisitions or Cataloging, a job in itself often requires long training, knowledge of languages, and a mastery of a complex series of routines related to Library of Congress classifications or bibliographic searching. This kind of specialized work may or may not have related supervisory responsibility, but should in itself merit a superior position for anyone capable of handling it.[28]

A.

Let us now suppose a research library that defines its own slots (positions) for its nonprofessional staff (clericals) and see what it might set up.

First of all, there is terminology, by which this staff might be called such things as clerical assistants, technical assistants, library assistants, library clericals, etc. Probably, some terminology with "library" in it is best, to keep the personnel descriptions in the library distinct by title from those of university clerical workers. Perhaps the arbitrary classification of "library assistant" will do as well as any.

The number of ranks for clericals with such a title then becomes a matter for consideration. I myself favor a relatively small number of ranks, say, three or four—i.e., LA-1, 2, 3, and 4. My experience has been that institutions ranking clerical employees into (as an example) ten groups (1-10) tend to make the higher levels of rank almost impossible to achieve and, in effect, under-rank and underpay their clericals. In such institutions we often find a host of clerical employees in the 4-6 range and almost none in the 8-10 range. If we wish to retain our suggested three or four ranks, there could be steps within each; but cost of living and merit raises without an excessive number of steps within a rank would be fairer and would make for easier upward movement from rank to rank.

B.

If we assume, arbitrarily, three library assistant ranks, we can then set up job descriptions for each. A fourth rank, LA-4, would simply be more of the same in depth, complexity of work performed, and years of service. I think that half-time personnel should be as entitled to any of these ranks as full-timers, since such a corps of experienced, qualified half-time employees on a regular schedule can be vital to the success of operations in Acquisitions.

LIBRARY ASSISTANT I

1. MINIMUM EDUCATION AND EXPERIENCE QUALIFICATIONS

Graduation from college; or two years of college and one year of clerical experience; or an equivalent combination of education and experience. *[Within the library itself, everyone should understand that occasional exceptions can be made here. For example, one might encounter a sophomore with no clerical experience, but with an exceptional academic record or foreign-language competency.]*

2. CHARACTERISTICS OF POSITION

The Library Assistant I is the entry level class for subprofessional library work. Positions in this class differ from Senior Clerk and Senior Clerk Typist in that the work performed by an LA-1 requires knowledge of library practices and procedures.

3. SUMMARY OF DUTIES

Under supervision, the LA-1 performs routine subprofessional library work in acquiring, processing, recording, filing, and/or circulating library materials according to prescribed procedures and/or definite instructions; may supervise the work of others; and performs other related duties as required.

4. EXAMPLES OF EXPECTED WORK PERFORMANCE

Charges and discharges books; maintains statistics; prepares overdue notices; and answers library information questions.

Types catalog cards; order cards from prepared (straight copy) or un-prepared (dealers' catalogs, books, announcements) sources; borrowers' cards; and interlibrary loan forms.

Files catalog cards with revisions; without revision, files LC proof slips, order cards, and circulation charge cards.

Does preliminary checking for catalogers or library holdings checks for bibliographers according to clearly established techniques.

Performs simple searching for missing books and serials.

Prepares routine claims for non-receipt of library materials.

Prepares materials for binding.

Makes specific changes on catalog cards with revision; annotates library records.

Does routine file marking for shelving government documents.

Enters continuing serials on checking cards.

Accessions (receives and records) monographs and bound volumes of serials.

Adds volumes and additional copies to existing records, and sets up Shelflist cards for catalog maintenance.

LIBRARY ASSISTANT II

1. MINIMUM EDUCATION AND EXPERIENCE QUALIFICATIONS

Graduation from college and one year of library experience; or two years of college and three of library experience; or an equivalent combination of education and experience.

2. CHARACTERISTICS OF POSITION

Positions in this class differ from Library Assistant I, in that the library tasks performed are more difficult, require exercise of judgment and initia-tive in order to perform them, and require that incumbents have not only procedural knowledge but comprehension of the practices of librarianship involved. Positions which are allocated to this class solely on the basis of supervision require responsibility for the training and work assignment of three or more full-time-equivalent employees.

3. SUMMARY OF DUTIES

Under direction, performs difficult sub-professional acquisition, cataloging, classification, circulation, and/or reference work that requires knowledge of library procedures and an elementary understanding of the practices of librianship; or supervises a small organization sub-unit; and performs other related duties as required.

4. EXAMPLES OF EXPECTED WORK PERFORMANCE

Participates in planning, assigning, and reviewing the work of clerical staff and Library Assistants.

Supervises the circulation desk staff; interprets library rules; and adjusts complaints.

Supervises filing done by Library Assistants.

Supervises claiming procedures; and prepares complex claims for non-receipt of library materials.

Supervises the shelving and stack maintenance.

Supervises binding preparation.

Supervises accessioning of monographs and bound serial volumes.

Supervises the preparation and distribution of completed sets of catalog cards.

Supervises, under general direction, the maintenance of records for reserved books.

Does bibliographical work of complexity, working with a variety of national bibliographies and trade tools.

Files catalog cards with complicated entries, such as those in Oriental languages, without revision.

Enters new serial publications on checking cards.

LIBRARY ASSISTANT III

1. MINIMUM EDUCATION AND EXPERIENCE QUALIFICATIONS

Graduation from college and three years of responsible library experience; or two years of college and five years of library experience; or an equivalent combination of education and experience.

2. CHARACTERISTICS OF POSITION

Positions at this level differ from Library Assistant II in that work performed requires a highly specialized knowledge or a thorough comprehension of a basic library function developed through years of library experience or undergraduate or graduate courses in librarianship. Positions allocated to this level solely on the basis of supervision require responsibility for the training and work assignments of at least eight full-time-equivalent general clerical and Library Assistant employees; or a staff of three or more Library Assistants including at least two full-time-equivalent employees at the Library Assistant II level (staff with almost professional knowledge of library procedures, functions, or techniques).

3. SUMMARY OF DUTIES

Under general direction, performs complex and difficult library work requiring highly specialized knowledge or a thorough comprehension of the practices and procedures of a basic library function; or has responsibility for the supervision of a complex organizational unit; and performs other related duties as required.

4. EXAMPLES OF EXPECTED WORK PERFORMANCE

Plans, assigns, and directs the work of a section within a library department (Acquisitions, Cataloging, Circulation, Reference, Special Collections, Documents, etc.).

Does bibliographic work of considerable complexity in Western European, Slavic, Oriental, or other difficult language areas.

Catalogs, with little revision, certain classes of library materials which require cataloging knowledge, technical skill, or specialized subject or language expertise.

Assists in the identification, processing, and preservation of Special Collections material.

C.

Salaries are, of course, determined by the economic conditions of particular geographical areas. But I must again emphasize the absolute necessity for Acquisitions (and for that matter, Technical Services as a whole, Reference, Special Collections, and so forth) having some kind of reliable staff of nonprofessionals if it is to function properly (call this kind of staff "career nonprofessionals" if you wish). And it should be obvious from the job descriptions in B., above, that any clerical capable of the LA-3 duties as outlined is worth far more to a research library—initially and for some time thereafter—than a novice M.L.S., and that this LA-3 should be drawing a salary substantially beyond that of a new M.L.S.

That such equity often does not exist in research institutions, and other kinds of libraries as well, argues not against the validity of the argument for fairness, but for the inability of many library administrators to comprehend fully the facts and economics of, say, Acquisitions, where a truly competent nonprofessional can do the work of two less efficient clericals if motivated by a solid salary that would still be considerably less than that of the two less capable employees combined. Staff turnover is a bane of Technical Services efficiency; and the constant retraining required by such turnover is not only disruptive of procedures but wearing upon everyone caught up in the stress of training new and inexperienced personnel. All in all, it may be easier to fight for decent nonprofessional salaries than to withstand the buffets of constant staff revision.

D.

I think that there is now enough in hand here to enable anyone who so desires to think effectively about the construction of job descriptions and equitable salaries for clericals. We should all remember, however, that when anyone is put on a payroll or given a promotion, not only salary and rank will have to be justified, but a description will be expected of what percentage of time an individual gives to his various tasks—that is, 25 percent bibliographic work, 15 percent record-keeping, 20 percent supervisory routines, and so forth. Such figures are easy to come up with; so there is no point in belaboring them here. It is, on the other hand, impossible to over-stress the necessity for proper job descriptions and proper pay for the individuals who fit these descriptions.

As a final note, I am going to emphasize a fact of life in Acquisitions: any professional in such work who fails to deal with nonprofessionals on a human basis and can not provide a reasonable financial expectation for them is going to find himself working under exceedingly difficult, if not impossible, conditions.

II.9

HOW TO PREPARE
USEFUL FORMS

Acquisitions sometimes seems to be a world largely composed of forms. The request card is, after all, a form; and the MOF, with all of its parts, is an ever-present fact of Acquisitions life. In fact, I have a "book" before me as I write this—a book made up of some eighty-eight xeroxed pages of forms (not including MOF's) used by the Monographs, Serials, Order, and G&E sections/departments of a medium-sized institution. The title of this book is, simply, "Forms"; and I am sure that none of us wants to delve too deeply into its contents.

What I would like to suggest, however, is that certain forms in Acquisitions can be valuable as devices to eliminate the time-consuming process of informing numbers of different people (usually other librarians, academic faculty, and dealers) about the same point time after time. For example, the "Order Procedures: Summary" included in the Checking Manual (II.2.A.8.) is really a rather lengthy, and important, form—created to save an Acquisitions staff from the dreary task of explaining verbally to departmental secretaries, over and over again, the correct procedures for submitting typed request cards.

The few forms which follow below will, hopefully, demonstrate some approaches to some problems that may commonly arise again and again, and will suggest how to construct other forms to deal with other repetitive problems that develop. Acquisitions departments of individual institutions will, of course, have to develop forms related to the repetitive patterns which will occur in each.

A. FACULTY FORMS

1. APPROVAL PLANS

Notice of establishment of such plans should, certainly, be sent to all relevant faculty. However, professors don't usually read library missives closely; and the odds are high that the few who do read them will soon forget the contents. Some form of written reminder is, hence, almost a necessity. The abbreviated sample which follows is for a very simple approval program; but if anyone were to try to explain even such a simple approval plan by typed letter or phone to, say, even a hundred faculty, he would have little time for anything else. More approval plans and a larger faculty merely intensify the need for such a form.

*Memorandum:*_____
(date)

TO: Professor _____[29]

FROM: Chief Bibliographer _____

SUBJECT: Approval Plans

Please submit request cards only for titles not normally received on the Humanities and Social Sciences and the Physical and Biological Sciences approval plans.

The Humanities and Social Sciences approval plan was initiated in _____, and provides the services listed below.
(date)

Humanities and Social Sciences

Provides books published by *ALL* American university and college presses; *and* Oxford, Cambridge (Clarendon), and London (Athlone) universities presses; *and* the following commercial publishers and additional university presses:[30]

Aldine
Bollingen Foundation
Brookings Institute
Columbia University, Bureau of
   Publications, Teachers College
Human Relations Area Files Press
Huntington Library
Investors Intelligence
Labor Policy Association
Metropolitan Museum of Art
Museum of Modern Art
New York Graphic Society
North Holland

. . .

The Physical and Biological Sciences approval plan was initiated in _____, and provides the services listed below.
(date)

Physical and Biological Sciences

This plan provides the following materials: texts, treatises, dictionaries, laboratory manuals, and similar publications of an *advanced nature*—that is, junior and senior level and above.

This plan includes *ALL* American publishers, *and* foreign publishers with domestic outlets.

2. INCOMPLETE REQUEST CARDS (TO BE SENT TO ACADEMIC FACULTY, LIBRARIANS, DEPARTMENTAL SECRETARIES, ETC.)

The_____Library   *Date:*_____
　　　　　　(name)

The enclosed request cards do not contain sufficient information for bibliographical processing. Please note the following points about order information.

1. The request card should have the author's name (last name first), title, place of publisher, date, edition (if other than first), number of volumes (if more than one), number of copies (if more than one wanted), price or price estimate, and series information.

2. Unless more than one copy or more than one volume is ordered, leave copy and volume spaces blank.

3. It is exceedingly important that an author's *full name* (first names as well as last), the title of the book, and its date be given wherever possible and as accurately as possible, since error or omission can cause considerable delay. Also, inaccuracy sometimes results in unwanted duplicates.

4. Copies of "Order Procedures: Summary," explaining in detail the correct format for request cards, *are available on request* from the Acquisitions department.

> *Chief Bibliographer*
> Acquisitions Department

3. REQUEST CARDS NOT TYPED (TO BE ENCLOSED WITH FORM 2., ABOVE, IF NECESSARY)

*Dear Professor*_____

Acquisitions can not process handwritten request cards. Will you please have your secretary type and return to us.[31]

> Thank you,
>
> *Chief Bibliographer*

4. REQUESTS FOR LIBRARY REQUEST CARDS (WHERE DEPARTMENTS CONTROL THEIR OWN LIBRARY FUNDS) AND BUDGET REPORT (TO DEPARTMENTS CONTROLLING THEIR OWN FUNDS)

A. REQUEST FOR A&S CARDS (BEGINNING OF FISCAL YEAR)

TO: *Professor* _____
    Library Representative, Department of _____
The new fiscal year is now under way, and all departments concerned are asked to submit request cards for books to be purchased on their A&S funds.

Chief Bibliographer

B. REQUEST FOR A&S CARDS (END OF FISCAL YEAR)

TO: *Professor* _____
    Library Representative, Department of _____
FROM: *Ted Grieder*
    Chief Bibliographer, Acquisitions
Subject: A&S Budget Report
This is to advise you that the state of your A&S budget is as follows on this date _____:

Allocation $_____
Unencumbered Balance $_____

In order to spend this unencumbered balance by the end of the fiscal year, your Department will have to purchase about _____ books. Since the Library has about half the titles requested by departments, you would normally plan to submit _____ request cards. It is desirable that you submit these cards *as soon as possible.*

C. BUDGET REPORT: A&S BALANCE, EXCLUSIVE OF APPROVAL PLAN RESERVES

Date: _____

PROFESSOR _____

Library Representative, Department of _____
    Exclusive of the funds reserved for Approval Plan purchases, your A&S balance available for the purchase of monographs is as of this date approximately $_____

Chief Bibliographer
Acquisitions Department

5. ANTIQUARIAN (O.P.) DEALERS' CATALOG FORMS

*A. INSTRUCTIONS TO FACULTY AND/OR SUBJECT
SPECIALISTS FOR SELECTION FROM ANTIQUARIAN
CATALOGS (TO BE STAPLED TO CATALOG WHEN REFERRED
TO SELECTOR)*

DEALER CATALOG INSTRUCTIONS
(Please Staple To Catalog)

REQUESTOR

Circle the item number in the catalog. Write your last name next to the desired item. One day service can be given if selection is limited. The Acquisitions department can handle approximately 25 titles per catalog per day.

Please forward catalog to your Library Representative immediately.

LIBRARY REPRESENTATIVE

1. Review selection.
2. Forward catalog with this instruction sheet stapled to front. Please *do not* have cards typed, since this delays processing of the catalog.
3. Authorize purchase by signing below, noting date, name of dealer, and catalog number.

AUTHORIZATION: _____ Dept. of _____
                        (Library Representative)

Name of Dealer _____Cat. No. _____

Date _____

*B. CATALOG DATA SHEET (TO BE STAPLED TO CATALOG BY
CHECKER; NOT A "FACULTY FORM," BUT DIRECTLY
RELATED TO A., ABOVE)*

Catalog _____   Date or No. _____

Date Cat. Rec'vd _____   Date Checked _____

Checked By _____

Fund _____   Requestor _____

No. of Items Checked _____   Number of Items Reserved _____

How Reserved_____   Date Reserved_____

6. REFERRAL FORM (WHERE DEPARTMENTS CONTROL A CERTAIN BUDGET (HISTORY, ENGLISH, GEOLOGY, ETC., AND SOME FACULTY MEMBER HAS SUGGESTED THAT A PURCHASE BE PLACED ON ANOTHER DEPARTMENT'S FUNDS)

TO: *Professor* _____,
        Library Representative, Department of _____
The enclosed cards are referrals to be approved by you for purchase on your
A&S funds. In the authorizations space on the cards, initial ONLY those
cards for titles which you accept on your A&S funds.
Please return all cards and this form to the Chief Bibliographer.

>   *Chief Bibliographer*
>   Acquisitions Department

B. DEALERS' FORMS

Forms to dealers are nearly infinite in variety. I give below only nine that
are perhaps typical and of some interest in demonstrating some of the
routines in the Monographs (the Separates, the Bibliographic Checking)
section/department. We recall that Serials will send out some forms that are
similar.

1. REQUESTS TO BE PLACED ON MAILING LISTS FOR PUBLISHERS' AND BOOKSELLERS' CATALOGS

If your Acquisitions department has not prepared and mailed out large
numbers of such requests, it should do so. Files of in- and out-of-print
catalogs (in-print includes reprint) are vital resources for the verifying (pre-
cataloging, searching) and retrospective collection development work of
any Acquisitions department. And alphabetical-by-publisher/dealer files of
these essential tools should be as extensive as possible, particularly for
antiquarian dealers and foreign and domestic trade publishers *not* in *PTLA*.

A. PUBLISHERS

>   *Date:* _____
        University of _____

The Library [letterhead]

Gentlemen:

Please place us on your permanent mailing list to receive copies of your
catalogs and announcements of publications as issued. Our orders for your
publications will be placed with our regular order agent.
Our official mailing address is as follows:

Acquisitions Department
The Library
Etc.

Thank you for your courtesy.

Sincerely yours,

HEAD
Acquisitions Department

B. ANTIQUARIAN BOOKSELLERS/DEALERS

Date: _____

University of _____

The Library [letterhead]

Gentlemen:

We would like to receive your catalogs to assist us in building our out-of-print and antiquarian collections. We would be most grateful if you would please send your current catalogs and future listings as they become availalbe.

We always particularly welcome advance catalogs, special offers, and special lists.

Our official mailing address is as follows:

Acquisitions Department
The Library
Etc.

Thank you for your courtesy in this matter.

Sincerely yours,

CHIEF BIBLIOGRAPHER
Acquisitions Department

2. CLAIM LETTER

University of _____
The Library [letterhead]   Date: _____

TO: Your Reference _____

Gentlemen: Dated_____

Will You Please:

____ *REPORT* on your ORDER # _____dated_____for the item below.

____ *REPORT* on our request to SEARCH dated_____for the item below.

____ *SUPPLY* item below on our ORDER # _____dated_____.

____ *NOTE THAT WE CONFIRM* our ORDER # _____dated_____.

____ *ADVISE OUR PURCHASE ORDER NUMBER* for the item(s) listed below. We are unable to identify it as our order.

ORDER #   DATE ORDERED   AUTHOR AND TITLE

Thank you,

HEAD
Acquisitions Department

3. CANCEL ORDER OR SEARCH

University of _____
The Library [letterhead]   Date: _____

TO:

Gentlemen:

Will you please CANCEL our ORDER or request to SEARCH for the titles listed below.

ORDER #   DATE ORDERED   AUTHOR AND TITLE

Thank you,

HEAD
Acquisitions Department

4. INVOICE CLAIM

University of _____
The Library [letterhead]   Date: _____

TO:

Gentlemen:

Will You Please Supply:

_____ *AN INVOICE* in *quadruplicate* listing our *ORDER NO.,* for the title(s) listed below. The order has been received, but we have not been billed. If your records do not agree, please notify us.

_____ *AN INVOICE* in *quadruplicate,* listing our *ORDER NO.,* for the attached charge. We are unable to identify it as our order.

_____ *A CREDIT MEMO* in *quadruplicate,* listing our *ORDER NO.,* for the title(s) listed below.

_____ *A CORRECTED INVOICE* in *quadruplicate,* listing our *ORDER* for the title(s) listed below (SEE attached copy of your *INVOICE NO.* _____ *DATED* _____).

ORDER # AND DATE   DATE RECEIVED   AUTHOR AND TITLE

Thank you,

HEAD
Acquisitions Department

5. QUOTE (QUOTATION) LETTER

University of _____

The Library [letterhead]   Date: _____

Gentlemen:

Please advise availability, price, publisher, and date of publication for the title(s) listed below. *Enclosed* is an *extra* copy of the list for your convenience in replying.
Thank you.

TITLES

Sincerely yours,

HEAD
Acquisitions Department

6. REQUEST PERMISSION TO RETURN MATERIALS

University of_____

The Library [letterhead]   *Date:*_____

TO:

We *REQUEST PERMISSION TO RETURN* the following for

_____ exchange
_____ replacement
_____ credit

REASON:

EXCHANGE	*REPLACEMENT*	*CREDIT*
____ wrong title supplied	____ imperfect binding	____ not our order
____ wrong edition supplied	____ imperfect text	____ extra copy
____ wrong volume supplied	____ damaged book	____ order canceled
		on _____
		____ duplicate purchase

Sincerely,

HEAD
Acquisitions Department

7. RESERVE LETTER AND FOLLOW-UP PURCHASE ORDER

A. RESERVE LETTER

University of _____

The Library [letterhead]   *Date:* _____

Gentlemen:

Will you please RESERVE the items listed below, if they are still available. Our *purchase orders* will be forwarded when your reply is received. If these titles are no longer available, will you please notify us. Enclosed is an *extra copy* of our order for your convenience in replying.

Thank you,

Chief Bibliographer
Acquisitions Department

Catalog #   *Item or Page No.*   *Author and Title*

B. FOLLOW-UP PURCHASE ORDER (ENCLOSING PURCHASE-ORDER SLIPS FROM THE MOF [SEE II.3., ABOVE] FOR TITLES RESERVED)

University of _____

The Library [letterhead]   *Date:* _____

TO:

Enclosed are our purchase orders for the items we reserved from CATA-LOG #_____ on _____, which items you replied were
                            (DATE)
available.

Thank you for your courtesy.

CHIEF BIBLIOGRAPHER
Acquisitions Department

C.

Although I do not include them here, a number of forms are required as well by any G&E operation—chiefly standardized forms for letters asking about the possibility of gifts from institutions or individuals or the possibility of exchanges with institutions, and forms thanking individual or institutional donors for gifts rendered. It is important to note, however, that forms for letters to individual donors should generally be only guides for secretary/typists to use in acknowledging routine gifts, and that such letters are best typed individually *unless* a donor is, as it sometimes happens, to be discouraged. Large gifts require, and should receive, elaborate and personalized responses (see II.4.).

D.

I hope it is now clear that "useful forms" are an important part of life in Acquisitions. Such forms as those in B.2.-5., above, or varieties of them, are common enough. However, such forms as those in A.1.-6., above, are far too uncommon. It hardly does for a librarian to rail at professorial unawareness about library procedures on the one hand and be, on the other hand, either too lazy or too fearful to supply professors with forms that will instruct and improve them. Master copies of all useful forms should be kept, by the way, at the typing station/pool in coherent order in a separate, marked file. Finally, *the content of forms should be thoughtful.* A bad or misleading form can be worse than no form at all.

II.10

HOW TO PRESENT
EXPLANATIONS AND
DEFENSES OF OPERATIONS

On occasion, every administrator in an Acquisitions section—Bibliographic Corps, Separates, Serials, Order, G&E—will be called upon to exposit his or his group's activities, defend them, request more help, or deal with some kind of procedure or problem in some kind of a report or memorandum. I give three examples of such expositions/requests below to demonstrate possible approaches, all of which I think may give the student or practicing librarian some insights into particular problems and ploys. A reader might, however, wish to adjust some of the statements into forms of expression perhaps more akin to his own "style" in librarianship.

A.

The memorandum below is a reaction to an erroneous budgetary statement by a library administrator in charge of finance (see II.7., above, which elaborates the kinds of records and statistics that can support defenses and expositions of operations). Sometimes, such administrators fire a shot simply to test the target; sometimes, other motives urge them to the attack. The experienced acquisitions librarian can only respond honestly and factually, relying upon his arsenal of records and statistics. As a matter of fact, financial officers sometimes criticize correctly, in which event the acquisitions librarian does well to acknowledge, and suggest solutions for, difficulties arising within his lines of administrative responsibility.

Date: _____

TO: Mr. A., Financial Officer
FROM: Dr. G., Chief Bibliographer
SUBJECT: Mr. A.'s figures for production in the Bibliographic Department.

Mr. A. has questioned productivity and costs in the Bibliographic department. This is properly his function, although I do not agree with his figures. For him to state that it is costing the Library $49.00 in time-per-title order is, at best, outré. To put it on the line, I am not entirely certain that the library administration or the university administration has ever faced up to the fact that a correctly run Technical Services, Acquisitions department, or Bibliographic corps costs money. More specificially, I am not entirely certain that the library administration is fully aware of what a Bibliographic corps is or does, even though it bought and, to some extent, paid for one.

This is neither the time nor the place to get into a discussion about the function and cost of a Bibliographic corps in a research institution; but I can say that we now have the humanities and social sciences under control and that the Romance language, Spanish language, and Germanic and Slavic departments all view our work with some enthusiasm. Moreover, we have now worked out successful liaisons with the department of English and the department of History, the two largest Arts and Sciences disciplines which were the most unhappy, vocal, and difficult before our bibliographical presence here. My concern at the moment is, however, to present a statement of activities and statistics.

When I arrived at_____University, we set up my own one FTE of responsibility in humanities, one in social sciences, one in Spanish language, one in Romance languages, and one in Germanic and Slavic (five FTE). We were given five clerical FTE as backup (some purists call for two clerical FTE for each bibliographer). We are now speaking of a total of ten FTE. I did not, however, realize that a typing pool would have to come out of the five clerical FTE; so we can now remove two FTE for this duty, leaving three clerical FTE as backup for holdings checks and so forth. I am myself working directly in my subject area only half time, what with supervision, revision, liaison with faculties and dealers, and so on. What we are, then, talking about for selection and precataloging activities are 7½ FTE (and we must remember that the 4½ professional FTE are also reading journals, surveying collections in their disciplines and language areas, executing faculty liaison, etc.). Further, I take 7½ FTE only for expository purposes, since, as Mr. A. is well aware, the social sciences bibliographer has been on half time and pursuing his Ph.D. for 80 percent of the time period which we are discussing.

This "7½" FTE costs $93,600 per year (clerical average $7200; professional $16,000). Taking the month of May as an example, this group initiated or received 4570 requests and precataloged and placed 3724 orders. May has twenty-one working days; so we get a figure of 177 orders placed per day or 23.5 per FTE (seven-hour day), a figure very favorably comparable to other operations I have seen. Accepting this "7½" FTE in operation, we get a time cost of $25.00/order, not the $49.00 cited by Mr. A., who appears to be nearly 100 percent off the mark. Furthermore, 20 percent of these orders were for antiquarian titles, which necessitated reserving desired titles by cable or phone, placing firm orders, selecting and ordering titles from catalogs from which the return was not 100 percent, and going through a good many more logistics than those of merely selecting current titles from national bibliographies.

Having, I trust, explained our statistics in relation to those of Mr. A., I think I should add that all of our bibliographers should be largely into retrospective work and monitoring approval plans. Further, Mr. Y., head of Technical Services, and the library administration have now had before them for two months approval plans for U.S., British, French, Italian, German, Russian, Spanish, and Latin American academic titles. These have been worked out in great detail at a cost of considerable professional and clerical time (the time for typing the necessary correspondence has been perhaps half that of the two clerical FTE associated with the Bibliographic corps). In other words, all of the materials for setting up these approval plans have been prepared and have now been in the hands of the administrators who can authorize them for two months. Once these plans are in operation, the time-cost-per-title selected, precataloged, and ordered will drop dramatically. May I anticipate the library's early action on these approval plans?

If Director Z., Mr. A., Mr. Y., or anyone else, has any further questions or figures to discuss, I am more than willing to cooperate, as is my staff.

Cordially,

Dr. G.
CHIEF BIBLIOGRAPHER

cc. Director Z.
Mr. Y.

B.

The following expository protest was written to get on the record the fact that a certain number of acquisitions personnel can do only so much work. If a monographs budget increases or there are backlogs of requests, extra personnel are required to deal with these situations. Such a statement seems self-evident, but not all of us in the profession are gifted with the ability to see the obvious with clarity. This memorandum protest concerns the kind of Bibliographic Checking work station with which the reader is now familiar (the chief bibliographer here could as well be called head of Separates or head of Monographs), *not* the kind of formal Bibliographic corps dealt with in A., above.

I also enclose the response to the chief bibliographer from the head of Technical Services in B.2., below, because it was written by an able librarian.

A reader might wish to test his grasp of irony by seeing if he can pick it up in the tone of the response.

1.

Date: _____

TO: Mr. Y., Head of Technical Services
FROM: Dr. G., Chief Bibliographer [Head of Separates or Monographs]
SUBJECT: Staff at the Bibliographic Checking point in relation to the budget for the coming year.

1. *General Statement*

As our discussion of 29 May 197— has made apparent, total FTE at the Bibliographic Checking point will be 5 for the coming fiscal year. The total budget to be spent at the Bibliographic Checking point will be $206,567.00—exclusive of special funds. Total FTE at this work station was 5.5 last year; total budget that had to be spent—exclusive of special funds—was $151,000.00.

What this means at the Bibliographic Checking point is that funds to be spent for monographs have increased 27 percent while staff has decreased 9 percent. The result is that this work station will be roughly 36 percent less equipped to spend the budget in the coming year than it was last year; and this figure does not take into account time lags, such as the month that will be lost between Ms. T's quitting and Mr. J's arrival; nor does it take into account the anticipated increases in departmental funds for both DNC and cataloged titles.

To keep an equivalence in the relation of bibliographic staff to budget for the past year would require an increase of 2.25 FTE beyond what is at present scheduled for the coming year.

2. *Some Observations*

Such a situation will lead inevitably to certain conditions, a few of which I now wish to get on the record. Doubtless, a number of other little unpleasantnesses, which I cannot foresee at this time, will arise as well.

a. We will not be able to undertake any special projects for the coming year. Already outstanding are history, geology, and heraldry projects, which will probably not now be possible. I suggest that you begin preparing the concerned academic faculties.

b. Efforts somewhat touched with heroism have at present reduced the staggering backlog of 22,000 request cards—accumulated by Mr. D. before his termination and my arrival on the scene—to only 3,000. It is, however, predictable that a new backlog, perhaps one surpassing his achievement, will exist by the end of this next fiscal year. As you know, such a backlog creates some rather nasty difficulties with the academic faculty.

c. It will be impossible to run more than a fraction of the catalogs submitted by the academic faculty after July 1. We will endeavor to set up a system whereby every department will be treated equitably, but some protests may arise. To maintain such a time-consuming service at all (to which we have been heavily, and I think correctly, committed in the past) will cut into already insufficient staff time.

d. It will be impossible to spend out the budgets for some Arts and Sciences departments. Some unhappiness may result.

e. It will not be possible to devote any intensive efforts toward spending out the remaining special funds. For example, a great deal of attention has been given to Spanish and French special monies, and to continue to do so is not now possible.

3. Some Conclusions

Given that the acquisition of monographs has a degree of importance, to increase the book budget while concomitantly decreasing staff in Acquisitions might seem somewhat illogical to a disinterested observer. To put an ever-increasing work load on a staff that is decreasing in size can only prove to be demoralizing in the long run, as it has proven to be in the past. To philosophize about the causal factors resulting in the current reduction of staff at the Bibliographical Checking station and generalize them into the realm of campuswide, statewide, etc. policy seems to me to be rather begging the question. The situation which I have described will exist for at least a year right here, at the University of _____. Ultimately, the situation will have to be solved right here, at the University of _____.

Cordially,

Dr. G.
CHIEF BIBLIOGRAPHER

cc. Mr. L., Director of Libraries
    Mr. M., Associate Librarian

2.

Date: _____

TO: Dr. G., Chief Bibliographer
FROM: Mr. Y., Head of Technical Services
SUBJECT: Your Memo of _____.

Dear Ted:

This is to acknowledge your memorandum of _____, with reference to the staffing problem for the coming fiscal year. Associate Librarian M. has advised that your letter has been forwarded to Director L. in Italy.

For me to suggest that the next fiscal year will present any significant amelioration in work load would be both cynical and dishonest. The single ray of hope suggested by M. is that salary and other savings may be effected in sufficient quantity to augment your staff. M. has now placed your section at the top of the "additional staff" priority list.

Allow me to underline my comments given in our recent discussion. There is no correlation intended between the book budget increases and the staff decreases. We will not press the bibliographic checkers to make up somehow for this deficit in help, but will continue with our philosophy of buying the best books, in the most efficient fashion, at the best possible price, with the greatest possible speed.

Your view of the situation is both astute and restrained. I wish to express my gratitude for your interest and concern, and say how appreciative I am to count you as a colleague.

Cordially,

Willy Y.
HEAD OF TECHNICAL SERVICES

cc. Director L.
    Associate Librarian M.

C.

The following report, or something like it, would be expected from any acquisitions librarian or bibliographer sent on a book-buying trip. Such professionals as agents are to be preferred to the academic faculty, since professors are by and large unfamiliar with acquisitions procedures, the nature of book dealers and the book trade, library holdings, and so forth. The real trick is to explain in dollars and cents to university administrators the value of such trips by librarians. By using professors travelling abroad in summers or during sabbaticals, university administrators are ever hopeful of getting free expertise, although the difficulties and confusions caused by the use of such inexperienced agents are a part of the lore of Acquisitions. Librarians should, on the other hand, endeavor to get themselves as exclusively as possible into the act by whatever persuasions are necessary.

The report which follows is directed at a particular audience. Moreover, it sells pretty hard and, for our own purposes here, may provide a reader with some food for thought and some insight related to the procedures for and the values of such book-hunting junkets. A librarian may never make such a voyage; but if he likes books, even the imagined participation in such a peregrination ought to be enjoyable. The writer of this report is, by the way, attempting to set a sound precedent for similar excursions by other librarians.

Date: _____

REPORT TO PRESIDENT _____ and DIRECTOR _____

BOOK-BUYING TRIP TO BRITAIN,
SEPTEMBER-DECEMBER, 197____

I spent twenty days in London, about five weeks in English provincial cities, one week in Scotland, and a fortnight in Dublin. I visited some 100 book dealers and purchased 8,000-10,000 books, with other negotiations still under way. The cost for all material purchased will amount to some $75,000.

The trip cost about $3,500 for transportation and per diem expenses. By purchasing collections on the spot at reasonable prices, we paid some $20,000 less than the same materials would have been priced at in the U.S. (if they could have been found here at all). In other words, I believe that this trip has actually saved the University about $16,500 from the funds so generously granted the library by the President.

Several collections were purchased *en bloc,* but many individual books were selected one-by-one from the stocks of various dealers. Selections were based on specific "Want-Lists" supplied by many of our faculty, plus my own general "feel" for what is needed to support our academic programs here. Almost without exception, the books selected are out-of-print, antiquarian titles. We, through our faculty, had been looking for some of these books for years. Most of the books purchased are solid, scholarly works in the humanities and social sciences. However, several important publications in science have been located. Some of the collections purchased, and those for which negotiations are still under way, are described in the following statements.

1. Franciscan Priory

4,000 volumes for $28,000 were obtained from_____ of London. This library belonged to a Franciscan Priory near Woodshale, England. Most of the material in it was published from the seventeenth to the nineteenth centuries in English, Latin, German, Flemish, Italian, Portuguese, and Spanish. Some 80 percent of these books were published before 1800. The collection includes dictionaries and reference works, philosophical and historical treatises, works of important Catholic authors, and commentaries. These books will be of great value for students and faculty working in history, literature, and philosophy. The price per title of $7.00 is extremely low, considering the early date of publication and the scarcity of most of these books. As it turned out, many other libraries were interested in this unique collection, but I was very fortunately on the spot and was able to act quickly. The acquisition of a collection of this scope and richness at such a price can be considered as a *coup* for us. The collection has been carefully packed and is now on its way to us by freighter.

2. Medieval History and the Reformation

These 350 volumes were originally in the libraries of Canon Tucker of Cambridge University and the famous Dr. Arnold of Rugby. The cost was

$1,800. These important resources were obtained from_____ of Oxford.

3. Modern Fiction

These 600 volumes of individually selected English and American fiction for $2,000 represent a tremendous bargain. Most of these titles will fill in some of our own better holdings in literature; and a few were deliberately selected, because of the extremely low price, to provide duplicate copies for the students in one of our largest departments.

4. Scottish History

Mr._____, the best-known dealer in Edinburgh, assembled a good basic collection on this subject for us. He has committed himself to offering us priority on further individual titles and collections. The lack of Scottish materials has been a difficulty for our History department, which focuses on English history; and all members of the department are most enthusiastic about this acquisition, as we all are about the unit cost of $10 for these 1,000 volumes.

5. English History

Some 500 volumes on this subject were obtained from various dealers, the majority from_____ and _____'s in London. Professor _____ supplied me with a list of specific titles, and I was lucky enough to find some 75 percent of them at a cost of $20 per selected volume.

6. English Literary Criticism and Biography

Some fine books, 500 volumes in all, were assembled from various dealers: _____ of Staffordshire, _____ of Chichester, and _____ of Penrith. The cost of $4 per volume is nominal.

7. Drama

Some important theatrical material fell my way—including manuscript prompt books, books on stage design, and an interesting collection of memorabilia—and was purchased from_____ in London. As you know, the Drama department is particularly interested in theatrical staging, and Chairman _____, in particular, and the department in general are quite enthusiastic about this unique gathering, which was purchased for only $1000.

8. Music

Negotiations are under way for the possible acquisition of an important library of music theory and a manuscript collection of music from

_____ of London. Our musicologists—namely, Professors _____ and _____—are actively assisting us in working out this purchase.

9. Economics Collection

I was able to purchase some 2,500 volumes of academic works published over the last 35 years for $20,000. These books are from an enormous library assembled by a lecturer at the University of_____, in Lincolnshire. The beauty of this collection is that Mr. _____ of Greenwich, the agent, permitted us to select from lists he gave me and allowed our Economics department time to screen from them, thus entirely avoiding the problem of duplicating our own strong holdings. Personal contact was vital here.

10. Irish History

A friend of mine in Dublin, Mr. _____ of the National Library of Ireland, was very helpful in this project. For example, he arranged interviews for me with the Historian of the National Library and with several book dealers specializing in Irish history. As a result, I was able to make arrangements for the assembly of this extraordinarily good collection of scarce, though fundamental, historical books, several runs of important historical and literary journals, and an almost complete file of clippings from contemporary newspapers related to the national and historical implications of the Abbey Theatre, along with an almost complete file of Abbey Theatre programs. Part of the material, some of which had not been on the market for many years, had just been assembled by the firm of _____. I viewed it only a day before it was to go up for auction and was able to skim off the cream, so to speak. The final price is now near settlement; and Professors _____, _____, and _____ feel that the sums under discussion are almost unbelievably low.

The results of this book-buying trip can be summarized as follows:

1. The Library was greatly enriched by the acquisition of some 10,000 important, and many rare or scarce, books at most reasonable prices.

2. Many book dealers in the British Isles now know about us and our interests; and having met a representative from our library, a number of them have expressed a willingness to assist us in our programs of collection development.

3. A great deal of information about the book trade in Britain is now available to our Acquisitions department. Such information has already proven to be very useful and will continue to be in the future.

4. Because of the success of this trip, I recommend that we plan more of the same. A visit to the Continent would also be advisable.

Respectfully,

Mr. H.
HEAD OF ACQUISITIONS

Copy also to:

Associate Director ____
Head of Technical Services ____
Chief Bibliographer _____
Professors ____, ____, ____, etc. [all appropriate academic faculty involved
   or named in any of the preceding statements]

D.

For the reader, the results of the above explanations and defenses may
be of factual interest. Under A., above, the financial officer concerned went
back to his drawing board and did not target Dr. G. again; most of the approval plans mentioned were subsequently put into effect. Under B., above,
Dr. G. received "priority" and the 2½ FTE requested. Under C., above,
buying trips continued in the institution concerned—most, however, to
New York and other centers of the U.S. book trade, rather than to Britain or
the Continent.

II.11

HOW TO ACQUIRE THE
BASICS OF THE BOOK TRADE

While it is beyond dispute that certain individuals have an aptitude for becoming bookmen, no one can pretend to learn anything about the book trade—in- or out-of-print—without reading books; reading about books; looking at a great many in-print, trade catalogs and o.p., antiquarian catalogs; looking at books; and handling books (see also II.10.C. for a description of a book-buying trip, a fine way to learn about the book trade). As a matter of actual fact, it is also much easier to get somewhat into the world of books if one lives in, say, Manhattan, a center of the U.S. trade, than if one resides in, say, Winslow, Arizona, my hometown. No matter where they are located, however, most research institutions of any size possess substantial antiquarian holdings in their Special Collections and subscribe to both in-print publishing and reviewing organs (*PW, BPR, New York Times Book Review, New York Review of Books, Times Literary Supplement, Library Journal,* and *Choice* are some obvious offhand examples of such titles) and subscribe to such antiquarian, o.p. publications and listings as *Antiquarian Bookman, Book Collector, Library Bookseller,* etc., and each day receive numbers of antiquarian catalogs and listings from dealers all over the world. There is, thus, little excuse for any acquisitions librarian in a research library not being up on both the current, in-print trade and the antiquarian, o.p. trade as well (see also I.5., which should be reviewed at this time, since it deals with some of the subjects in hand).

A. IN-PRINT TITLES

Here we must distinguish between two kinds of books (and serials): academic or scholarly and, for want of a better term, creative (belletristic). By and large, any research library—as the approval plan formats in II.6. indicate— would want all U.S. publications of a solid academic nature in the humanities, social sciences, arts, and sciences. Here, discounts are low and not reallly a matter to haggle about. Any jobber supplying this type of book is working on a low discount from the publisher and can not usually give much more than a 10 percent discount, if that. Normally, such academic titles are ordered by libraries long before the formal, academic reviews appear: so there is little more involved than a somewhat mechanical, though necessarily thoughtful, application of the various procedures of selection we have considered before.

Although I do not wish to stress unduly the simplicity of acquiring scholarly monographs in the various disciplines, it is a fact that a little learning, some experience, and some common sense will enable any acquisitions librarian to select such monographs correctly more than 90 percent of the time. Anecdotally, I can recall an instance when a group of subject specialists in the physical and life sciences was unable to review a large number of science titles that had arrived from various approval plans. Time being of the essence, as it were, I finally reviewed all of these books myself and sent them on to Cataloging after the usual verifying (pre-cataloging) routines. Two days later, the science specialists arrived; and three of them re-reviewed the same several hundred titles, finally deciding that I had erred in three instances. The point is that without particular subject specialty I was able successfully to identify acceptable approval-plan titles in mathematics, physics, biochemistry, physical chemistry, biology, botany, and so on. With such academic monographs, the depth of approach in a title is the determining factor, one more easily ascertained than is the present or ultimate research worth of creative literary efforts.

Acquisitions of contemporary creative work suitable for the development of study and research collections in the literary arts is another matter. It is, of course, difficult to make aesthetic judgments; but there are certainly many works of prose, prose fiction, poetry, and drama that can be eliminated from consideration through the use of review publications or a personal perusal of various titles. On the other hand, taking poetry as an example, many contemporary poets of great promise or real merit are simply not reviewed at all in well-known journals, which tend to be highly establishmentarian and not infrequently a good many years behind the times. With such poetry, it may be that Special Collections has some kind of program for acquiring such work, in which case it should certainly not be ordered for the general library. A conference among selectors who might be working with contemporary creative writing is definitely indicated. Moreover, I think we should all remember that Keats, Whitman, Edward Fitzgerald, Frost, and many other authors of current repute were once avant-garde, underreviewed or attacked, and, for all practical purposes, unknown. Fitzgerald's *Rubáiyát* was brought to public attention only by Rossetti's chance discovery of it in a bookseller's bargain barrel; Housman had to pay for the publication of *A Shropshire Lad;* Carlos Williams' early books required subsidies from his own pocket; and so on.

I would say, finally, that if *one* creative title is judged worthy of acquisition, serious consideration should be given to acquiring all other books by the same author. As a rule, one and two-book author collections help neither under-graduate study nor graduate or postdoctoral research. Reading and subject interest must come into play here—a knowledge of contemporary literature is gained by work and thought. Through his own reading and thinking, that of colleagues, and that of faculty, the acquisitions librarian can draw up some guidelines for this somewhat perplexing field. Such guidelines will be partly inductive and partly intuitive.

The question of paperback versus hardcover copies of academic or cre-ative monographs of any nature is a particular subject in itself, and one that can only be touched upon briefly here. It used to be that Acquisitions nor-mally ordered a hardcover copy of a title, even though a paperback was a-vailable. At that time, the thinking was that even if a paperback could be bound by the library (and many do not lend themselves to library bindings because of narrow margins, quality of paper, etc.), the cost in time of the binding pro-cesses plus the cost of the binding itself rendered the price differential be-tween hardcover and paperback copies either nonexistent or negligible. At present, however, two things have occurred: the price differential between paper and hardcover books (which used to be called cloth cover) has wid-ened; and many of the hardcover books of today are not sewn—boards of cardboard or some other material are simply slapped onto the sheets of a monograph and glued to form a somewhat feeble kind of casing. Further, a glance at BIP will show that a quality paperback priced at $5 can cost $12, $17, or, even, $25 in hardcover.

I believe that most publishers are aware of the institutional preference for books in hardcover, and that this awareness is a factor in the discrepancy between paper and hardcover prices. In view of this existing situation, I think that every Acquisitions department should formulate some kind of policy about purchasing hard or paper covers. The actual cost of binding by a library binder plus some kind of staff-time-cost figure can be worked out; and if this actual cost plus the cost of a paper copy (given a quality, bindable title) is still several dollars less than the cost of a hardcover copy, it seems evident that binding paper copies will save a good deal of money.

The ice may be thin here, but I would at least like to suggest that any bind-ing policy that is worked out should consider the possibility of acquiring and processing paperbacks onto library shelves without any binding at all. I do not wish to get into the details about what not to bind, but multiple reserve-room copies of assigned texts and readings seem one obvious category of candidates for non-bound paperbacks. Popular fiction may be another, un-less an author is being seriously collected as part of a planned program. Fi-nally, decision making about paper or hardcover, and binding or not binding, involves a great deal of money. Whatever the final decision in Acquisitions, it must be based on correct facts and figures, and followed consistently.

B. REPRINTS

As we know from our previous discussions, reprints make available a great many retrospective materials which are o.p./antiquarian and not available in original format through the publishing trade. Any acquisitions librarian worth his salt will have on hand a complete international file of reprint catalogs and reprints-in-print tools cumulating lists of reprints available; and he will select *expensive* reprints—monographs, sets, and serials—*with care.* The reasons for this care in selection are two: (1) a number of titles have been reprinted by more than one company, at various prices, of which the lowest will usually dictate the proper source of purchase; and (2) o.p. monographs, sets, and serials are frequently as available through o.p., antiquarian dealers as are reprints of these titles, sometimes at lower prices (condition being good, a cheaper o.p. title would be preferred to a reprint).

We must, however, note that the *cost in time* for staff involved in the process of weighing the price of a reprint against a possibly lower o.p. price must be taken into account. This cautionary statement applies more to the selection of individual monographs than to the selection of more expensive sets and serials, where cost in time for decision making is usually more justifiable on a dollars-and-cents basis. For example, if I am considering the purchase of a $3000 reprint of a serial, it is obviously worth my while to check with dealers specializing in o.p. serials backfiles to see if they can give me a price for this serial. On the other hand, if I say it is ridiculous to pay $15 for a reprint of what I believe to be a common o.p. monograph, I then have to involve myself and my staff in the time-consuming processes of communicating with o.p. dealers and possibly spending a good deal of time initiating a search for this particular title. And it may turn out that what I thought to be a common book is in fact not available at all through antiquarian, o.p. channels, or is available only at a price near that which I judged to be too high. My approach to the acquisition of this monograph may, thus, have cost my institution a good deal more than the reprint price which I rejected.

Deciding whether or not to purchase a reprint or look for an o.p. copy of a given title is a process which will develop efficiency through experience. A rule of thumb (which must be applied with common sense) is that the higher the cost of any reprint, the more justifiable the time spent checking o.p., antiquarian sources for price comparisons.

C. ANTIQUARIAN /O.P. TITLES

In a few paragraphs we can deal only sketchily with the subject of antiquarian books. But I would like to cite the thesis that there are two groups into which all librarians can be divided, one relatively large and one relatively small: the large group, consisting of librarians who don't care about books as books (if not actually disliking them except as units, numerals, or statistics) and view them merely as merchandise—marbles, pies, nuts and bolts, etc.; the small group, consisting of librarians who do care about books as books and take an interest in the aesthetics and the history of the book. In this latter group will certainly be found special collections librarians, and ought to be found bibliographers and acquisitions librarians engaged in the selection, acquisition, and processing of books for building both current and retrospective collections.

To see which of these two groups may be more congenial to him, a student can take a course in library school in the history of the book. But anyone, apprentice or journeyman, can read a few books *about* books to see how they strike him. I have no fixed guidelines in this matter (any syllabus of a course on the book in a library school will list a great number of possible titles), but would suggest that any interested person can take a simple self-test by reading a few of the very many books written about books: Svend Dahl, *History of the Book* (1958); Douglas McMurtrie, *The Book: The Story of Printing & Bookmaking* (1938); Alfred Pollard, *Fine Books* (1912); Nolie Mumey, *A Study of Rare Books* (1930); Charles Sawyer and F.J. Harvey Darton, *English Books, 1475-1900* (2 vols., 1927). I would cap off this reading by perusing a most interesting biography of a notable bookseller, *Rosenbach* (1960), by Edwin Wolf and John Fleming. One would surely wish as well to poke around in *Antiquarian Bookman* and *The Book Collector,* two bookmen's journals. If first flights among these few titles plunge rather than soar even feebly, I think a modern Icarus might wish to consider specialties outside Acquisitions.

I by no means, I hasten to add, wish to exclude such disciplines as education, history, economics, mathematics, the physical and life sciences, and so forth from the realm of the bookman, since there have been notable bibliographers, collectors, bookmen, and librarians working in these and many other disciplines, which may have been slighted by my overly literary reading suggestions. I would say, in conclusion, that anyone who reads through a span of *The Book Collector,* which touches a number of disparate disciplines and tastes united by a common interest in the book, and finds nothing stimulating might be self-defined as a member of the majority group of librarians, which is, after all, where the power lies.

On the other hand, if one does discover an incipient interest in books and the antiquarian trade, what to do? The first and most obvious thing is to visit bookshops, if there are any around. The second is to read more books about books in some kind of historical sequence—that is, those dealing with incunabula and other early printing, with the history of printing and bookmaking in various countries, and with the ins and outs of genres for collecting, such as early American imprints, modern authors, detective fiction, Victorian three-deckers, a particular social science, a particular physical or life science, etc. (there is a world out there on any of these subjects and an almost infinite variety of others). Third, I would select a particular subject/genre of interest— poetry, the history of a physical or life science, pedagogy, drama, music, whatever—and would study numbers of antiquarian catalogs and listings relevant to my interest. Here, we must keep in mind that although acquisitions librarians should have *specialties,* they must as well be *generalists* if they are to work most effectively with the materials necessary to develop collections for all present or planned academic programs at a given institution.

To overemphasize the importance of *reading* and *studying* booksellers' catalogs is simply not possible. Critical readings of such catalogs will reveal a great many discrepancies among listings, both in the descriptions of and the prices asked for any particular book. Why? When one can answer this question, a bookman is in the making. These discrepancies and variations suggest the operation of such factors as a deep desire for money, laziness, and sometimes a genuine lack of knowledge. On the other hand, if a bookseller lists a book—say, a modern novel or an early American medical work—at some outré price, and an acquisitions librarian buys it, who is to say who knows the game better. To be fair, we must keep in mind the fact that while there are roughly set norms for pricing great, landmark books, most o.p., antiquarian titles are worth exactly what a dealer can get for them.

D.

To recapitulate, if you think you like books, go to bookshops and to your own special collections area. Look, ask questions, and don't hesitate to plead ignorance. Those who know one important trade—say that ours is now Acquisitions—can afford the luxury of admitting to be a novice in another.[32] The bookseller who knows everything about early Italian printers' devices would be as a helpless infant if thrown into the welter of procedures and routines which we have looked at together in this guide.[33] He has his trade and you have yours, both highly honorable. So ask, and listen away in bookshops.

If you are in what may be politely referred to as the hinterlands, your research library—if it truly is such—will still have substantial holdings in Special Collections; so there will be no excuse for not handling books and studying the many bibliographies and specialized reference guides which any sound Special Collections will have on hand. To be honest, special collections librarians may sometimes, like booksellers, present a somewhat formidable front, and some *are* formidable; but most are usually willing to spend a surprising amount of time with fellow professionals who appear to be sincerely interested in learning about books.

Librarians are not only the keepers, but the *acquirers* of books. Such is the special profession of Acquisitions. And it seems self-evident that professors of Acquisitions must know a good deal about the reprint, in-print, and out-of-print book trade if they are properly to perform their function. Why should the fishers of books be any less knowledgeable about the tools of their trade or any less dedicated to pursuing their prey than the Izaak Waltons who ply mere water?

II.12

HOW TO STATE
COLLECTION DEVELOPMENT
(BOOK SELECTION)POLICIES

The subject of collection development—namely, the art of building collections by the careful and correct selection of current and retrospective books, sets, and serials to support the present and anticipated teaching and research needs of any particular institution—has been discussed a number of times before in this guide (see especially I.4.-5. and II.5.-6.); and if these various discussions are kept in mind, we already understand the various methods for approaching current and retrospective selection/acquisition in relation to academic programs and budget for materials and staff (see also II.7.-8., 10.). Recently, although the vogue may have peaked, it has become very much *à la mode* to put the methodology (the procedures and functions) of collection development into formal, written statements, some relatively simplistic and some detailed and extensive.[34]

It seems to me to be logical that the university community should have a desire to know what the library is doing with the funds for the purchase of monographs and serials. However, interested faculty who deal directly with the library's selectors do in fact know in considerable detail what is going on in the collection development related to their particular interests and disciplines; they are most helpful in assisting in this collection development, and play a very important role in directing it toward its proper goals. Any formal collection development policy statement appears to me to be, thus, executed chiefly to inform only the very members of the university community who know the least and care the least about the library and its functions—namely, the academic deans and the academic faculty who do *not* take the time or make the effort to establish liaison with and work with professional library selectors in their work of collection developments.

I would be less concerned about the production of these written policy statements had I not viewed firsthand the enormous cost in expert time it takes to produce them. In time-cost, simplistic statements of collection development policy are gold; detailed and extended statements of such policy are platinum. In these present times of budgetary stress on library monies for materials *and* jobs for librarians, it may occur to a disinterested observer to wonder how much expensive jewelry the profession can afford.

Not all of us, and certainly not any neophytes, will ever be directly engaged in constructing statements about collection development policy; but as we rise in the ranks, some of us may one day have to tackle such an assignment. Let us now, therefore, look at two such policy statements, below. The first is relatively simplistic and is given pretty much in its entirety; the second is a detailed and extensive statement, presented only as an abbreviated outline to show what such a statement would contain. I think that a look at both of these will be helpful in demonstrating approaches to the subject in hand and perhaps one day providing guidelines for an acquisitions librarian faced with the necessity for executing such a professional task.

A. RELATIVELY SIMPLISTIC COLLECTION DEVELOPMENT POLICY STATEMENT

This statement is composed of two different documents, given in 1. and 2., below. It is concerned *only* with the disciplines and schools serviced by the main, general library of a particular institution. Professional schools—such as dentistry, medicine, law, the graduate school of business, etc.—and affiliated institutes are *not* its concern. In 3., below, I include a brief statement explaining how the library determines overall allocations of book budget money; this statement is directed at academic deans and their faculties.

We must always remember that behind all procedures and programs in collection-development statements is the ever-present fact of the *size of the budget* for the purchase of materials—always, or at least commonly, referred to by librarians and academic faculty as the "book budget," a blanket term to describe the money allocated to the library to purchase monographs *and* serials in any format. *The fact* of the size of the "book budget" lies watchdog behind any statements about collection-development policy, since no policy, simple or complex, can proceed beyond the fact of economics—namely, the amount of money available to support that policy.

1.

*Date*_____

_____UNIVERSITY: GENERAL LIBRARY

COLLECTION DEVELOPMENT POLICY STATEMENT NO. 1

Collection Development is headed by a committee—Mr. B., Dr. F., and Dr. G.—appointed to this function by Director N. They are assisted by an advisory group of seven subject specialists representative of the various disciplines and schools which the General Library serves and with a considerable time of service with the faculties of these disciplines and schools. All of these collection-development personnel have examined a great many policy statements from U.S. research institutions and applied their abilities toward evaluating them and working out COLLECTION DEVELOPMENT POLICY STATEMENT NO. 2, which is the specific implementation of the methodology which is the concern of this POLICY STATEMENT NO. 1. Both statements must be understood as two essential parts of *one whole approach* to collection development in the general library.

At the present time, we have some thirty subject specialists selected from our professional staff. Each of these has demonstrable experience and educational background in his subject or language area. Each of these subject specialists is a "generalist," with special expertise in his particular areas of selection. Under our present budgetary limitations, such specialists can not devote full time to selection, having a number of other professional duties as well. However, each has been allocated no less than 20 percent of his time for current and retrospective collection development.

The subject specialist (1) evaluates his present collection(s); (2) makes recommendations for purchases both independently of and in conjunction with the advice of his faculty; (3) serves as liaison for relations between the library and faculty and students; and (4) develops particular selection policies for given areas of responsibility after evaluatively surveying his collection(s), consulting all appropriate bibliographies, and seeking the advice of all members of his academic faculty. Library of Congress proof slips and reviewing journals in their disciplines and areas of responsibility are important resources in the work of these selectors.

The Collection Development Committee, in consultation with the advisory group noted in paragraph one, is also responsible for budgetary allocations to the various schools and their disciplines, using such specific criteria as enrollment points, numbers of graduate students within a particular discipline, numbers and nature of degrees offered, numbers of faculty within particular disciplines, present and planned programs by the university administration and the academic faculties, teaching and research needs, and evident strengths or weaknesses related to these programs. Of course, the library budget for collection development is a basic determining factor in the area of selection.

Finally, our collection-development policies directly reflect the stated emphasis of the university administration on research as divergent from, though not necessarily opposed to, basic instructional needs. This emphasis seems only logical in view of the large number of doctoral programs within the university and the heavy research productivity of the academic faculty.

2.

Date _____

_____ UNIVERSITY: GENERAL LIBRARY

COLLECTION DEVELOPMENT POLICY STATEMENT NO. 2

1. Purpose

A. To give aims and guidelines to the subject specialists who ultimately determine the content of the library's collections.

B. To make these aims and guidelines known as well to the whole library staff.

C. To implement the curricula by supplying the study and research resources required by students and faculty.

D. To emphasize President _____'s community goal of a scholarly research library in the highest 10 percent of excellence.

2. Methodology

See COLLECTION DEVELOPMENT POLICY STATEMENT NO. 1, dated _____, for the composition of the Collection Development Committee and the activities of library subject specialists. Also see 3., below.

3. Selection Policy for the General Library

A. *General Statement*

The Collection Development policy for the General Library is a spelling out of the methodology for acquiring monographs, serials, and other materials to support the teaching and research functions of the university and, as well, to enhance the cumulative scholarly resources of the area's academic communities.

The most significant portion of selection involves the planned acquisition of materials best qualified to strengthen the university's resources for instruction, research, and cultural preservation. The importance of careful selection has increased with the continuing growth in the number of titles published and the costs of acquiring, cataloging, housing, and servicing them. In many of the schools, faculty have been appointed as library representatives. Their recommendations are valued and vital. However, the library's subject specialists have ultimate responsibility for ordering current and retrospective publications, and must take responsibility as well for coordinating the collection-development programs as a whole.

Like any other, the Collection Development policy statement is a flexible guideline, necessarily subject to constant review and informed revision. The direction of any library's growth must be responsive to immediate and projected needs and/or changes. The quality of our collection development is particularly important, since the fixed space of the General Library demands careful selectivity, consolidation of materials wherever feasible, and close attention to technological advances in systems for bibliographical control.

B. *Guidelines for Overall Policy*

(1) New Programs

The Collection Development Committee and its advisory group must be informed of new course offerings, research projects, and departmental changes in academic goals and programs. No new programs can be instituted without provision by the university of adequate funds for the purchase of library materials, *adequacy* to be determined after in-depth consultations between CDC members and appropriate subject specialists.

(2) Materials to Be Acquired; Materials Not to Be Acquired

a. Books, serials, basic data tapes, microforms, and other relevant forms that may develop should be given full consideration by subject specialists. Because of space limitations, microform will, when practical and satisfactory, be considered as a substitute for hard copy.

b. Textbooks per se are not purchased.

c. Multiple copies of any title are not purchased for location within the General Library, except when demonstrated to be imperative in such areas as reserve, reference, and special collections.

(3) Limitations of This Statement

Since our professional schools and institutes have their own libraries and expert selectors, materials falling within the disciplinary ranges of these libraries are not normally purchased by the General Library.

(4) Area Resources

The proximity of the university to a number of other solid research libraries is an important consideration in our book selection activities. It would be illogical for the General Library to begin to develop large new subject strengths, purchase extremely costly monumental sets or backfiles of serials, or acquire rare materials if access to these is only a few minutes away. However, these other libraries cannot be viewed as surrogates to enable us to escape our own educational and research obligations to our university community.

(5) Budgetary Guidelines for Selection

Our annual evaluations of graduate and undergraduate studies serviced by the General Library—considering overall point enrollment, graduate enrollment, faculty size, and M.A. and/or Ph.D. programs in operation or developing—dictate the financial allocations per discipline which serve as monetary guidelines within which each discipline can be developed each year.

C. *Guidelines for Selection*

(1) Definitions of Levels of Collecting

Needs and demands differ in various subject areas. To indicate how far the General Library can go in meeting these needs and demands, we recognize several degrees of depth in the development of collections.

a. General Collection

A general collection is one which serves to introduce and define the subject and to indicate the varieties of information which are available, including some dictionaries, encyclopedias, selected editions of the important works of major authors, historical surveys, biographies, and serial publications presenting the basic scholarship in the field.

b. Instructional Collection

An instructional collection is designed to meet all teaching needs within its scope and should include a wide range of basic works, complete collections of the works of important authors, yearbooks, handbooks, a wide range of representative serials, and the fundamental bibliographical apparatus pertaining to its subject(s).

c. Comprehensive Research Collection

A comprehensive research collection is adequate for the independent research of both graduate students and faculty, and includes all current publications of research value as well as retrospective publications deemed desirable by the faculty. Such a collection includes all of the important or useful works in the field and the important editions of them, as well as an extensive body of critical and biographical works, documents, complete files of serials, and extensive bibliographical resources.

d. Exhaustive Research Collection

An exhaustive research collection includes, insofar as possible, all relevant publications of research value, including such marginal materials as manuscripts, archives, and ephemera. At present, such collecting in depth is undertaken only in the two disciplinary areas endowed beyond General Library budget allocations—that is, American and English literature (the _____ and _____ endowments) and labor history and economics (the _____ endowment).

(2) Responsibilities of Subject Specialists

a. Careful attention to the four levels of collecting, noted in C.(1), above.

b. Evaluation of present collections.

c. Selection of library materials within a clearly defined area, including monitoring of all individual orders and approval-plan titles.

d. Liaison with faculty and students.

e. Development of detailed, _written_ policy statements for subjects and areas of responsibility.

D. _Subjects and Specialists_

See the attached list which follows on a separate sheet for current subjects/disciplines and the subject specialists working with them.

SUBJECTS AND SUBJECT SPECIALISTS:_____
                                          (DATE)

Subject	Specialist
American History	-------
American Literature	-------
Anthropology	. . .
Art and Art Education	
Astronomy	
Biology	
Business and Commerce	
Chemistry	

. . .

3.

Date_____

EXPENDITURE PER SCHOOL OF TOTAL LIBRARY

MATERIALS BUDGET: REPORT TO THE UNIVERSITY

LIBRARY COUNCIL AND THE ACADEMIC DEANS

This report bears only upon expenditures for library materials and not upon overall library costs for selecting, ordering, receiving, cataloging, and servicing these materials.

School	Percentage of Budget Per School
Arts and Sciences (the University College and the Graduate School)	29%
School of Education	23%
College of Business and Public Administration	11%
Graduate School of Public Administration	9%
School of Continuing Education	9%
School of the Performing Arts	11%
School of Social Work	5%
Incidentals (reserve texts, replacements, etc.)	3%
TOTAL	100%

It must be realized that the above table of percentages for the various schools is an approximation. However, it is based upon demonstrated patterns of book expenditures, allocation of funds, and studies of student use of materials, and is probably accurate within a 2 percent margin.[35]

The broad percentage of the budget charged against Arts and Sciences and Education, grouped together, is a reflection of heavy graduate use plus the large enrollment in both schools and the large registration point count there. These two schools in the last fall, September_____, accounted for more than 50 percent of the total registration points of students served by the General Library.

The large percentage expended by A&S (including the University College and the Graduate School) reflects a variety of factors, among them (1) demand for the most current information which can only be supplied by serials, (2) costly items for the sciences—for example, *Biological Abstracts, Chemical Abstracts,* and *Physics Abstracts*—together with overall higher prices for books in the sciences, and (3) the broad reading spectrum of the humanities and social sciences, as well as the expensive indexes and abstracts for these disciplines. The percentage expended for A&S would have been higher except that its faculty teaches a number of basic courses attended by students from all undergraduate schools of the university; and these courses as a rule require only textbooks and reserve readings.

The percentage of expenditure for Education reflects not only costs of the technical and the educational training materials unique to the field, but of purchases of materials in Arts and Sciences vital to its teaching curricula and indispensable to any Education library, whether art, music, psychology, history, and so forth. Education's needs, thus, cut across virtually all fields of selection for arts and sciences. In addition, nearly a thousand periodicals oriented directly to Education's curricula must be supplemented by some of the basic serials in the arts and sciences.

The General Library continues to maintain extensive book holdings (large enough to have functioned formerly as a separate library) and to subscribe to more than a thousand serials directly related to the College of Business and Public Administration. The library buys extensively in business administration, marketing, and economics, and also subscribes to the customary business informational services.

Graduate Public Administration utilizes the materials of our documents center, as well as those materials gathered for a variety of courses in the sciences and social sciences. Social Work has heavy usages in the documents center, the sociology collection, and current reference material.

The students of the School of Continuing Education have demonstrated an increased use of the library in the last year, particularly in the last semester. Their demands seem to be general and wide-ranging, but fall into a concentration in the fields of applied knowledge, from real estate management to foreign languages.

The School of the Performing Arts has required substantial support, since it works in many areas—cinema, dance, television, and theatre—

not initially well represented by the General Library's collections. Performing Arts also utilizes many of the holdings directly related to the individual humanistic disciplines.

B. DETAILED AND EXTENSIVE COLLECTION DEVELOPMENT POLICY STATEMENT

Having looked at a relatively simplistic policy statement in A., we would expect that a more detailed and extensive statement would differ from it only in degree; and such is the case. If a school of librarianship is situated in or near a *large* university library system, the student, like the librarians themselves, may have such a policy available in the library for study. Let me, however, sketch some of the considerations about structuring such a policy.

1.

The *Introduction* to a Collection Development Policy Statement will explain the following: (1) *why* such a policy statement has been constructed, (2) *what* it aims at, and (3) *what* its limitations are—not necessarily in that order. An outline of this introduction would be something like the following:

(1) The very large number of current titles of possible interest to the University Libraries within a given year (ca. 600,000) and the large number of antiquarian/o.p. titles which we consider in a given year (ca. 120,000) make some kind of collecting guidelines imperative, since (a) only some 360,000 of these titles fall within our areas of collecting interest and (b) we are budgeted under the amount which would be necessary to purchase even these 360,000 titles.

a. Further close inspection will reveal half (180,000) of these 360,000 titles as being the most central to our areas of vital interest.

b. With an eye to the budget, we can contemplate the purchase of perhaps two-thirds (120,000) of these current and o.p. titles.

(2) A collection development policy aims at setting forth guidelines—discipline by discipline, subject by subject, or area by area, as the case may be—to assist us in our practice of attempting to select the best possible books relevant to our teaching and research programs, present and planned.

a. Such guidelines must not be too detailed, lest they too soon become outdated.

b. Such guidelines must not, on the other hand, be too broad or indefinite; for they will then lose any functional worth.

(3) Any statement about collection development policy must be understood to be limited by budgetary conditions and to be as well only a statement of an ideal—that is, the statement must be understood to present guide-

lines for what we are now trying to do to the best of our ability, and must not be understood to be an evaluation of the strength or worth of any existing collection as it has evolved from the past into its present status. Strengths and weaknesses of collections will, of course, be taken into consideration by our subject specialists and bibliographers in their retrospective collection development activities.

2.

The Introduction will be followed by some kind of explanation about procedure—that is, *how* this statement was put together. It will be obvious to all of us that any kind of a detailed policy statement will have to come from academic faculty and subject specialist input. But in order to control this input, it should be equally obvious that someone—namely, librarians—will have to construct some kind of a guidance device for the faculty and subject specialists. It follows that since we need questions to get input/answers (and we need a number of answers), we will have to formulate some kind of questionnaire (a reader should, at this point, review II.6., *especially* II.6.D.2. where the German-language approval plan is set forth; approval plans *are,* after all, *collection development policy statements to approval-plan dealers* for their guidance in the kinds of current materials to supply).

Any such questionnaire will have to ask several things: (1) What is the *aim* of your present collection development work? (2) What are your *chronological guidelines* (are there limitations or certain periods to be collected, developed, or omitted)? (3) What *geographical areas* are to be included (or excluded)? (4) What *restrictions,* if any, are there for materials in *non-English languages?* (5) What *types of materials do you collect?* and (6) *What types of materials do you exclude?*

The introductory explanation of procedure should not only tell what questions were asked by a questionnaire, and how responses were collated by librarians, but should also list a sequence of "Guidelines for Selection" (such as in A.2.C., above) to describe various levels of collecting depth. These levels must be formally stated here (as in A.2.C., above).

3.

The *logistics* for handling these large numbers of questionnaires and the responses to them can get somewhat complicated. Such being the case, whoever is in charge of putting together a final, detailed and extensive Collection Development Policy Statement will have to delegate responsibility to a great many librarians within the university libraries (we are not dealing here with only one, general library) and will have to make each selector/subject specialist/bibliographer responsible for (a) getting questionnaires to every member of his faculty or faculties, (b) getting the questionnaires back again,

(c) compiling and summarizing them, and (d) applying the "Guidelines for Selection" within his areas of responsibility in collection development.

This delegate will *then* have to put his collated information onto some kind of a written form, the structure of which will be dictated by the nature of the questionnaire, and prepared by the library; *then* indicate levels of depth of collecting for all subdivisions of disciplines within his areas of responsibility; *then* let his faculty review his statements before he finalizes them and turns them into the designated receiving station in the library, where all of these different, final, individual statements will then be put together, prefaced by the appropriate remarks, and welded into a final, overall statement of collection development policy for the university libraries system.

4.

The *procedure* for putting together the final policy statement immediately gets one into the problem of grouping into one logical and coherent whole the numbers of individual policy statements. For our purposes here, I think we can say that all disciplines and areas *funded* by the main, general library should be listed alphabetically under that library, whether or not these disciplines and areas are housed in the general library or in a discrete library located physically outside the general library. For example, there may well be a geology, engineering, biology, education, etc. library housed physically outside the general library; but if these disciplines/subjects are funded by the general library through its budgetary allocations from the university, these disciplines should, along with others whose holdings are primarily or entirely located in the general library, be listed under the heading of "General Library" or "University Library." In other words, the general library listings will represent *funding lines* not necessarily representative of location of materials or of administrative lines for libraries or collections housed elsewhere.

The libraries of professional schools, research institutes, research stations, etc., *not funded* by the main library should be grouped separately under their appropriate general headings and then alphabetically by title of the individual libraries for the professional schools (dentistry, graduate school of business, law, medicine, and such), institutes, research stations, and so forth.

5.

One picture being worth the proverbial one thousand words, let us look at one individual collection development policy statement for one discipline. This statement is intended as an example only, and does not pretend to deal knowledgeably with its particular discipline.

It should be added that not all of these individual reports will conform exactly to one another. The subject specialist responsible for finalizing his report or his faculty may choose to report in greater or lesser depth, *within* the structure of the form used.

GENERAL LIBRARY

Date _____

Collection Development Policy Statement:
Philosophy

Subject Specialist:

_____
(NAME)

A. *Purpose of This Policy*

The purpose of collection development in philosophy is to build holdings able to support teaching, from basic through graduate level to the Ph.D., and research from the graduate level through the Ph.D. into postdoctoral research in considerable depth.

Undergraduate courses tend to focus chiefly on the basics of ethics and logic and on general approaches to art and religion. There is also an emphasis on the historical—that is, philosophy from classical times to the present, including developments within particular chronological periods and the study of the thinking of individual philosophers within these periods.

More specialized and advanced undergraduate and graduate courses inevitably include some of the historical approaches and attention to individual figures noted in the preceding paragraph, but continue on in depth into aesthetics, language, metaphysics, phenomenology, set theory, systematic studies, theory of knowledge, etc. At the advanced levels, the thrust is on language and mathematics: mathematical linguistics, mathematical models, psycholinguistics, theories of language, etc.

In modern philosophy (seventeenth century to date), and certainly in twentieth-century philosophy, there is a heavy interdisciplinary collaboration in collection development with the departments of Linguistics and Mathematics, as is the case in the collaboration with Classics for the earlier periods.

B. *Chronological Guidelines*

We have no chronological limitations in our collecting policy.

C. *Geographical Areas*

We collect relevant materials no matter where published.

D. *Language Restrictions*

We collect in all Western European languages, although we do attempt to acquire the definitive major editions/translations for all subjects and authors in English, if such are available. It almost goes without saying that we attempt to secure all important editions for all subjects and authors with which we are concerned in the original language published and in the original language and other Western European languages thereafter.

E. *Materials Collected*

Monographs and Monographs in Sets
Serials
Manuscripts and Ephemera (by gifts only)

F. *Materials Not Collected*

Those not relevant to our interests, and media tools, such as AV materials of any kind.

G. *Guidelines for Selection*

Specific subjects as enumerated in A., above, are collected within the general period and subject ranges listed below.

Subject	*Depth of Collecting*
General Studies	B (instructional level; the reader should refer to A.2.C., above)
Classical Period	C (comprehensive research; the reader should refer to A.2.C., above)
Christian, Medieval, Renaissance Periods	D (exhaustive research; the reader should refer to A.2.C., above)
Modern Philosophy to ca. 1900	C
Modern Philosophy 1900-	D

6.

We have now looked at some of the procedures, considerations, and problems related to the construction of a *detailed and extensive* collection development policy statement. I think we can all see that to put together such a policy statement requires a great deal of thought and time on the part of a great many well-qualified librarians and academic faculty. A reader should now be able to take one of his own particular subject interests and cast it in the form of one of the individual collection development policy statements that combine together in logical sequence (usually alphabetically by name of each particular discipline/subject) to form the main body of the whole, final policy statement. I think, further, that we should now be able to discuss the nature of collection development policy statements and make knowledgeable observations about their purpose and utility.

II.13

HOW TO CHOOSE A *JOB*

Once upon a time, as I was setting off into life in the postdoctoral reality of the professorial mills, a respected and realistic mentor remarked with some degree of asperity that I appeared to be seeking an institution of Ivy-League status, located in the Sierra Nevadas but within a stone's throw of San Francisco, and basing promotion in academic rank solely upon classroom performance without emphasis upon academic publication. He correctly observed, further, that I was seeking the impossible, both geographically and professionally, and might be well advised to begin to come to grips with some of the truths of my chosen vocation. And it may be, similarly, that beginners in the professional ranks of librarianship—and more experienced professionals as well for that matter—will not at first find what might be viewed as ideal placements in Acquisitions. Whoever has followed this text to this point knows, however, a good deal more about Acquisitions than it is common practice to teach in schools of librarianship, and will not, thus, have to enter blind into any Acquisitions department. We can now look at a few considerations related to the adventure of choosing a job. Others will doubtless occur to any thoughtful reader.

First of all, any sound Acquisitions department will have an *organizational chart* showing the prospective slot to be filled and the job responsibilities and duties of that position in relation to the activities of the entire department. There should as well be a detailed and written *job description* of the slot to be filled. Beyond this, anyone would wish to ascertain as specifically as possible (a) salary scales, (b) opportunities for advancement, and (c) the degree to which he might in the present or future be able to enter into current and/or retrospective collection-development activities.

As a corollary to this general, overall investigation of the kind of a job that is being offered, and its place in the microcosms and macrocosms we have looked at earlier, I would be remiss at this point if I did not stress the subject of *faculty status* for librarians as something for all of us to keep in mind. If a job offered brings with it faculty status, any beginner and any experienced librarian not familiar with academic procedures for promotion in rank and for the granting of tenure would be well advised to find out specifically what obligations the possession of faculty status will entail. The dreadful academese of "publish or perish" is now surfacing in the panels, symposia, and literature of librarianship. Any librarian would be foolish to accept the "benefit" of faculty status without determining exactly what is expected of him in return. If the presentation of formal papers to professional bodies and publication in professional and scholarly journals is a formal requirement for advancement for a librarian, he should understand that he is committing himself to a great many late nights, lost weekends, and annual vacations spent in the mines of professional academic research and writing, and in the effort to get that writing accepted by professional and academic publications.[36]

Second, anyone interested in Acquisitions should seek *as strong a commitment as possible for thorough on-the-job training.* If it is at all practicable, any beginner in the discipline of acquisitions should pursue bibliographic checking and order routines in monographs for several months, since such routines must be mastered if training in acquisitions is to be successful. Some time should be spent in the mailroom, more at the Kardex, and still more in the Serials and G&E sections. It is, I think, impossible to overemphasize the importance of substantial and detailed on-the-job training if a librarian is looking for the professional satisfaction that comes only from his own knowledge that he knows what he is doing and is doing it well.

I would guess that most of us in the trade believe that good acquisitions librarians are made, not born, and that the first few formative years of training in the particular discipline of acquisitions are of vital importance, both to a newcomer to the profession and to the more experienced professional who might wish to pursue the techniques of acquisitions after moving from another area of professional activity. A lack of training or incorrect training in acquisitions can have serious consequences: personal, in removing the possibility of the satisfaction that comes from the knowledge of a job well done; professional, in causing enormous difficulties in the central programs of verification (pre-cataloging), order procedures, and collection development. These professional consequences in relation to the overall functioning of the library itself are not to be underestimated.

A third important consideration is that of the adequacy of *clerical backup.* Each professional in Acquisitions should have, for example, the backup of four or five FTE clericals; an *organizational chart* with these FTE spelled out should be available for inspection. Among these nonprofessionals, there should be a number of capable and experienced, preferably career, personnel. Educational standards for clericals are important here. Also, *very important* is the presence of a clear-cut salary scale providing for the fair treatment and advancement of clericals within the library. Almost any library worth its salt will have control over its own clerical salary scales and job descriptions, so that salaries and advances in rank will be free from the bureaucratic entanglements of university-wide labor pools, whose administrators are not noted for flexibility.

An obvious corollary to the importance of adequate clerical backup is that there should be *sufficient professional staff* for these nonprofessionals to support. If we see G&E without a professional, or we see a large serials operation without at least two professionals, something is wrong. A careful look at charts, production records, and lines of responsibility will clarify this particular consideration. There can, of course, be too many professionals in an operation; so we must weigh the balance of the lines of responsibility, the budget, the numbers of professionals, and the numbers of clericals.

Fourth, the existence (or nonexistence) of a planned and up-to-date *bibliographic center* is certainly worth inquiry. And we should also check to see the *depth of working tools* in Acquisitions itself. There should be a number of these: bibliographic checking manuals, order procedure manuals, serials manuals, G&E manuals, and so forth—all vital guides to orderly procedures and routines. The *quality* of the manuals with which they work often reflects the quality of the Acquisitions departments which use them. The kind of request card used and the structure of the MOF, both of which we have looked at in some detail, often mirror the nature and functional efficiency of an Acquisitions department.

Fifth, the matter of possibly extant *backlogs* should be looked into. It should be obvious that significant numbers of requests and request cards not processed, orders not sent out, incoming books not unpacked or still standing shelved but untouched, MOF slips unfiled, and so forth—all such conditions will indicate an operation that is losing ground or, possibly, going under. Backlogs are sometimes a sign of mismanagement, but more often a definite indication of insufficient staffing. Further, we know that a staff adequate for handling daily demands may prove to be insufficient when it comes to the task of reducing backlogs. And we should know, also, that some librarians have an unfortunate tendency to hide backlogs away, certainly not to speak of them to potential candidates for employment.

Finally, and as we conclude this text and our present subject, it seems to be mentor day. I would myself like to say, be patient and learn the techniques of acquisitions. I doubt that capable acquisitions librarians will ever be a drug on the market. I think we should also recognize the facts of professional life: it would be wonderful if all of us—including ourselves and present and potential colleagues—were intelligent, industrious, pleasant to hear, and beautiful to see; but in the world as it is and as it gives substantial evidence of continuing to be in the future, we must consider ourselves fortunate if those with whom we work simply know what they are doing. If colleagues also possess a sense of humor, we should not risk the wrath of the gods by demanding anything more.

NOTES

1. I am writing in a time of severe financial stress for institutions of higher learning. following upon the bright, go-go years of the sixties, when it seemed to many such institutions that very generous state and federal funding would be provided into the foreseeable future. In the late seventies, severe budgetary restrictions extending far into the future now seem almost inevitable.

2. The use of LC slips is particularly helpful to the Catalog department, since these slips by definition establish LC entry. The entry for any title for which there is a slip can be punched into such a computer source as OCLC (see I.7.) to determine whether or not a particular title has already been cataloged and recorded in a data bank; if it has, a request to print a set of cards with LC classification can be punched into the computer and a set of LC cards produced and received within a week. I should add that if a title is not in the OCLC bank, it can be cataloged within a library and then punched into the computer and a set of cards requested and duly forthcoming.

3. There is a good summary of machines at work in various libraries in Connie R. Dunlap's "Mechanization of Acquisitions Processes," in *Advances in Librarianship,* 1 (1970), 37-57. This 1970 volume is already somewhat dated, but the first three articles are still worth reading for observations about hardware and technical services processes. The fourth article, Helen Tuttle's "Standards for Technical Services Cost Studies," is a good summary of the subject and reenforces, I think, my point about *the difficulty* of getting solid cost studies for machine versus manual operations, although this is not the author's specific subject. This serial to date as well contains other articles about machine procedures; the footnotes of all *Advances* articles provide particularly useful lists of other studies in their field.

4. The reader should see II.8. for descriptions of clerical ranks and positions that will expand upon this paragraph.

5. The reader can see that in this library the various academic departments control the funds allocated to them. It should be clear as well that when departments "own" their library acquisitions budgets, Acquisitions is required to go through many more referrals of requests and watch fund allocations much more carefully than it would in a library which controlled all funds itself.

6. In holdings and verification procedures, it is useful if checkers use black pencil for normal notations on request cards/forms, red to call attention to particular points, and green to indicate markings to be omitted by those typing MOF's.

7. The reader should refer to "Useful Forms" (II.9.A.5.), if he wishes to get a better picture of forms related to the processing of antiquarian booksellers' catalogs.

8. The reader is here referred again to I.7. in this text. Learning to play with an acquisitions terminal has the considerable merit of simplicity, which any procedural manual makes clear. That this learning should be confused with any kind of full comprehension of acquisitions or bibliographical techniques has no merit whatever.

9. A number of terms are used in various libraries to describe personnel doing bibliographic checking—checker, bibliographic checker, bibliographic assistant, assistant bibliographer, bibliographer, searcher, precataloger, etc. I have used some of these descriptives interchangeably in this section on verification to familiarize the reader with some of these terminologies.

10. In a manual in actual use in an Acquisitions department, b.(2) would simply be crossed out in all copies *or* the old page removed and a new, correct one inserted, with the details of a now invalid acquisitions technique omitted. I have retained the material here, with notes to our hypothetical bibliographic checkers, so that the reader can see the historical sequence from a service willing to search and clear copyright for one-shot reproduction, to the adoption of a searching fee for such service, to the demise of the service altogether. No commercial company can, no commercial company should be expected to, retain a service that proves to be economically unsound.

11. See "Useful Forms" (II.9.A.) for such a listing of approval-plan trade publishers for the information of faculty and librarians.

12. "Order manuals" are, as I have observed earlier, more commonly at hand than "checking manuals" in most Acquisitions departments. Any good library-school library will possess a number of representative order manuals from various institutions. The reader who has followed this text thus far should now be able to peruse such order manuals with comprehension, even though some of them are indeed long and complex. Moreover, the functions of the Order section department should be further clarified by the treatment in subsequent sections of Part II of this text of such subjects as gifts, approval plans, useful forms, statistics, and so forth.

13. This discussion *must* be understood to deal primarily with gifts of library materials. Monetary gifts, unless peculiarly restricted, are always welcome; difficult to come by in significant amounts; and, if involving large sums, lie usually in arenas of negotiation beyond the pale of the G&E librarian's areas of control.

14. For orientation, the reader should here refer to "Organizational Charts," II.2. A.2., in this text.

15. The *Checking Manual* in this text describes such routines, II.2.A.5.A-B.

16. Bibliographical and order-record processes are described in detail in II.2. and II.3. of this text.

17. I do not wish to get in depth into the still-existing national plan in which a number of libraries send unwanted materials to a central depository, which then lists its holdings, so that contributing libraries can peruse various lists and from them request and acquire "free" materials. If we count time as money and think about the logistics of such a plan, common sense reveals that it costs a good deal of money by such a method for a participating library to get rid of unwanted materials (*discards*, really) or to acquire other materials—what with the packing, shipping, selecting, receiving, etc. involved.

18. For reasons perhaps best known to lovers of the occult, LC originally terminated the eighteenth century at 1770 and the nineteenth century at 1890. The revised *Schedule* gives 1770/1800 and 1890/1900 as terminal dates.

19. *American Literature, English Literature, and World Literatures in English: An Information Guide Series* is currently under way by the Gale Research Company (1974-) and will ultimately span this range of subject matter in period-genre sequences.

20. The necessity for these sometimes-elaborate machine-produced profiles may be questioned, since all that is actually needed is a clear exposition of what an institution wants and does not want, and someone with the aptitudes of a bookman to follow instructions at the jobber's end.

21. Almost any library going into approval plans will already have standing-order plans with various academic and trade publishers to acquire all of their publications. When an approval plan is initiated, Acquisitions must decide *either* to cancel these standing orders with other dealers and have the approval-plan jobber supply such titles *or* to instruct the approval-plan agent *not* to supply titles from presses with which the library already has standing orders, *and* provide the agent with a list of the presses whose publications he *should not* supply.

22. At the moment I am writing—and, I think, into the predictable future—teaching and research in foreign languages in the United States are experiencing serious problems. Any figures for expenditures for materials in non-English-language areas are, thus, subject to constant *downward* revision. These foreign-language problems have been argued at length in *PMLA,* the professorial organ of the Modern Language Association of America (MLA), with somewhat inconclusive results. At any rate, the acquisitions librarian and the bibliographer must be aware of the present decline in the studies of such languages in the U.S.

23. A final weapon in the kind of argument a reader has been following (omitted here because it can confuse a non-technical mind) is that European dealers, unlike those in the U.S., traditionally give no trade discounts. The services which they will provide as approval-plan jobbers are, thus, in reality a kind of discount not otherwise obtainable.

24. G&E, as we know, processes materials not acquired by purchase. We should note, further, that the bindery, usually a sub-station of Serials Acquisitions, must also keep statistics on volumes bound, cost, etc. I do not plan here to deal with the activities of a bindery operation, but the serials acquisitions librarian must decide about binding backfiles, and see to it that the various titles whose issues are to be bound annually—as is the general practice—are called in punctually, bound correctly, and returned to the library's shelves as soon as possible. Attending to bindery activities is an important duty, the difficulties and importance of which must not be underestimated.

25. A good many experienced acquisitions librarians believe that the detailed work of a bibliographic checking lends itself better to part-time effort than to full time, since seven or eight hours of such work can be mentally and physically tiring and can yield markedly reduced production in the later hours of the day.

26. A production of 20 verified, polished cards was later established as a fair and rather absolute minimum for the kind of work we are speaking about (as described in the *Checking Manual* II.2.A.5.). *It is important* that the reader remember that these production figures are for routines which demand that a bibliographic checker establish LC-type entries, assign dealers, verify or estimate prices, submit polished work, etc. Simpler checking routines require less time per request.

27. In the present difficult budgetary times, a number of research libraries have felt compelled to cancel some of their subscriptions. This is a policy with which I generally disagree, although I have no doubt that there are many instances of serials subscrip-

tions that should never have been placed and were placed without sufficient evidence of need and/or rational comprehension of future cost.

28. It is interesting that this problem of the ranking and salaries of subject specialists and experts in bibliographic techniques, in relation to the ranking and salaries of administrators, has not yet been ironed out among librarians themselves in a number of research institutions—thus, in my opinion, still leaving the librarian vulnerable to serious probings about his right to be viewed as an academic professional, much less as a faculty member.

29. Try to avoid "Mr." and "Dr." title distinctions when dealing with academic faculty and address them all as "Professor." No instructor will object. If a departmental secretary requests such a form as a guide, simply send it with professorial name omitted.

30. Some details of this form are repetitious. But as any reader who has followed this text to this point knows by now, no experienced acquisitions librarian takes for granted any outsider's ready comprehension of procedures and routines in acquisitions.

31. Even if the professor does not have a secretary, to suggest that he has one readily at hand lends a mollifying element to this statement. Footnote 29 also touches upon academic protocol.

32. I once sold my home to a delightful and very wealthy rancher who kept calling me a biographer (bibliographer just didn't fix in his mind). When it came to the final details of real estate, he simply knew everything and handled the affair beautifully. I readily admitted my own ignorance, which was obvious, and praised his expertise. "Hell," he said, "forget it, I can't even say right what you do."

33. A very fine bookman recently gave an "acquisitions" course in a well-known library school, and maintained that *only* former booksellers could ever become good acquisitions librarians. Not one of his students called him on his contention because they, like the "professor," knew very little about acquisitions. The exact opposite of his thesis is true:an antiquarian bookseller, like any member of the academic faculty, would be totally lost amidst the acquisitions procedures which we have looked at together and, I am sure, would hate or fear them, as is our common reaction to the unknown or the difficult.

34. As nearly as I can figure it out, the academic deans and some of their faculties directly and personally—or through the intermediary voice of some kind of "University Library Council"—put pressure upon the directors/deans of libraries, who in turn put pressure on their bibliographers/selectors/subject-specialists to produce something in writing, to satisfy these academic forces that they are being taken care of by the library and are getting their fair share of attention and monies from the library and its professionals.

35. This kind of document, which may seem superficial at first glance, must give enough detail to satisfy, but not so much that it confuses its audience. There is also a fine line here between what is and what is not appropriate to reveal about library procedures before a mass faculty audience. This fine line is usually determined by experience and a "feel" for the situation with a given audience, in a given institution, at a particular time. No library deliberately conceals the details of its budgetary allocations, but it is better to explain them to interested faculty on an individual basis than to throw such easily misunderstood money matters into the Roman arena of general academic debate. A document like this is, thus, often much more difficult to construct than a casual reading of it might lead one to believe.

36. Although it seems a self-evident fact to some of us that thirty-five or forty-hour weeks and eleven-month working years are not conducive to the production of professional and academic publications—equal to those produced by the academic faculty, which has far more free time as well as teaching assignments directly relevant to its research work—this self-evident fact is not so clear to a good many university administrators. My own opinion, which may of course be erroneous, is that the profession of librarianship has not entirely come to grips with the matter of faculty status, with the responsibilities it can bring, or with the logistical hard fact of time being essential for solid academic and professional publication. Acquisitions work properly done is hard work; and time applied toward scholarly or professional writing after a day of such work is hard time indeed.

SHORT LIST OF ABBREVIATIONS

An effort has been made in this text to explain abbreviations as they are used. However, this brief list is added to refresh the reader's memory in the event of need. This list is by no means comprehensive, and "Definitions of Terms" (II.2.A.3.) and the "Index" should also be consulted.

AC	Added Copy
ALA	American Library Association
AV	Added Volume
BAL	*Bibliography of American Literature*
BBIP	*British Books in Print*
BIP	*Books in Print* (U.S.)
BNB	*British National Bibliography*
BPR	*Book Publishing Record* (cited in Sheehy under *American Book Publishing Record*)
BUCOP	*British Union-Catalogue of Periodicals*
DNC	Do Not Catalog (not to be cataloged)
FTE	Full-Time Employee (½FTE is a half-time employee)
G&E	Gifts and Exchanges Section of Acquisitions
ILL	Inter-Library Loan
LC	Library of Congress
LC Cat	Library of Congress Catalog (1942-1952; for full information on the LC-NUC sequences, also see Sheehy, AA92 ff.)
LEV	*Libros en Venta* (Spanish-language BIP)
MARC	Machine Readable Cataloging
MCC	Main Card Catalog (also PC, Public Catalog)
MOF	Multiple-Order-Form
NCBEL	*New Cambridge Bibliography of English Literature*
NST	*New Serial Titles*
NUC	*National Union Catalog* (1953- ; for full information on the LC-NUC sequences, also see Sheehy, AA92 ff.)

NYP	Not Yet Published
OCLC	Ohio College Library Center
O.O.	Orders Out or On Order
O.O. File	Orders-Out File or On-Order File
O.P.	Out of Print
PBIP	*Paperbound Books in Print*
PC	Public Catalog (also MCC, Main Card Catalog)
PTLA	*Publishers' Trade List Annual*
PW	*Publishers' Weekly*
RBR	Reserve Book Room
Sheehy	Eugene Sheehy, comp. *Guide to Reference Books.* 9th ed. Chicago: ALA, 1976.
SO	Standing Order
ULS	*Union List of Serials*
UNV	Unverified
USGPO	U.S. Government Printing Office
VLB	*Verzeichnis lieferbarer Bücher* (German-language BIP)

INDEX

Initials in this Index—for example, BIP, O.O., U.S.—are alphabetized as one word. It should be noted that there is extensive cross-referencing ("indexing") within the text itself. Those readers who have followed the text will understand that it aims at methodologies and procedures in Acquisitions, and not primarily at formal, analytical descriptions of individual bibliographical titles, although some such titles are dealt with in some detail. When only the last name of the author by which his bibliography is commonly known is cited in the text itself—Lowndes is one of a number of examples—his name is so cited in the Index. The reader or student may go to Sheehy for a full description of Lowndes' bibliography, or any others, and profit from the exercise. This index may, thus, be viewed both as a reference and as a study guide, providing both answers and keys to questions for readers interested in thinking about and getting involved in the methodologies, procedures, and terminologies of Acquisitions.

About the Author

Dr. Grieder is the curator at Fales Library and Special Collections of New York University. He has published numerous books about libraries, as well as *Corpus* and *A Student's First Aid to Writing*. His writings on librarianship and his literary criticism have been published in many journals.